SIMONE WEIL AND THE SPECTER OF SELF-PERPETUATING FORCE

SIMONE WEIL

AND THE

SPECTER

OF

SELF-PERPETUATING

FORCE

E. JANE DOERING

University of Notre Dame Press
Notre Dame, Indiana

Library of Congress Cataloging-in-Publication Data

Doering, E. Jane.
Simone Weil and the specter of self-perpetuating force / E. Jane Doering.
p.   cm.
Includes bibliographical references (p.   ) and index.
ISBN-13: 978-0-268-02604-2 (pbk. : alk. paper)
ISBN-10: 0-268-02604-1 (pbk. : alk. paper)
1. Weil, Simone, 1909–1943.
2. Violence—Moral and ethical aspects.
I. Title.
B2430.W474D64   2010
194—dc22
2010007652

∞ *The paper in this book meets the guidelines for permanence and
durability of the Committee on Production Guidelines for
Book Longevity of the Council on Library Resources.*

To Bernard Doering,

who is my *sine qua non,* without whom the challenge of

studying the mystical philosophy of Simone Weil would

never have attained its full promise.

CONTENTS

PREFACE

This study traces Simone Weil's unwavering desire to lay bare to her readers the reality of seductive, death-dealing brute force, with the dreadful consequences that follow when one counters violence with violence. Through her exploration of history, sacred texts, literature, and close observation of contemporary events, as well as reflection on her mystical experiences, she sought a resolution to the paradox of God's love for his creation and the terrible vulnerability of human bodies and souls to destructive force perpetrated by other human beings. She came to the conclusion that only openness to God's love, accessible to all, provides sufficient courage to face heart-rending situations with the actions that stem from Christ's commandment "Thou shalt love thy neighbor as thyself" (Matt. 22:35). This good force of supernatural origin can block the self-perpetuating spiral of devastating force. Her intellectual insights and her mystical experiences revealed to her that a reliance on the eternal criterion of "good," whose source is outside this world, allows one to "read" universal truths in the melee that comprises all human situations. She believed that every person has access to this "good" by being open to the love of God, whose grace will inevitably descend, bringing the pure good of love to diminish the extant evil. Her study of the Bhagavad-Gita in Sanskrit gave her a reassuring response to her quest.

Following the path of her determined search for ways to counter violence and yet not be contaminated by it, I have analyzed her essays, including many of her lesser-known works from her earlier years, which contain the seeds of what eventually became her unique mystical philosophy, a philosophy that closely interweaves thought and action. I show pragmatic applications of her ideas by three moral philosophers, who never knew her but were taken with her insights into force: Dwight Macdonald, Nicola Chiaromonte, and Albert Camus.

The essays presented here amplify the richness of her thought and rhetorical skill. With pleasure, I have delved into all her notebooks, recently annotated and collected into four volumes and published in *Simone Weil: Oeuvres complètes* by the Gallimard Press. This study brings her personal notations to a wider English-speaking public. Until these volumes were compiled, only extracts had been available to the public, and still fewer had been translated into English. All my primary sources for understanding her thought have been studied in the original French.

My method has been to address the earlier essays in chronological order because her thought was developing in a linear fashion. After her forced exodus from Paris, however, a sense of urgency becomes apparent in the parallel threads weaving through all her writings, making the sequence of her work less pertinent. Because the years in which she lived were critical to the formation of her thought, I have placed her ideas against the backdrop of the violent events of her times. The chaos of the Second World War, with its prelude in the Spanish Civil War, brought her to the realization that the ideology of pacifism did not suffice to protect humankind, so her reflections on war led her to a variation of a just-war theory that has a unique and unapologetic spiritual element. She used historical examples to illustrate and persuade her readers of her point of view, and I use her historical times to shed light on the evolution of her thinking.

I have often used the masculine forms of nouns and pronouns in translating her words because that was her style in the days before the valid stress on gender-neutral language.

ACKNOWLEDGMENTS

My fascination with Simone Weil's social and political thought began with my initial reading of her first "chef d'oeuvre": "Réflexions sur les causes de la liberté et de l'oppression sociale." Since that time, I have joined annually with scholars around the world to discuss her intense desire to diminish social, physical, and mental oppression imposed on human beings. My sincere appreciation goes to all the generous colleagues who have listened to and commented on my numerous articles and presentations. The members of the American Weil Society, led by its able president, Dr. Eric O. Springsted, and the international Weil scholars in the Association pour l'étude de la pensée de Simone Weil, presided over by Professor Robert Chenavier, merit a heartfelt "merci."

For their confidence in my ideas and the direction I was taking from the beginning, I thank Ruthann Johansen, president of Bethel Theological Seminary, and Florence de Lussy, former curator of the Fonds Simone Weil at the Bibliothèque Nationale. To the Weil scholars who read through the whole of my manuscript in its varied roughshod forms, I give a "purple heart" for contributing above and beyond the call of friendship: Larry Schmidt, Ann Pirruccello, and Vance Morgan. My husband Bernard gets an additional medal for his multiple readings. Equally important were scholars who read parts of the manuscript that dealt with a particular specialty: professors Brad Malkowski and Michael Crowe. I thank both Lisa Hardeker, the copy editor of my initial drafts, and Elisabeth Magnus, the final copy editor for Notre Dame Press, for their perceptive comments and suggestions, which enhanced my ability to communicate Simone Weil's ideas. Julia Douthwaite and Maureen Boulton gave vital support at critical moments, as did Peter and Ann Walshe.

The manuscript would not have arrived at this point without the financial support of the Institute for Scholarship in the Liberal Arts at the University of Notre Dame, whose mission is to sustain distinguished work in the arts, humanities, and social sciences at Notre Dame. The Florence Gould Foundation, in its goal to further French and American active relationships, gave immediate and valued support to the very successful 2001 international symposium on the campus of Notre Dame, which brought many French and American scholars together to discuss the work of French philosopher and mystic Simone Weil. That meeting initiated many ongoing fruitful dialogues. My theme for this manuscript received its impetus from that memorable meeting of fine minds, and my continued relationship with those scholars has allowed this manuscript its full fruition.

My dear husband, Bernard Doering, the fixed foot of my compass, to whom I am eternally indebted, fits into all the above categories of valued support.

Introduction

*Everything submitted to contact with force is debased, whatever the
contact. To strike or be struck results in the same corruption.
The coldness of steel is equally mortal at the sword hilt or point.
Everything exposed to contact with force is susceptible to perversion.
All things in this world are exposed to contact with force,
without exception, save love.*

Simone Weil, "Of What Does the Occitanian Inspiration Consist?"

On June 13, 1940, while Simone Weil was shopping at an open market
with her parents, Nazi troops rolled into Paris, declaring the capital
under German control. In the past, Simone had theorized about the effects of force imposed on the vulnerable but had not physically endured
it. Now she was a war refugee within her own country. She felt anguish
for her fellow Frenchmen, her native country, and the world. Confronting social violence with effective counterforce had been her constant
concern, but she saw no means of checking the violence spreading
throughout Europe. She had lost her confidence in pacifism. Peaceful
means of stopping Hitler had been tried and found wanting, and she
firmly believed that no one could control unleashed force, which would
spiral until its energies were fully spent. Her overriding question was:
If, as Thucydides argued, "All beings, whoever they are, exploit to the
fullest extent all the power in their command," how could human
beings, either as collectivities or as individuals, limit force? From embracing integral pacifism to accepting the reality that force must be

met with force, she sought a counterforce with strict parameters that could prevent the contamination of both victor and vanquished.

Weil knew that brute force manifesting itself in human inter-actions brought defilement to those who dominated and those who suffered subjugation. Her anxiety over the vulnerability of the indi-vidual in society led her to warn early on against a highly centralized state run by an anonymous bureaucracy that facilitated the role of a totalitarian dictator. Weil wrote constantly to alert her countrymen to be vigilant to the luring call of force and to explore noncontami-nating methods that could allow force to be used successfully against an oppressor. The paradox of force being both necessary and debas-ing left her distraught. She sought to resolve the mystery that God's love for his creation coexisted with the self-perpetuating mechanism of force that catalyzes force in others, forever encumbering human relations. Her rationale that even war could have moral and spiritual justification—on rare occasions—adds useful nuance to our contem-porary discussion of a "just-war" theory. All her compositions had a specific audience but were written in a philosophical style that revealed fragments of the truth she so earnestly sought to uncover. This study brings to the forefront Weil's works that attempt to illuminate innova-tive ways to thwart the persistent human tendency to covet power.

FORMATIVE ASPECTS OF SIMONE WEIL'S LIFE

On February 3, 1909, Simone Weil was born into a middle-class Pari-sian family of Jewish origins but with no active religious affiliation. An impressionable and compassionate child, Simone was five years old when Europe plunged into the First World War. Her father's wartime medical responsibilities gave her full opportunity to observe war's dis-figurement of human beings. Her parents, who prized intellectual achievement, supplemented Simone's education with tutoring at home, particularly since she suffered from fragile health. Her ado-lescent and young adult years were plagued with severe migraine head-aches for which no one had a remedy. From an early age she despaired that she would always remain on the threshold of truth and never be among the privileged who were granted entry. Being in the shadow of her admired and brilliant older brother, André, who became renowned among twentieth-century mathematicians, reinforced this feeling.

After preparatory classes in the select Lycée Henri IV, where she studied under the guidance of philosopher Alain (Emile Chartier), Simone gained admittance, through a stiff competitive exam, to the academically elite École Normale Supérieure (ENS). At nineteen, she held her own as the only woman in her class of bright, well-prepared, and intellectually driven men. She specialized in philosophy, as was rare for a woman at that time. Although Weil was thoroughly at home in the ENS academically, as a young woman who disregarded traditional societal expectations she endured demeaning attitudes and cutting remarks from her male counterparts and professors.

Weil had a strong sense of goals and oriented her life around three guidelines: (1) to critically analyze any given question; (2) to write down her reflections; and (3) to take appropriate actions. She wrote constantly, setting down her ideas and empirical observations in her notebooks for later incorporation into her carefully crafted essays. The multiple facets of her ideas, her varied fields of inquiry, and the wide range of her activities were dazzling. The theme that held them all together was her intense compassion for vulnerable human beings, which made her explore solutions for the unjust treatment of common people by pursuing the causes of social inequity.

For Weil, theory was never separate from action. She believed that the validity of any commentary required an empirical knowledge of the conditions to be analyzed, so she always verified her philosophical theories by her readings and her personal life experiences. Each time she entered a milieu unusual for persons of her background, she brought away new insights that attentive readers still find valuable. Each endeavor involved skills of persuasion and, occasionally, sly means to gain access to places where she ordinarily would be refused. To the end of her days, by all the means within her power, she aspired to know the truth.

After receiving her *agrégation*—a diploma qualifying her to teach in French secondary and university education—Weil became a philosophy professor in various girls' lycées. She spent her weekends designing and teaching courses in math, science, and language skills for workers as a step toward helping the downtrodden to fight oppressive workplace conditions. She encouraged workers to consider their own best interest, which, to her thinking, entailed maintaining their human dignity by using their minds and energies in ways far beyond fighting for higher salaries. Through her activist presence and her many articles in workers' bulletins, she supported working-class demands for equitable treatment and at one time attracted public scorn by participating in a strike of the unemployed.

Her first projects engaged questions concerning exploitation in the workplace, such as what the dangerous machinery and the long hours in the factories did to workers' sense of self-worth. To know their situations firsthand, she took physically demanding work assignments in three different metallurgical factories and later performed laborious farmwork. After initially fighting against the hazardous work environment imposed on industrial factory workers, she widened her horizons to include all who suffered under the yoke of dehumanizing force. When the Spanish Civil War broke out, she enlisted as a soldier in the Colonna Durutti, an anarchist brigade. Her last project—never set in motion—was to form a corps of nurses to be transported into the thick of the fighting, bringing first aid medical treatment and a caring human presence to wounded soldiers in the field. In a manner quite consistent with her nature, she felt the need to bear the full brunt of battlefield violence if she were to theorize about the perils of war for individual souls.

THREE ENCOUNTERS WITH CHRISTIANITY

In the second half of the 1930s, three mystical contacts with Christianity reoriented Weil's thinking and gave an explicitly Christian spiritual basis to her political and social engagement. Few people knew about these occurrences at the time. She described them in 1942 to her spiritual mentor, Father Perrin, by saying that Christ had come down and taken possession of her.[1] Each mystical event occurred within the framework of what she had always held essential in the condition of being human: age-old cultural traditions, the humility of the poor in spirit, and a surrounding of natural beauty, which she came to consider a form of God's implicit love.

The first mystical contact took place in a Portuguese fishing village, probably shortly after her factory work. Observing a mournful Saints' Day procession of women carrying candles and chanting ancient religious canticles as they circled the fishing boats in the light of a full moon, she understood that "Christianity is the religion of slaves par excellence, that slaves cannot not adhere to it, and I too along with the others."[2] Her use of the word *slaves* in the framework of Christianity implied total submission through willing consent to God's love, even when the material conditions imposed intense suffering. This idea became a dominant theme in her final writings. The second experience took place in Assisi. She wrote to Father Perrin: "While alone in the small Romanesque twelfth-century chapel of Santa Maria degli Angeli—a marvel of incomparable purity, where Saint Francis often prayed—something stronger than I obliged me for the first time in my life to kneel down."[3]

The third experience came during some crushing headaches as she was reciting George Herbert's poem "Love," which, for her, had the virtue of a prayer. She had been introduced to Herbert's metaphysical poems by a young man she had met during Holy Week in the Benedictine Abbey of Solesmes, which was renowned for the beauty of its Gregorian chant. In the same letter to Perrin, she wrote: "When suddenly Christ took possession of me, neither the senses nor the imagination had any part; I felt through my suffering the presence of love, analogous to the love seen in the smile on a beloved face."[4]

Weil came to consider liturgical services as another form of the implicit love of God. Although drawn to the Catholic Church, for complex reasons related to her insistence on absolute integrity she rejected Father Perrin's request to baptize her or to be a member of the Catholic Church. She held firmly to her freedom of thought, wanting to bear witness to all who had never had the chance or desire to know the historical Christ. In this letter of farewell to Father Perrin, she affirmed her belief that many venerable religions had valid contacts with the divine. In addition, she explained that the Church's refusal to acknowledge past transgressions, such as the Inquisition and the Crusade against the peace-loving Albigensians, was incipient totalitarianism. The authoritarian approach of the Church had led to the practice of *anathema sit*, a formula in former Church practice that imposed excommunication on anyone who refused to accept Church dogma. She believed that "to function properly the intelligence requires total freedom, including the right to deny everything, and no domination whatsoever."[5]

Christianity, nonetheless, impregnated her life and thinking, with the passion of Christ holding the focal place. Her journal entries reveal admiring echoes from the Gospels, a source of great beauty for her. The *Iliad*, which she knew so well, took on a new illumination when colored by a profound Christian interpretation. Weil wished to know the truth conveyed by the sacred scriptures of long-standing religions, and she found solace in the beauty of Hindu sacred literature during her intense study of ancient Asian texts. Her reading of the Bhagavad-Gita resonated with Christian undertones, which are revealed in her Marseilles and London notebooks.

Intimations of the pervasive presence in Weil's thought of her mystical experiences can be inferred from her later writings. Her life, thought, and writings wove an intricate tapestry from beginning to end, and her mysticism added significant texture to her life's design. Her mystical encounters intensified her attraction to Christianity and reinforced her desire to orient humankind toward love of neighbor rather than toward paths of violence. When Christ's presence became manifest to her, Weil had already moved on from militant worker activism, without ever diminishing her deep interest in improving the lot of the disinherited members of society. Her understanding of human suffering, however, received new illumination related to the sacredness of the human person—every human person.

Her contacts with Christianity, spanning the last half-dozen years of her life, heightened her perspectives on the essential roles of beauty, humility, and suffering in the human condition. For Weil, beauty attracted human beings toward God, while brute force crushed human souls and destroyed all that was precious. Humility allowed one to be fully attentive to another's needs by mindful listening. Suffering, accepted in the love of God, could be purifying; Christ's humble acceptance of his passion remained the supreme model for humankind. All suffering that could be eliminated should be; no one could ask for suffering, nor should violence ever be imposed. Human beings had the obligation to see that their neighbors did not suffer the deprivation of the vital needs of soul or body. In innovative fashion, she delineated those needs in a prelude to her last work, *The Need for Roots* (*L'enracinement*).

A PHILOSOPHER'S DEATH

Weil died on August 23, 1943, in a sanatorium for tubercular patients in Ashford, England. The prior year, she had accompanied her elderly parents to safety in the United States, with the resolve, nevertheless, of returning to France, but she got only as far as London. Given hazardous wartime conditions, even getting that far took relentless determination. She was torn by the thought that she had abandoned her native land in its time of need. Her fragile health and extreme disappointment at not getting permission from the Free French Forces to reenter France led to a physical breakdown with tubercular complications. A cure was rendered impossible by her refusal to eat more than what she believed was available to the most deprived of her compatriots in occupied France, or to accept rich foods—considered the remedy for tuberculosis—while the British were short on rations. The rigor of her thought imposed a harsh consistency on her lifestyle. Up until her death, she continued writing to fulfill her self-imposed mission of describing a postwar society in which compassionate people would reject social oppression by assuring an equitable, impartial justice enlightened by supernatural love.

SIMONE WEIL'S INTELLECTUAL LEGACY

Weil's thought merits attention in the twenty-first century. Her writings reveal the evolution of a gifted mind that illuminated traditional wisdom with fresh perspectives concerning the plight of human beings in the world. As a philosopher, she strove ceaselessly to gain insights into the unequal and unstable relationships of force that allowed the powerful to dominate the vulnerable. Her keen observation of human behavior, her first-rate intellect, and her practical application of concepts advanced by great thinkers qualify her work as a genuine source of theoretic and pragmatic ideas. She had a profound human-ism, a deep love for her fellow human beings, and a talent for clear, accessible prose. Her mental probing was always open-ended, and her rhetorical queries suggested further provocative lines of thought. She exacted constant verification of the insights gleaned from either contemporary events or her reading. At the ENS, she pursued her search for truth while interacting with intellects of equal stature, all given great latitude in their studies. That excellent academic training reinforced her drive to understand the human condition and honed her ability to express her findings with lucidity.

Weil's habit of underpinning theoretical ideas with a form of praxis makes her work a unique approach to confronting the decline of compassion in today's world. The horrendous conditions of her time provided an impetus and a framework for her pursuit of effective ways to confront and block the use of force in the social sphere. She began her intellectual and activist engagement in the struggles between social classes but then moved to conflicts between nations. Her mysticism infused her reasoning and enlightened her thinking with a new radiance. Toward the end of her life, Weil's political, social, and mystical approaches to human existence meshed into one philosophy, founded on the sacredness of human life.

Weil believed that philosophy's role was to uncover an already existing truth, not to create a new system. Consequently, her philosophical inquiry gave close attention to the physical world, literature, sacred texts, and contemporary ideas. After scrutinizing each new concept carefully, Simone Weil incorporated what she intuited as true, but she never ceased delving further. Although she did not find a definitive response to the enigma of force ever present in the human condition, she laid out parameters adaptable to the contextual contingencies for action. Her quest to know the teleology of human existence had no limits.

Along with great literature, the works of notable social and political philosophers, past and present, nourished her thinking. Alain, who had a formative influence on her, had an original style of teaching in which he drew philosophical conclusions from literary works. Weil continued this method in her own studies and teaching. She absorbed ideas from others and then incorporated them into the fabric of her philosophical theories without specifically identifying their source. Her custom was to take the basic idea and then push the thought further, making innovative applications, where useful, to contemporary problems. She read widely and voraciously, at times entering sources in her notebooks, but many times not. Nevertheless, the allusions, for the most part, have been pinpointed and studied by Weil readers. Many authors held an important place in the forefront of her thought: Plato, the Greek playwrights, Homer, Heraclites, Kant, Rousseau, Spinoza, Marx, Alain. The list is by no means exhaustive. Others have made excellent analyses of the relationship between Weil's ideas and those of other eminent minds.[6]

HER WRITINGS

We are fortunate that, despite the upheaval created by the occupation of France in 1940, Weil's friends and neighbors, aware of the extraordinary quality of her contributions, were able to salvage the major part of the multiple papers left in her apartment or in others' keeping. Beyond her many finely crafted essays, Weil left a broad legacy of thought in rough-hewn fragments jotted down in notebooks (or *cahiers*). These entries furnish a rich store of information that she had gleaned from her reflections, her readings, and her observations of the interconnectedness of humankind, the world, and the divine. Her manifold reflections bring to light the process by which she sharpened her thinking and developed ideas for future essays. For the reader, they yield a wealth of material, exceedingly dense, with many themes interspersed, and display the processes of an extraordinary mind guided by the unquenchable desire to know the truth and reveal it to others.

Over 90 percent of her notebook entries were written during the last three years of her life while she had to be continually on the move: in Marseilles, on the seven-week transatlantic passage, in New York, and finally in London. She used school copybooks, labeled them, tore out pages to rearrange them, and sometimes kept more than one notebook at a time for different purposes. Marginal comments added a later thought to the original notation or served a different function entirely. Ideas were packed together, with separate strands of thought moving in parallel fashion, and the pages and covers were overlaid with script, diagrams, and formulas.

These notes, written for her personal reflection, are now part of the Fonds Simone Weil at the Bibliothèque Nationale in Paris, along with her manuscripts, still being prepared for publication through the Gallimard publishing house. The exacting scholars who edited her *cahiers* for the *Oeuvres complètes* have masterfully detected their chronology from the type of paper used, the mention of a book or an event, and the notebook's appearance. These indications have helped the editorial team to arrange the entries in sequential order for the four annotated volumes of her notebooks, which supply readers with new sources for exploring and weighing her significant contribution to social and political thought. They also reveal a Simone Weil hitherto unknown— not different but fuller—with a wider range of intellectual pursuits than had been imagined from her finished articles. Because of her short life span of a scant three and a half decades, many ideas noted in her daily writing were never shaped into polished essays, so this raw material offers precious glimpses into her thinking. My study has made maximum use of Weil's notebook comments, of which only a limited number have been translated into English, to explore her formative insights into both the nature of a ubiquitous ruthless force and her representation of a countering positive force.

SCHOLARLY CONTRIBUTIONS OF THIS STUDY

Through this work, the English reading public will gain easier access to those writings of Simone Weil that portray the full range of her ideas on exploitative force and its opposite: an efficacious counterforce for the good. I have sorted out her meaning of the term *force* in many different contexts, whether she was referring to "any natural agent capable of effecting change in matter" or to the unjust social pressures exerted for personal self-aggrandizement and exploitation by the dominant over the subservient.[7] Despite her preference for precision in word choices, her use of the term *force* has multiple applications, all of which reflect the uniqueness of her insights. After beginning with the word *oppression* during her social activist period, she shifted to the term *force* when referring to the increasing National Socialist threat. To further complicate the issue, she often conflated the scientific terms of *force* and *energy* when speaking of transformations in physical matter. She concluded by referring to supernatural grace as the sole good force to counter evil.

By presenting Weil's fresh reading of Homer's *Iliad* and her particular interpretation of the Bhagavad-Gita, this book traces the progression from her early commentaries on oppressive social conditions to her proposed resolution for the dilemma of how to deploy force without being perverted by its contamination. I show how the wisdom and beauty of the Hindu philosophical poem offered her consolation in her reluctant acceptance of a justified use of force. The insights Weil found in this ancient mystical poem concerning her critical question involving judgments to be made when confronting violent behavior helped her to delineate guidelines necessary to any fruitful use of force. The notebooks are our source for knowing the revelations she saw in the Gita, for these conclusions never found their full expression in essay form because of her untimely death.

Two lesser-known pendant essays, one on reading or interpreting a situation and the other on a system of values, are highlighted as connecting links to her ultimate conclusions on ways to counter force effectively. One must read one's fellow human beings objectively and measure the choice of reactions against an eternal criterion of the good. Weil's Project for a Corps of Frontline Nurses receives a fresh analysis to give it its worthy place as a fitting and ultimate praxis for her theory on the radiance of good actions.

Finally, I examine how a New York meeting in 1946 of three social philosophers—American, Italian, and French—provided the primary impetus to the diffusion of Weil's writings. Little has been written about the initial circulation of her ideas after World War II. After her early activist polemics written for educators and workers, she seldom focused on publishing her work. The encounter of three journalists, agnostics by their own account, is presented for the first time as a crucial springboard for the spread of her ideas throughout North America and Europe.

A MESSAGE BEQUEATHED TO HUMANITY

Very near the end of her life, Simone Weil wrote to her mother that she had a message of pure gold for humankind but feared that no one would be inclined to hear it. She had sought confirmation for this perceived message in the physical universe, in human psychology, and in classic and sacred texts. Her experiences had shown her that recognition of the potent self-perpetuating capacity of force, inherent in human relationships, would require new social strategies in view of a more comprehensive understanding of the spiritual dimension in human beings. She wanted others to be aware of this reality.

Her mystical encounters with Christ had revealed to her the impersonal sacredness of every individual, which dwells invisibly within every person and does not depend on any personal or random attributes. Although this sacred part of every human being that goes through life expecting good to be done to it is vulnerable, it is within this sacred aspect of every human being that obedient consent to God's love occurs. The community must protect this fragile center of the individual, which can be reduced to impotence by cold indifferent force. Because knowledge of the supernatural is transmitted through all the great traditional religions and their cultures, concern for the well-being of one's neighbor means that everyone has the obligation to preserve these civilizations from annihilation.

Weil's message dealt with the constant imperative of keeping force checked because individuals' lives were at risk, as were the traditions of civilizations that transmitted valuable facets of the supernatural. The churning violence could be quelled only by persons who acted selflessly for a higher good and who accepted the sacrifices required. From her anguish for others' suffering, Weil brought out a new understanding of the human condition. She desperately hoped her message would be heard. This study follows her tortuous path from her early recognition of the self-perpetuating autonomy of violence to her final resolution of the continual struggle to constrain brute force from destroying humankind's vital bridges to the supernatural.

CHAPTER ONE
Simone Weil's Rejection of Pacifism

War denies the very idea that the individual human
person has the highest value in this world.

Weil, "Reflections on the Civil Service"

In her years as a pacifist, Simone Weil condemned war for the terrible
physical destruction it wreaked and for the oppressive domestic policies it required. For her, only freedom and peace could sustain the
value of every individual. In the decade before Hitler flouted the Munich Accords by marching into Prague, Weil tried every means within
her power to sue for peace. She extolled the value of work that made a
civil contribution and of education that developed skills for critical
thinking. She denigrated the overextension of power that came with
authority and the hypocrisy of arguments that used hollow slogans to
give primacy to ends over means. She detailed the corrupting effects of
deploying force to achieve a goal and pleaded for coherence in the rationales for or against violence. In doing so, she held a mirror up to the
foibles that are all too present in human nature.

Having seen firsthand and at a very young age the mutilation of
the French male population wrought by World War I, she wrote her
first pacifist piece at nineteen, on the value of civil service as an alternative to military service. In the years that followed, she strove to give
an explicit pacifist direction to the French League for the Rights of
Man, promoted antiwar petitions, composed polemics against war and

the preparation for war, and wrote letters of pacifist persuasion to people in positions of influence. Using her prodigious writing skills, she stripped the veil from emotion-laden words and misleading pretenses for waging war. The human readiness to surrender individual liberty and submit to those in command provoked her to apply the ideas of the eminent sixteenth-century political theorist Estienne de la Boétie to contemporary events. Until Hitler invaded Prague in March 1939, she had advised appeasement to avoid the terrible throes of war. But once the black swastika flew over the palace in Bohemia, she disavowed total pacifism and ruefully accepted the existence of force as an inherent part of human nature. Her intellectual journey from pacifism to an advocacy for a strictly limited use of force constitutes the focus of this chapter.

EARLY ACTIVISM

*The idea that negates war is the idea that the
human person has the highest value in the world.*

Weil, "Reflections on the Civil Service"

In the summer of 1928, before entering the École Normale Supérieure (ENS), Weil prepared a piece valorizing a civil service option that would allow one to perform manual labor for a constructive cause instead of drilling in the armed services. In Weil's philosophy, physical work gave meaning to human lives, whereas war negated the value of the individual. Work contributed doubly to the good of society by heightening the sense of personal dignity, as well as the awareness of others' dignity. Weil wrote: "I can feel the value of the individual human person only in so far as I feel my own value; and I feel my value only in so far as I take action. Work alone brings peace."[1] She increasingly stressed the importance of work that contributed to the common good, a theme that became central in her philosophy. But her personal intention to participate in the Civil Service Organization by doing the same hard digging as the men evaporated when she found that all women were relegated to kitchen duties.[2]

The following year, she and some of Alain Chartier's other follow-ers energetically campaigned for reorienting the goals of the League of the Rights of Man. They wanted the League, which had been created around the time of the Dreyfus case to defend victims against anti-Semitism and a too-powerful state, to actively advocate political initi-atives for peace.[3] When the League's president, Victor Basch, asserted that the League should not take a political stand but remain impartial for greater effectiveness, Weil drew up a public rebuttal, reasoning that impartiality was not an option, since a priori a government in power wanted to stay in power, even at the cost of injustice. Hence, close monitoring of authorities and systematic opposition to power should guide the League's decisions aimed at safeguarding the people's right to peace. "In particular," she wrote, "for questions of peace and of war, the League, which recognizes the right to peace as one of the rights of man, must support all initiatives—no matter how radical—that tend toward peace, provided only that they be just."[4] She and her fellow ac-tivists had only minimal success in reorienting the League toward a politically assertive stance, for Basch and others refused to support a pacifism that incorporated a methodic opposition to power and au-thority.[5] Basch's moderate stand, however, did not defend him against the power of the occupying forces, who dissolved the League as one of their first acts. Four years later, the Vichy militia assassinated Basch, at age eighty-eight, for his participation in the Resistance movement.[6]

Peers and professors did not always appreciate Weil's sharp tongue and single-minded determination. Her dogged work for just causes alienated many who were on the receiving end of acerbic comments when they ignored her requests. In the beginning of the 1928–29 aca-demic year, she circulated a petition (written by her friend René Châ-teau) critical of the military. Petitions drafted by students were com-mon at the time, but this one attracted unfavorable attention in the Parisian press, creating much aggravation for the directors of the École.[7] The petition asked that the obligatory officer military training at the ENS be made optional. Young male intellectuals were asking not to be relieved of service but to be allowed to enroll as simple recruits with no privileges.

The request reflected the pacifism in the air and a genuine desire to be on equal footing with the common conscript, but it also delivered a rebuke from the young French intelligentsia to those who commanded the military. Although as a woman she was not subject to military service herself, Weil aggressively solicited signatures, reproaching those who refused to sign. The assistant director of the school, with whom she had locked horns before, told her bluntly to mind her own business.[8] Undeterred, she helped the men garner signatures from half the male student population—no mean feat, since if the request were granted they would receive far fewer privileges and much harsher military assignments. The petition fell by the wayside, however, when the minister of defense dismissed it as an adolescent passing fancy.[9]

SIMONE WEIL AND THE MARXIST IDEA OF REVOLUTION

> *It is evident that the Marxist tradition presents neither*
> *unity nor clarity in questions concerning war.*
>
> Weil, "Reflections on War"

Having completed her academic studies in 1931, Weil became an activist on behalf of oppressed workers. Logical thought took center stage as the most pragmatic means of finding a way to oppose force imposed by abusive social structures. She insisted that the workers must have every opportunity to develop their ability to reason and to express their needs effectively. To her way of thinking, an accurate assessment of problems, along with a rational approach toward potential solutions, could encourage reorganization of the workplace and bring positive benefits to both management and workers. Without illusions about whether individuals do indeed maximize their intellectual capacities, she believed that the mind was a potent force for good.

To this end, Weil briefly supported the Marxist idea of revolution—that is, an abrupt upheaval in society—as an effective tool to change the working environment. But she faulted Marx for his failure to seriously address the capricious role of force in human interaction. While recognizing that the workers' living and working conditions augmented or diminished their capacity for resisting oppression, she never considered men as pawns of their environment. Seeing the ruinous effects of overreaching power and oppressive force wielded by tyrannical leaders, Weil eventually superseded Marx's basic notion that economic need is the guiding principle of human interaction with her concept that human beings tended to exert brute force wherever possible. She believed that workers with the necessary skills could bring about a beneficial social transformation, but she also knew they needed guidance to decide what would accord them a place of dignity. In addition, the realization that her role as a catalytic agent might lead to bloodshed and great suffering for others caused her serious misgivings.

Workers needed education, which would give them the tools to determine first what social structures would permit their humanness to flourish and then to think through effective means of creating them. A key element was to build up the workers' pride in their vital contribution to France's economy and national heritage, so she tirelessly supported and taught challenging courses for workers in the sciences, language, and mathematics in order to give them the intellectual tools to assess what was possible for them and the verbal skills to express their needs. She reasoned that since all persons could have access to the truth of the human condition through freedom of thought, society must provide the means for improving everyone's mental proficiencies. To know the workers' situation from the inside in order to help them acquire the appropriate skills to achieve their goals, she worked side by side with industrial machine workers, trying to replicate their living situation with all its pressures and deprivations.

For similar reasons, she traveled to Germany in 1932 to evaluate the potential of the much-extolled German workers on whom the communists had pinned their hopes for a workers' revolution. Her observation of the situation in Berlin, however, dispelled any illusion that a social revolution would come from the fractured German workers' groups. She found that, although robust and competent, the German workers had become dupes of underhanded subterfuges devised by authorities determined to maintain positions of control. She had to accept that being skilled or knowledgeable was not sufficient for the marginalized in society to gain equality with the powerful elites; more was needed. Although she ceased using the word *oppression* in her reflections on the consequences of abusive social constraints, its presence still pervaded her writings in a variety of forms. Her terms shifted to *power* and *force* as she began exploring the use of force in a broader context than the oppression of one social group by another.

The situation in Germany exposed, for Weil, the utopian quality of the hope that workers would effect international change. On her return to France, she accused Marx of having made the empty idea of revolution the opium of the people. Her French communist comrades poured vitriolic criticism on her negative appraisal of the potential of the German workers to initiate a revolution.[10] In retrospect, her analysis of the partisan power struggles between the National Socialists, the communists, and the bourgeoisie, fomented covertly by Nazi and Soviet manipulators, was proven to be accurate. Indifferent to the scorn heaped on her by her leftist comrades, Weil espoused a series of gradual social reforms, insisting that not even Marx was more important than the truth.

REFLECTIONS ON WAR

Only those who are in the battles win them,
while only the powerful profit from them.

Louis de Saint-Just, quoted by Weil in "Reflections on War"

In 1933, the year Hitler came to power, Weil composed an in-depth analysis of the idea that workers could improve their situation through violence. Entitled "Reflections on War," it contains themes that she continued to develop throughout her life's work.[11] The first of Weil's writings to be translated and published in the United States, it still has relevance for our contemporary discussions of war. In it, she highlighted the lack of rigor and clarity of the multiple and contradictory rationales for violence. History's long list of revolutions and counterrevolutions proved that war and fascism had always enjoyed a close relationship. The French Revolution, Napoleon's imperial reign, and the Russian Revolution had all led to unending struggle and deprivation for the common people. These violent changes and their aftermaths showed that a revolution brought on by weaker elements in society succeeded only in replacing one group of oppressors by another.

Any theory supporting war or any other violent change that privileged ends over means had an inherent faulty premise, she claimed. Essential to all questions of whether to go to war, Weil argued, was a consideration of how war would affect the country's internal politics and its social and economic conditions. Readiness for war implied tight political and military control over a nation's people, so the decision to go to war was decided more often by carefully orchestrated internal politics than by external relations (a familiar theme for Weil). The control achieved by the state inevitably ground down people's lives, for "arms manipulated by a sovereign state bring liberty to no one."[12] Weil's rationale for safeguarding peace was founded on the importance of honoring one's own dignity and that of every individual, as one could not do during times of social disorder. "In any circumstance," she maintained, "the worst possible treason consists always in accepting one's subordination to the [administrative, police, and military] apparatus and in serving it by crushing underfoot human values: one's own and those of others."[13]

Weil always assessed a situation honestly, in person where possible, in order to imagine alternative behaviors. In 1936, when General Franco's army invaded Republican Spain, Weil wanted to observe the interaction of forces on the battlefield. By siding with those whom she considered "starving peasants [struggling] against landed proprietors," she hoped to participate in the Republican defense of liberty and democracy.[14] To her dismay, however, she soon found a complex mix of admirable and reprehensible behavior on the part of her Republican comrades. Criticizing the Republican means of fighting for justice as seriously tainted, she faced her disillusionment frankly. Her stay was cut abruptly short when she tripped over a camouflaged pot of boiling oil set in the ground, badly burning her leg. Her parents, in France, having heard the alarming news that Simone was seriously hurt, found her in a Catalonian hospital just in time to ensure that she received proper medical care and avoided having her leg amputated.

Her short stint in Spain with an international unit of anarchist militias had been long enough for her to accept the disheartening fact that brute force corrupts both sides. Those who are given a gun and free license to use it brandish their dominance over the vulnerable, scarcely concerning themselves with questions of justice or any pointless spilling of blood. She concluded: "In this, there is a contagious impulse, indeed, an intoxication, impossible to resist without an exceptional strength of soul."[15] The militias she observed had succumbed to this debasing intoxication and had lowered themselves to the level of their adversaries. Their behavior corroborated for Weil the ineluctable contamination of force.

A RESPONSE TO ALAIN'S CHALLENGE

The power to start or end hostilities is exclusively
in the hands of those who do not fight.

Weil, "Reflections on War"

Weil's overriding anxiety about a widespread European conflagration, despite her ardent desire for solidarity with the Spanish workers fighting to preserve their democracy, buttressed her approval of the French government's refusal to send arms to the Spanish Republicans. The bloody internecine struggle had swiftly exhibited every sign of being the prologue to an armageddon between Russia, Germany, and Italy. The notion of pacifism had not yet released its hold on her, but, in this perilous atmosphere, Weil continued to probe the corrosive nature of force.

In 1936 Weil's admired philosophy professor Alain threw down the gauntlet to French intellectuals by publicly asking them several questions in view of Hitler's provocative act of occupying the Rhineland, and Weil was among those named to respond. Weil chose to respond to the question: "Are the [leaders] who hold honor and dignity to be more important than life ready to be among the first to risk their lives in opposing Hitler? And if not, how should one consider them?"[16]

In her response, Weil dealt with practical questions bearing on all wars: Who decided that a country would declare war? Who actually went into combat? Who profited from war conditions? Who risked los-

ing everything? She wanted to apply consistent criteria to policy decisions concerning crucial questions about war that would equally apply
to a nation's treatment of its own disenfranchised members. She posed
a rhetorical question about whether a nation had a moral obligation to
aggressively counter a perceived humiliation that had damaged its
prestige or sovereignty when this directive did not also apply to that nation's own humiliated working masses. If so, arguments for war over
an affront to a nation's "honor" reeked of hypocrisy and exploitation,
for wartime restrictions inevitably gave full rein to a nation's authority
to exploit those in the lower social ranks.

Weil argued that for a nation to avoid hypocrisy, the criterion of
alleged humiliation for declaring hostilities would have to apply to internal as well as external politics, and the disinherited would be justified in rising up against their perpetual humiliation. That, however,
she suggested sardonically, would subvert the established social order.
Thus the masses, compelled to endure humbling circumstances, were
conscripted into the military and obliged to endure subjugation and affront. Afterwards, they returned home to situations where their dignity
too often suffered at the hands of those who had become rich with
little risk.

Weil singled out the words *honor* and *dignity* as the most blood-
stained in the language, reminding her readers that Poincaré's vacuous formulas "Peace with dignity" and "Peace with honor" were
preludes to the senseless slaughter following 1914.[17] She held these
pre–World War I slogans, along with the men who had proclaimed
them without going to war themselves, responsible for the desecration
of human lives. Dignity, signifying self-esteem, was contingent exclusively upon freely decided actions; honor also depended on a free uncoerced resolution, in this case to put one's life in danger for a greater
cause. Authorities who declared war impelled others to go to battle.
Consequently, she argued, men in power could not honestly base their
call to arms on an appeal to honor or dignity, for both depended on the
liberty to make unconstrained choices. As for the noncombatants, neither their honor nor their self-esteem was at stake in war because, in
theory, they had little share in the dangers. As a result, logically one
could conclude that, because war did not engage anyone's individual
honor, no peace could be considered dishonorable.

Weil's principal point here was to underscore the hypocrisy of leaders who argued that protection of a country's dignity and honor obliged them to declare war and, by consequence, to conscript those who were forced to submit to indignities every day within their own country. Her accusation had a factual basis in the debasing treatment of thousands of colonial subjects who nevertheless supported France's cause in World War II. Similarly, African American servicemen in World War II suffered humiliating treatment both in the service and at home after fighting to defend the United States.

In this concise essay, Weil philosophically brought a higher principle to bear on the subject of war, which was integrity in applying criteria for major decisions involving violence. She exposed the dishonesty of authorities who cavalierly sent men off to war and, by proclaiming empty slogans, deceived them into believing that some lofty phantasmal goal merited the supreme sacrifice of their lives. She declared that war, in both its preparation and its conduct, was a mechanism of internal oppression founded on inequality. Therefore, the hypocrisy could be dispelled only by the radical decision to honor peace over war. Weil's arguments for nonviolence had a revolutionary tone in that they advocated equality in human relationships and an unemotional, honest, and pragmatic discussion of whether the cause merited the terrible human sacrifice. Her careful dissection of the question of what is and is not a justified reason for going to war had pertinence in the twentieth century and still does in the twenty-first century.

At this point in her life, Weil saw conditions of peace as the only safeguard of human values. She was not alone: between the two wars, pacifism was a widespread, understandable reaction to the futility of the destruction inflicted on the French population during "the Great War." Of the eight and half million Frenchmen mobilized in the First World War, only a fourth of them returned home relatively unscathed: a million and a half died, while almost five million were wounded, imprisoned, or missing in action. The total French casualties were 73.3 percent of their armed forces.[18]

Even after Hitler introduced conscription in 1935, marched into the demilitarized Rhineland in 1936, and formed a pact first with Italy, then with Japan, Weil and others continued to plead for propitiatory negotiations and against preparing to fight. She proposed that a credible assessment of the potential loss of lives and cultural heritage would show that the costs of war surpassed by far the liabilities of concessions. She was sure that proper mediation could prevent a military confrontation and the consequent weakening of individual liberties. Innovative techniques in diplomacy retained a major role in all her attempts to stave off violence. At this point, rationality was still the strong card in her suit for pacifism, but events soon convinced her of its inadequacy for stopping an adversary determined on forceful domination. She was right, however, about the sacrifices; the cost of World War II in human lives was horrific.

THE POWER OF WORDS

*To push men to the most absurd catastrophes neither gods nor
secret conspiracies are necessary, human nature suffices.*

Weil, "Let Us Not Recommence the Trojan War"

In the following year, Weil developed two of the key antiwar arguments in her "Response to Alain" and rewove them into a pragmatic discourse entitled "Let Us Not Recommence the Trojan War." In this 1937 piece she called once again for clear, hard thinking about rushing into war without rationally assessing the means, goals, and costs. She pursued her warning against rallying words, hollow in meaning yet charged with emotion, which gained treacherous momentum when the prestige of one's nation seemed sullied. To make her point about the role played by manipulative words in accelerating or slowing a nation's entry into fruitless conflicts, she called on an ancient classic tale: the *Iliad*.

Weil's first reading of Homer's epic poem—in the Lycée Henri IV with Alain—had captivated her with its beauty and forthright portrayal of human character traits. She reread the *Iliad* in Greek many times, translated long passages into French, taught the poem in her philosophy classes, and in several ways held the poetic narration of this ten-year war up to a new and unexpected light. Like Alain, she believed that great literature opened up philosophical insights by reflecting true aspects of human nature. More than anything else, she believed that looking attentively and objectively at human nature would encourage human beings to understand their behavior and their options.

The essay appeared in four parts during early April 1937 in *Nouveaux Cahiers,* a journal published by a study group of academics, civil servants, and industrialists, in which Weil was an active participant and contributor to the journal. Their discussions, focusing on contemporary problems of domestic and foreign affairs, inspired her to speak out once again against war. The title, "Let Us Not Recommence the Trojan War," is usually translated into English as "The Power of Words" because it initially appeared under the title "Le pouvoir des mots," which sums up its main theme. Weil had originally entitled her piece "For a Little Clarity," but after having seen and appreciated a production of Jean Giraudoux's successful play, extolled in the pacifist press, "La Guerre de Troie n'aura pas lieu," she chose to create a resonance with Giraudoux's title and with the impending threat.[19]

In her essay, Weil looked at the destructive use of new technology and placed the blame for it squarely on human beings. Human beings decided the use of resources, so they had to be fully aware of the consequences of their choices. "If the peril [of ruins and massacres] is so grave, it is without doubt, in part, because of the power of the weapons of destruction that technology has put into our hands; but these arms don't go off by themselves, and it is not honest to blame inert matter when we hold full responsibility."[20]

From here she launched straight into her topic: the manipulation of emotion-laden words flaunted as absolutes—*democracy, tyranny, communism, capitalism, nation, security, authority, order, freedom.* Words tossed about in this way became misleading, according to Weil. Like the gods in Greek mythology, impassioned empty words brandished as rallying slogans goaded people into conflicts that ultimately had no definable goal. Such words, left vague and undefined, were often starkly juxtaposed in pairs of opposites: *dictatorship* versus *democracy* or *honor* versus *shame.* In this fashion, they obscured what the actual goals of a conflict were and whether these were congruent with each other. But a conflict that lacked a specific goal or had incoherent goals had no criteria for either measuring success or negotiating a sensible compromise. The rationale for continuing it therefore ended up being the sacrifices that had already been made: past sacrifices perpetually called for new sacrifices, so the carnage rolled on until there was nothing left to sacrifice. "If we seize one of those words all swollen with blood and tears, in an effort to compress it, we find it has no content. Those words that do have a content and a meaning are not murderous."[21]

Weil construed the role of the abducted Helen as analogous to these empty mobilizing words. Other than Paris, no one on either side cared at all for Helen, but the relentless pursuit of illusory honor represented by this woman continued to its bloody and barren end. The value of the struggle was measured by the price each side paid. When the Greeks were tempted to return home, Homer brought in Minerva to evoke the sacrifices of the Greeks' dead compatriots, as if to suggest that the war could not be stopped because the dead did not wish it. (Here Weil again took a stab at Poincaré, who in 1917 had used the same argument.) Several times, reasonable warriors on each side proposed reasonable conditions for ending the carnage, but each time someone burst forth with an emotional tirade, clamoring for victory, war trophies, courage, heroes, honor, and so on. Spurred on by the gods or by human nature, the war could not be stopped: it had taken on a momentum of its own. "To push humankind to the most absurd catastrophes," wrote Weil, "neither gods nor secret conspiracies are needed, human nature suffices."[22]

For Weil, Homer's tale highlighted humankind's inability to deal rationally with force. She inveighed against the inability to apply elementary methods of reasonable thought to crucial social dilemmas. Though physical science had at its disposal a storehouse of refined intellectual mechanisms for applying criteria to its discipline, modern civilization appeared to have lost essential notions of limit, measure, degree, proportion, and necessary relationships between means and results.[23] Without the gauge of specified attainable goals, people lost sight of their own best interest. Even those in power could not imagine the wheel of fate turning against them, no matter how far they overextended their reach. In her conclusion, Weil insisted that for present-day problems one could not blame gods or international capitalist trusts or any other scapegoat; the fault rested with human nature. She wrote: "To clarify notions, discredit words congenitally empty, define the use of others through precise analysis, is, as strange as it might appear, a labor that could save innumerable human lives. [But] our era seems to be inept at this task."[24]

According to Weil, any decision making for or against war required reliance on explicit methods of evaluating the potential impacts of war and all its alternatives. Although *dictatorship* and *democracy* might appear to be polar opposites in the extent of order and freedom they each implied, the two terms had significance only in relation to a social structure. Democratic nations had elements of tight control over behavior even though a high degree of liberty was enjoyed, and dictatorships carried a heavy burden of historic baggage that affected the amount of control a despot could actually exploit.

While an adversary needed to consider how a particular dictatorship could be altered without resort to war, citizens of a democracy needed to realize that mobilization for war entailed severe restriction of freedoms. The people could find themselves living in an increasingly totalitarian state even as they fought to defend their freedom against outsiders. As a temporary sacrifice, such a situation might be accepted with sufficient goodwill, but the vital danger remained that despotic conditions could become permanent, as had happened in the past all too often. In Weil's choice of arguments, one reads alarm for her countrymen faced with the likelihood of having to defend their homeland by force. She wanted them to evaluate carefully all that they stood to lose, for they could lose a great deal.

Fresh from her activism against oppressive internal working conditions, Weil saw that basic principles from class struggle applied to conflicts in general, including those between nations. Since there was always social tension in relationships between groups within a society as well as between societies, there was a constant mutual level of wariness between those holding much power and those with little or none. She knew that a balance between those who commanded and those who obeyed could never be stable, nor should it be, for competition between unequals entailed exploitation. By the nature of things, each side had to grapple continually to retain or achieve more power. Those on top of the ladder strove to keep the status quo, where they had control. Those on the lowest rungs had to fight to keep their basic rights as human beings. This contest was endless, but it was not war. Society's delicate balance of powers had to be constantly realigned, and ways had to be sought to reorder ever-shifting relationships of stronger and weaker groups without resort to violence. A parallel existed in international relations between stronger and weaker nations. Nations had to endure an ever-present instability involving perceived power and prestige, just as workers had to insist unflinchingly on their dignity as contributing members of society.

To inspire her readers with the idea that struggles for dignity were perennial, Weil drew on historical incidents to prove that conflicts could be successfully resolved without resort to violent means. She had two favorite inspiring examples of success in competitive bids for equal treatment: the Plebeians' uprising in ancient Rome and the peaceful workers' occupation of the factories in June 1936—a luminous moment for Weil from which she often drew reassurance. Both rebellions eventually led to the respect and the concessions that the rebels had been seeking. When the Roman nobility faced an exterior threat at one point, the Plebeians adamantly refused to give any assistance to ward off a threatened enemy attack, knowing that once again their sole reward would be empty promises. Their determined preparations for immediate emigration forced the Roman noble families to concede to their demand for the election of tribunes of plebs (spokesmen) who could represent them in future cases of unjust treatment. Two millennia later, the same adamancy on the part of French workers earned them better workplace conditions, namely, paid vacations, more reasonable hours, and the right to send elected delegates to factory officials' meetings, a privilege that still exists in twenty-first century France.

Weil warned that prestige was illusory and limitless; no nation or people ever had enough or was sure of keeping any imagined glory. As shown in the *Iliad*, the situation was always tenuous. She explained: "If Priam and Hector had surrendered Helen to the Greeks, they could have incited the Greeks to sack a town so poorly prepared for its own defense. The Trojans would have also risked a general uprising in Troy, not because returning Helen would have incensed them, but because they would feel their leaders were not sufficiently powerful."[25]

Although slogans and abstractions were illusory, they caused pain for living, breathing human beings. Credulous followers became trapped in mortal confrontations because of unexamined assumptions of national pride. Modern techniques of propaganda, spread far and wide by modern media, hoodwinked the gullible, who in turn learned too late of their need to protect themselves from words that seemed to reveal a good but actually were designed to manipulate.

Weil saw that force throve on force in a spiral without end unless people came to their senses. In her observation, all modern nations sought to avoid the loss of prestige by improving their ability to wage war. This competition set in motion the ludicrous cycle of going to war to conserve and increase the means to wage war: that is, the man- power, resources, and armaments. France, she pointed out, had un- scrupulously risked war over Morocco in 1911, not for basic necessities, but for that particular North African colony's ability to keep the French economy viable, due to its raw materials, jobs, and human beings, who were exploited as cannon fodder in both world wars. Oil, she stated caustically, was much more likely to provoke war than was wheat. "In truth, if one examines modern history, one arrives at the conclusion that national interest signifies for each state the ability to wage war";[26] thus national security meant depriving all other nations of the capacity of waging war. No one knew why a nation had to continue to make war, any more than the Trojans knew why they had to keep Helen.[27]

National leaders subscribed to the hallucinatory goal of having the means to wage war, even though the expensive arms race belittled human life and rode roughshod over individuals. Weil suggested that a careful look into the word *nation* would uncover millions of cadavers, orphans, and war-mutilated survivors, as well as a great deal of despair and tears. She had no illusion that either unilateral disarmament or general disarmament was even conceivable, but she did want people to deal honestly with an essential contradiction in social relationships: "All social situations rest on a parity of forces, a balance of pressures analogous to that of fluids. Different countries' prestige cannot be equated; prestige has no limits, all pretensions of prestige detract from the prestige and dignity of others. Consequently, all prestige is insepa- rable from power."[28]

Absurdly, striving to maintain a nation's prestige could lead to its destruction if candid rationality were not brought to bear on the facts of the situation. Weil, in her resolute fashion, was alerting her countrymen and all her readers to the inanities that led to bloody conflict. She wanted to encourage clear thinking about crucial conditions that furthered war or peace and to warn against hasty solutions whose facile appeal to the emotions initiated a lethal spiral of violence. Her erudite but accessible "Power of Words" essay was aimed at fellow intellectuals, who would immediately grasp the significance of her allusions to ancient history and to recent European events and politicians, as well as to familiar, catchall phrases of propaganda.

The Trojan War served as Weil's framework to bring to the fore contemporary social, political, and economic struggles and their relation to questions of war and violence, as well as the use of inflammatory political language that pushed citizens toward war. She agreed with Heraclites that struggle was the condition of life. Therefore, to minimize their exposure to war people had to discern between the real conditions of their lives, which involved both a struggle for dignity and elusive dreams of prestigious power over others. To Weil, pacifist conciliation still made more obvious sense than returning force with force; hence, the tendency for people to allow themselves to be led into violent confrontations by leaders who manifestly did not have their best interest at heart remained an enigma, though one that surely had a solution.

THE FEW IN CONTROL OF THE MANY

In all that is social, there is force. Balance alone nullifies force.

Weil, Notebooks

As war grew nearer, Weil puzzled over the self-destructive lure of power. She intuitively felt that the laws governing human behavior could be uncovered and could facilitate setting up guidelines for more compassionate social behavior. She perceptively saw parallels in the physical laws of the universe and in human behavior: a falling body in the material world gained an increase of kinetic energy as it descended, and vile motives in humans had more driving energy than did higher motives.[29] Yet although gravity was the force par excellence in the universe, even gravity's downward pull had counteracting forces: for example, the energies of the sun's rays that made plants grow upward. These observations led to her pivotal conclusion that supernatural grace performed a similar elevating function against the downward pull of self-serving actions.

With these analogies, Weil tried to imagine a social organization that would allow members to amass radiant energies that would foster conditions of justice and liberty. But her progress in this theory was blocked by her inability to explain an absurd but all-too-common phenomenon: many individuals obediently submitted to the authority of a few (or to one), even when it was clearly to their disadvantage. To explore this phenomenon of willing subservience, Weil evoked the work of Estienne de la Boétie, a sixteenth-century political theorist. In her essay "Meditation on Obedience and Liberty," Weil incorporated two new elements into La Boétie's ideas on the vulnerability of human nature due to its pliability: the role of force in human relationships and the opposing role of grace, whether acting in the individual or—more rarely—in a massive peaceful uprising for justice.[30]

Weil recognized that moral gravity created a drive to exploit social inequality and that only powerful counteracting forces could restore fairness and justice to social imbalance. Weil found those positive forces in the human capacity for thought, love, and the freedom to consent to supernatural love (i.e., to actively seek the grace to love all one's neighbors). Because these positive forces superficially appeared weak, those who wished to bring some form of justice into the political domain had to go against the tide of public opinion. Consequently, suffering became an inevitable part of any efforts to rectify injustice.

The Moscow Purge Trials, conducted between 1936 and 1938 as a climax of Stalin's Great Purge, in which millions of Russians were executed, reinforced Weil's intent to explore the enigma of willing subservience. From 1936 through 1938, political rivals and critics of Stalin, both real and potential, were publicly condemned as traitors and executed on fabricated evidence. Stalin coerced prominent Old Bolsheviks into confessing nonexistent crimes, and millions of alleged "enemies of the people" were cold-bloodedly packed off to prison camps. Weil had long since lost any confidence in the Stalinist regime as a worker

state, but this wholesale liquidation of lives intensified for her the rid-
dle of civil obedience. Why did great masses of humanity obey even to
the point of allowing one man to make an entire generation bleed?
When compliance was as dangerous as rebellion, what pushed the
many to continue obeying? Weil noted cryptically in her notebooks:
"In all that is social, there is force."[31]

In her 1937–38 theoretical essay, Weil focused on the quirk in
human nature that allowed those in power, though limited in numbers, to keep exploitative control over their far more numerous subjects. She was confounded by the complicity of the deluded victims in
maintaining this injustice. Their collaboration, contrary to their best
interest, contradicted natural phenomena, for it was as if the gram
could weigh more than the kilo.[32] She wondered how man could be
subject to different rules than nature, and why.

La Boétie, in *The Politics of Obedience: The Discourse of Voluntary
Servitude,* had speculated on the same phenomenon, calling it simply
Contr'un (Against One). Echoes of the sentiments expressed by this
distinguished political philosopher resonate throughout Weil's writings, though she rarely mentions his name. She does refer to her tender attachment to a "young Stoic straight out of the pages of Plutarch,
La Boétie," in a 1937 letter to her friend Jean Posternak.[33]

La Boétie's two fundamental premises—rule rests on the consent
of the masses and natural liberty has great value—had Weil's full
agreement. But she reproached this sixteenth-century humanist for
leaving unanswered a basic question: Why did the mass of people
allow themselves to be shackled by the few? In addition, she rejected
his assertion that greater numbers made force; on the contrary, she insisted, "Despite what our imagination leads us to believe, number is
weakness."[34] She offered contemporary examples to prove her point:
twenty men in the street could easily beat up a single man, but it took
only one or two white men to mercilessly whip twenty Annamite
coolies.[35] This illustration from France's abusive rule in Indochina
(Annam) again showed her dismay over the evil effects of colonialism;
Weil never ceased advocating for the underdog. But she understood
that a small group had the ability to establish cohesiveness, whereas a
larger group remained a cumbersome juxtaposition of individuals with
little defense against tyrannous rule.

La Boétie's reflections on the nature of tyranny and on the natural liberty of the people to consent or not consent to governmental power led him to suggest a simple and obvious solution: since tyranny was grounded on general popular consent, the tyrant would fall if the people simply joined together to withdraw their consent to obey. Weil desperately wanted to know why did they not do so. She agreed with La Boétie that "if [men] really wanted [liberty], they would receive it" and that if human beings persisted in valuing and honing their ability to think rationally they could not be enslaved.[36] Since the capacity for thought could not be taken from individuals, why did they neglect to use it? This was a persistent refrain for both thinkers and one that pre-occupied Weil to the end of her life.

La Boétie stressed, as did Weil, that nature had made human be-ings all free, thinking individuals and that men would much prefer to be "guided by reason itself than to be ordered about by the whims of a single man."[37] The resilience of the capacity to reason was, however, subject to chance. "There is in our souls some native seed of reason, which, if nourished by good counsel and training, flowers into virtue, but which, on the other hand, if unable to resist the vices surrounding it, is stifled and blighted."[38] Weil also believed in the necessity of edu-cation and social support to guide a person to apply eternal values to decisions involving human relationships. Just as the love of liberty was tenuous, men got used to subjection and eventually did not find it bitter.[39] La Boétie added: "It is incredible how, as soon as a people becomes subject, they promptly fall into such complete forgetfulness of freedom that they can hardly be roused to the point of regaining it, obeying so easily and so willingly that one is led to say, on beholding such a situation, that this people has not so much lost its liberty as won its enslavement."[40]

La Boétie's reflections buttressed Weil's continued insistence on the need for apprenticeship in strengthening one's capacity to freely consent. Cherishing liberty was dependent on an early training that inculcated a love of freedom, for man instinctively followed the ten-dencies of custom, education, and example.[41] "The good seed that na-ture plants in us is so slight and so slippery that it cannot withstand the least harm from wrong nourishment."[42] Chaos in the social sphere disrupts the ability to calmly reflect and to maintain one's sense of autonomy and viability. Human beings, she wrote, needed constant protection from succumbing to this susceptibility to feeling alone and adrift.

The malleability of the human spirit in both the strong and the weak became an increasing concern for Weil. She noted the human tendency for the subservient to think it was in their nature to obey and for the powerful who commanded to believe that they were naturally superior. Each action of obeying and commanding reconfirmed these mutual but debilitating attitudes. She deduced from this trait of human nature the importance of exterior reinforcement, for the most heroic of intellects faced a great challenge to maintain a belief in his or her personal sense of value without external reassurances. This dangerous vulnerability in human nature explained in part the ability of the organized few to keep an iron control over a disparate mass of people.

La Boétie, referring to human pliability, wrote that custom could have more influence than native ability. "It cannot be denied that nature is influential in shaping us to her will and making us reveal our rich or meager endowment; yet it must be admitted that she has less power over us than custom, for the reason that native endowment, no matter how good, is dissipated unless encouraged, whereas environment always shapes us in its own way—whatever that may be, in spite of nature's gifts."[43]

The extraordinary could occur; some heroic figures did stand out despite all odds and reclaim their full dignity by refusing slavish compliance to another's arbitrary will. "There are always a few, better endowed than others, who feel the weight of the yoke and cannot restrain themselves from attempting to shake it off: these are the men who never become tamed under subjection. . . . Having good minds of their own, they have further trained them by study and learning. Even if liberty had entirely perished from the earth, such men would invent it. For them slavery has no satisfactions, no matter how well disguised."[44]

These were the individuals who kept the love of liberty alive, but they were few and paid a great price.[45] In Weil's mystical philosophy, they were consciously or unconsciously receptive to God's grace and were living this presence through their actions impregnated with love of neighbor. She knew that compassionate and pure political actions demanded a courageous selflessness on the part of valiant souls who would, nevertheless, be scorned by their contemporaries and by history. Only openness to God's grace could produce the miracle of steadfast support for the weak against the strong.[46] Not even Christ as a human being was exempt from experiencing uncertainty; Weil often gave the example of Christ on the cross, who, having momentarily lost the sense of his mission, cried out in despair: "My God, my God, why have you forsaken me?"

History shows that rare waves of inspiration can pass over a mass of humankind, inspiring men and women to rise up as one and claim their due. Such occasions made the powerful tremble. Weil's previously mentioned two examples, one ancient and one modern, often appeared in her writing as she presented them for different purposes. Tacitus, in book 1 of his *Annales,* described a nonviolent military mutiny by the aggrieved legions of the ancient tribes of Germany against the feared Roman centurions in 14 AD. "The strongest symptom of a wide-spread and intractable commotion, was the fact that, instead of being divided or instigated by a few persons, the [defiant] were unanimous in their fury and equally unanimous in their composure, with so uniform a consistency that one would have thought them to be under command."[47]

In describing French workers' peaceful occupation of the factories in 1936, Weil wryly observed that had the bourgeois factory owners remembered their history they would have seen that the workers' action, like that of the German legions in Tacitus, showed an inner discipline and no need of an outside agitator.[48] This successful mass action by determined and unruffled workers was a source of boundless satisfaction for Weil, but she realized that unfortunately the exhilarating power of such protests could not last among workers who had urgent everyday tasks to face. The remembrance of their moral and material success would linger, but eventually even that would fade. The new masters would quickly see the importance of forestalling and squelching all popular movements, for the subordinates' struggle for dignity was never-ending.

Weil concluded her "Meditation" with the frank assessment that all ventures of lucid thinking or unselfish love of neighbor, ambiguous as they might be, were considered subversive by despotic authorities who maintained social order by mystifying their right to rule. To break down demeaning social and political hierarchies, one had to demystify and desanctify the state apparatus through education and recognize values that were above brute force. Obviously, such values were the enemy of rulers who engineered, with alluring propaganda, the consent of the populace and who would severely penalize a maverick. Weil went beyond La Boétie by stating that force inevitably corrupted both sides but that constant struggles for power within a society were in the nature of things. "For whoever loves liberty, it is not desirable that these struggles disappear, but only that they remain within a certain limit of violence."[49] The formula of doing the least harm had to be applied with cold lucidity to any effort to remedy the misuse of social force.

For Weil, apprenticeship and education were essential for reducing the evil effects of moral gravity and for embracing the infinite worth of thought and love. Learning to confront aggression without violence takes courage and dogged patience. Weil's materialist reasoning and pacifism still held a central place in her thinking, so she was certain that rationality could thwart the fast-approaching war. She floated her last proposals for conciliation, one of which caused her deep remorse later on. At the same time, the foundation of her beliefs was shifting toward an affirmation that would eventually permeate her future writing and thinking: the supernatural destiny of humankind.

INJUSTICE FOR INJUSTICE

An injustice for injustice, since there must be one in any case,
let us choose the one that holds the least risk of war.

Weil, "Europe at War for Czechoslovakia?"

As a last resort, Weil proposed that Hitler be given rights over Sudetenland. She sensed that the coming conflagration would be so terrible that conceding certain injustices could preserve many individual souls and cultures from excessive harm. Peace was worth yielding to Hitler's immediate requests and rejecting any belligerent moves. In this mode she wrote her last polemic for pacifism, in which she sought alternatives to violent conflict. She wanted to believe that her fellow human beings, envisioning the inevitable dire consequences of violence, would go to extremes to avoid war, but she was losing heart. She railed against France's hypocrisy, inconsistency, and failure to support the rights of man doctrine, and she made a proposition for conceding part of Czechoslovakia.

In this essay, "Europe at War for Czechoslovakia?" written in 1938 for a review founded by her colleagues in the Committee of Vigilant Antifascist Intellectuals (CVIA), Weil pragmatically ranked potential reactions to Hitler's menace.[50] Reasoning that war and ways to circumvent it had to be honestly calculated in order to compare respective sacrifices and merits, she reminded her readers that military aggression was not only the least desirable response but also the most costly. Her succinct formula for causing the least possible harm led her to advocate a grave injustice in view of the situation. Given that the stakes were extremely high, she held all aspects of the dilemma up to the harsh light of logic, asking, Should France send her sons to their death for an incoherent principle or instead accept a humiliating erosion of her prestige?

In Weil's opinion, France's actions had already tarnished that illusory prestige because of past political decisions and the shameful conditions at home and in its empire. The French government's insistence that the treaty safeguarding Czechoslovakia be honored was to Weil a mockery because France had self-servingly broken her own agreement in 1911 regarding the status of Morocco. That breach of treaty had risked a war with Emperor William II of Germany. If France had broken her word then, Weil argued, she could as easily break a treaty now to avoid war. Weil wanted honesty from France so that it could once again provide the honorable leadership so badly needed in the joint efforts to prevent the coming conflict.

As a matter of honor, any nation telling others what to do should frankly examine and rectify its own moral failings. The fifty million colonial subjects who lived in quasi-slavery and the many oppressed people within France's borders undercut any claim to moral superiority. The hypocrisy of going to war for others' rights while not according rights to those within France's domain vitiated any claim of honor or of righteousness. By her prodding tone, Weil reminded her country-men that France's support of the rights of man needed more than just words. She believed that by responsibly observing the doctrine of human rights that had originated on its soil, France could once again be a much-needed beacon to other peoples struggling to preserve their unique sense of identity.

The crucial issue was whether the chance for peace would be in-creased by guaranteeing the borders of Czechoslovakia or by abandon-ing Czechoslovakia to its fate. Though Weil conjectured that only force would stop Hitler from taking over the border states, she questioned whether the French people were ready to sacrifice the blood of their young men for Czechoslovakia.[51] Her implied response, inclined to-ward giving peace an extended chance by not using military might against the Nazis, revealed her still slim hope that Hitler might be rea-sonable.

The reality of Hitler's intentions was another matter, however. Even though Weil knew that Hitler's racist ideology required periodic and brutal affirmations of power, she still opted to accept on good faith his claims for what was rightfully German territory. If Hitler wanted to regain the Sudetenland, which the Versailles Treaty had taken from the German nation, Weil philosophically proposed that he had some basis for that. If nations honestly supported Woodrow Wilson's Fourteen Points, particularly a people's right to self-determination, the fact that the majority of German speakers in Sudetenland had never had the op-portunity to decide their fate posed a real problem of consistency. This same indifference to a people's right to choose had occurred in 1919, when the fate of the Austrian German-speaking population had been decided for them without their consent. If a rectification of frontiers would satisfy Hitler, she reasoned, perhaps that should be granted. Since the victors at Versailles had unilaterally decided without a refer-endum to give part of Germany to Czechoslovakia, Weil suggested that by returning the territory to Germany Europe might extend the peace.

Weil even went to the extreme injustice of counseling that, given Hitler's anticommunism and anti-Semitism, the Czechs could agree to restrict communists and Jews to less important civil functions. She self-deceptively assumed that the safeguard of their culture, language, and ethnic characteristics could be assured. This hypothetical concession, entirely consistent with her method of first evaluating objectively all possible alternatives and then imagining their consequences, became a source of deep dismay for her when Hitler's full aggressive intentions became evident.

Weil understood the painful reality that the grand principle of "European stability" was constructed on war. If hegemony in Central Europe fell to Germany, the perceived balance of power between nations would be seriously altered. France wanted to keep its hegemony in Europe, but France could not, in good conscience, accept only its own hegemony without considering that of others. A modern nation was forced into the position of flaunting the illusory prestige of being the stronger or being taken for the weaker. Sadly, Weil acknowledged that the absence of any measure to gauge national power made armed conflict inevitable when two nations simultaneously felt the need to be the stronger. But there was a downside to being the dominating power, for hegemony created its own strain within a nation. Who could say that maintaining a position of power among countries would not eventually wear out a nation from the inside? Weil initiated the provocative idea of letting the country in a position of overweening authority run down its internal mechanism. She posited that Germany's sustainability in a position of domination might well not be durable; this experiment, not yet purposefully tried, would be far less costly than war.

"Europe at War for Czechoslovakia?" is a highly controversial piece of Weil's writing that benefits from being contextualized within her multilayered designs. Her concession that the Czech government should be allowed to marginalize Jews and communists, so hated by the Nazi regime, in order to keep the peace merits a harsh judgment. But what led her to this point was a willingness to weigh all options, not indifference to the well-being of others. She later condemned the limitations of her wholehearted commitment to peace. In light of the genocide that took place, what she considered at the time as a compensatory sacrifice to avoid the horrors of war appears reprehensible today.

Philosophically, by putting a mirror up to France, Weil wanted to shame her beloved country into facing publicly its own moral failings and to persuade readers that the rationale for this war could lead to endless wars. She, among many others, had not yet grasped the full extent of Hitler's megalomania. Many in both France and Britain—not only advocates of appeasement—had failed to discern that the riots and provocative incidents taking place among the German population in Sudetenland had been fomented on instructions from Berlin, with the intention of encouraging the impression that ceding the region to Germany might prevent war. Behind the scenes, "Hitler was using the Sudetenland as a pretext for the eventual takeover of all of Czechoslovakia."[52] Hindsight allows us a clearer evaluation of the various options than were evident in 1938–39. Weil's determination to look at all sides clearly and to confront candidly her own cherished homeland's abuses of power is an exemplar of probing reflection and some of its pitfalls.

To her profound dismay, Weil discovered that she had underestimated Hitler. Although her personal sense of guilt for having promoted the pacifist "ideology" was unassuageable, she never denied her own responsibility for having encouraged conciliation. Conscience-stricken, she acknowledged her miscalculation. She spurned pacifism as no longer having validity for the current circumstances and believed she had indulged in wishful thinking while terrible headaches muddled her mind. As always, she refused to hold onto an idea or theory after it was shown to be insufficient to serve a positive purpose.

She was not alone in realizing that the ardent wish for peace had done irreparable harm. There is evidence that advocates for appeasement may have given Hitler an inestimable advantage. Gordon Wright, a prominent historian of modern French history, suggests that the predilection for peace on the part of both politicians and the public allowed Hitler to seize the initiative in armaments and gain a lead of two or three years over the Western powers.[53] Wright explained:

[In 1936,] every one of the alternatives still open to France was either risky or potentially disastrous. Frenchmen were therefore quite naturally tempted to slip into a mood of wishful thinking, to avoid choosing any one of these evils and to hope that, after all, Hitler might be reasonable in spite of all appearances to the contrary. Even the leading figures of the Popular Front were affected by this mood. Although they were loudly and unanimously anti-fascist, in fact, they were divided into two camps: those who held that any concessions would be dangerous, and those who hoped that Hitler might behave if given a little rope.[54]

Ultimately, along with recognizing that force had a central place in the human condition, Weil accepted that sometimes, though only with carefully weighed good cause, men of goodwill had to deploy force. Hitler's aggression caused her to alter her direction and to attend to the urgent need of making others aware of the inherent place that power—and its consort, prestige—held in human aspirations. Nevertheless, war required explicit methods for evaluating ends and means; her insistence on this need was based on keen empirical observations of human behavior and knowledge of past history. A nation's constant need to display its invincibility could lead to endless war. At this point, Weil embarked on the quest for a new strategy to limit force's corrupting power when conditions compelled people to defend their homeland. In her concern over how to use force, yet keep it from spiraling out of control and demoralizing everyone it touched, she devised her own variation on a just-war theory. While she accepted the use of force in very limited circumstances, she never again advocated accommodation when faced with an unconscionable deployment of force.

CHAPTER TWO
The Empire of Force

The handmaid of war is despair; this despair
exists everywhere man is sacrificed.

Weil, Notebooks

Simone Weil now faced notions that were conflicting and difficult to reconcile: force is an inherent part of social interaction; force must be used, albeit on limited occasions; and force contaminates both wielder and sufferer. She began to explore this conundrum in her writing. In a brief sketch for an essay entitled "Reflections on Barbarity" she elaborated on the necessity of acknowledging the inherent human tendency toward barbarity (or brute force) if one were to effectively offset impending violence. In her "Reflections in View of an Assessment," she weighed the dangers pressing in on her country, while extracting insights from the tragedy of the breached Munich Accords. That defeat became her impetus for imagining innovative diplomatic techniques to employ in times when war appeared imminent. In an elegant literary essay entitled "The *Iliad,* or the Poem of Force," she made a strong case for the self-perpetuating capacity of brute force that could destroy men's souls. Her notebooks reveal her continued preoccupation with war as force par excellence, with bureaucracy as an anonymous, institutionalized form of force, and with finding ways by which force could be used as an instrument for the good. In this chapter, we examine Weil's adjustment to the reality that resorting to force was necessary at times and that choosing the means to attain the desired ends required lucidity, constant evaluation, and a true reading of the interior play of political tendencies within one's own nation.

REFLECTIONS ON BARBARITY

Except for an effort of generosity as rare as that of genius,
one is always barbaric toward the weak.

Weil, Notebooks

In "Reflections on Barbarity," Weil stated, "Barbarity is a permanent and universal characteristic of human nature and develops more or less according to the circumstances that give it play."[1] She elaborated that one society should not consider itself superior to another with respect to its potential for barbarous behavior, for the distribution of political power within a society decided the degree of barbarity unleashed. A centralized harsh authority, lacking firmly grounded ethical values, opened the floodgates for the tendency toward cruelty, which had an ingrained place in the makeup of every person and hence in every society. She considered that the real threat to the European people from Germany came in a form of oppressive colonization that would destroy their very souls. This tightly controlled type of civilization, devoid of moral criteria, substituted inferior values for those that had withstood the test of time. All people, therefore, had the obligation to protect the existence of their society, from which they drew spiritual nourishment through roots sunk deeply in its heritage.

Weil rejected in this essay her compatriots' patronizing judgment that the coming clash pitted the civilized forces of Europe against the brute force of Nazi barbarians. France's sense of superiority in relation to Germany came from not reading the situation accurately. A false sense of superiority clouded clear thinking, as did resorting to superficial labels. Neither *civilized* nor *barbarian* necessarily implied a quality for good or evil outside a specified context, so Weil wanted her people to accurately assess their own merits before choosing the best methods of self-defense. As defenders of human dignity and freedom, they had to be conscious that force was ever-present and thus continuously scrutinize their choice of means for achieving specific goals.

Weil blamed her countrymen's overconfidence in their level of civilization for giving them an unjustified feeling of self-righteousness. The terms *civilized* and *barbarian* referred to the complexity of society, she pointed out, not to its moral behavior. The form of cruel force implied in barbarity was inherent in human nature; historical evidence had unfortunately proved that advancement in civilization did not inspire humankind to forego indiscriminate slaughter. Individuals' perceptions of situations deeply concerned Weil, for a person's readings of events could inspire hope or lead to despair. The tendencies of one's thoughts either amassed vital energy or dissipated it.

According to Weil's observation, a civilized people who took for granted their moral virtues were particularly vulnerable to manipulation by shrewd propaganda and to utterly barbarous behavior. Nothing was more dangerous for a race, a nation, a social class, or a political party than to consider itself the proud bearer of civilization and, by inference, immune from committing acts of inhumanity. She alleged, "The acceptance of war in 1914 was rendered far easier because the people didn't believe it could be savage, since it was waged by men considered exempt from savagery."[2]

A civilized society with a high level of intellectual, cultural, and material development and with sophistication in the arts, sciences, and political institutions could impose its technology on others with a far more devastating effect than could a barbarian culture with its simpler level of social and economic organization. To Weil, Hitler was far from being a barbarian, as some of her scornful countrymen had categorized him; quite to the contrary, he astutely understood the phenomenon of capturing the imagination of his victims and paralyzing their ability to react. The real danger, in Weil's eyes, lay in his centralized bureaucratic state, organized around debased values that vitiated morality and subordinated the individual to society. Germany, for her in 1939, epitomized that menace.

Weil's analysis offered the hope of finding a better way to counter the recurrent menace to human values, in this case, from Hitler's National Socialism. In her way of thinking, if one observed how power was shared in a society, one could rank it according to a scale of human values in which brute force was considered an evil and its absence a good. For a variety of self-serving reasons, however, not everyone held this view. Agreement on it, a necessary preliminary for safeguarding a community's unique culture and for eliminating injustices, faced many obstacles, but then Weil set great store in the value of confronting a challenge. Understanding how power was exercised in a society accorded wholly with her maturing conviction, clearly stated in "Reflections on Barbarity," that "one cannot even begin to form any clear ideas on the relationships between human beings as long as one has not put the notion of force at their very center."[3]

This brief composition gives an intimation of ideas that Weil would elaborate in her prodigious output during her final three years: using an eternal set of values to read a situation correctly, rejecting the oppressive force built into a centralized bureaucratic government, and assessing the tensions of power within a society. With great anxiety for the future of France, she also began to articulate what would become the central theme of her final work: the importance of respecting the individual's vital need for roots. Each rooted community offered its members an essential bridge from the material world to the eternal: a gateway created and sustained by distinct traditions, culture, language, and rituals. Cultural ties to a specific past, with an orientation toward a future, were essential to being human. Manipulative, coldly calculated domination, such as colonization, put those ties at risk. The peril of a long-standing community's extinction was to be feared and deterred at all costs, even by the use of force. Brute force, in the service of either defending or destroying deep communal roots, spread corruption. Weil maintained that those who lowered themselves to the enemy's level of violence would have little chance of regaining the moral high ground. Continual self-scrutiny of means and ends was needed to oppose Hitler's skill in physically and psychologically overpowering his victims.

Events were moving very fast, and Weil worried about the inability of her contemporaries to concentrate in an atmosphere of fear. She urged negotiation and exploration of peaceable solutions that honored and protected the individual. In her opinion, the daily insecurity was affecting the spiritual and moral well-being of all. She wrote, "We are placed in conditions of existence such that disarray touches and corrupts all the aspects of human life, all sources of activities, of hope, and of happiness."[4] While total security would never be possible or even desirable for individuals, anxiety over a coming war that would leave nothing of their heritage intact was undermining everyone's abilities to think, to be courageous, and to plan for the future.[5] Weil wanted the defenders of their very lives and their cultural existence to abide by values "not of this world," values whose source was the supernatural. Her readers had the obligation to protect the country in which they had sent down roots, but their actions must comply with moral criteria.

"REFLECTIONS IN VIEW OF AN ASSESSMENT"

If ever politics consisted in being an art, it does now.

Weil, "Reflections in View of an Assessment"

Weil considered lucidity essential to gauge the moral quality and effectiveness of any action taken to meet international aggression. Those who could still think rationally had to systematically measure all potential courses of action against the menace of being colonized by Hitler's dictatorship. She estimated the threat to the continued independence of the European nations to be as serious as the peril the Greeks had faced when confronted by the Roman legions. Although extreme circumstances could require the use of force to hinder invaders, the deployment of force carried its own evil. New approaches to averting war had to be imagined and tried. Weil offered her alternative: a flexible give and take between adversarial nations that could extend the period of suspension between the state of peace and the "state of the danger of war" (a German expression that Weil appropriated). A primary goal was to keep the minds of her countrymen open to innovative diplomacy as a flexible strategy between giving in to subjugation and waging all-out war. Even if the technique failed, a reasoned purposeful negotiation based on firm moral grounds would sustain the dignity of individuals. Readers can discern in this essay her quickening interest in finding ways to affect interpretations or readings of situations that could nurture positive attitudes in a people. Realistic attention given to the fragility of one's nation and pride in its honest, consistent support of liberty could help it survive.

Weil composed her "Reflections in View of an Assessment" after Hitler's annexation of Czechoslovakia and Great Britain's decision to begin conscription (April 27, 1939).[6] Hitler's advance into Prague had demolished her cautious optimism after the Munich Accords; but the British conscription was also a harsh blow. She explored psychological aspects of national integrity, prestige, preparations for fighting, oppressive domestic policies, and international diplomacy.

Though Weil believed that individuals needed to maintain roots in a hereditary culture, she speculated over the paradox that the very existence of a nation seemed to give present-day war its perennial impetus. Since a modern nation's continued existence appeared to depend on war unlimited, peace could also be catastrophic if its parameters included an imperious need to ensure against all possible attacks from without. This condition implied the elimination of all adversaries who might imperil a nation's security, instigating perpetual competition between nations, each of whom wished to be the most formidable. She knew that "a nation never renounces defending its independence for ideological reasons, but only because it deems itself, rightly or wrongly, militarily powerless."[7] And since each nation had to acquire the prestige of being stronger than all other nations, it inevitably gave less attention to the well-being of its people. For their prestige, nations had to keep a facade of inviolate power that in fact could not be maintained, for reputation and power were illusory and inconstant. Given that full security through unassailability was not an obtainable goal, war had become unlimited because theoretically it had no obtainable object.

Appearing to be the strongest depended on the other states' willingness to believe it; thus prestige in international relations meant projecting virtual force. This virtuality ironically became a nation's undoing, for it incited envy. Nations had to negotiate from positions of power, for concessions in negotiations meant loss of power. If concessions signified weakness, and weakness diminished prestige, negotiations became the first step toward war rather than peace. Paradoxically, the goal of being the more forceful undermined a nation's security, for "once a nation appears to constitute a danger for the existence of other nations, its own existence is jeopardized."[8] Weil reminded her readers that it was impossible either for the Greek leaders to return Helen to the Trojans or for the Trojan warriors to refuse to fight for her. Both actions would have been read by their people and their adversaries as weaknesses and would have occasioned revolts from within and attacks from without. Consequently the Trojan War went on for ten bloody years until both opponents were annihilated.

With twentieth-century problems in mind, Weil probed into the psychology behind sparring adversaries. Because Hitler's opponents could not allow him to imagine achieving his goal of universal domination, Churchill's order for mobilization dismayed her on three counts. First, it gave hope to Hitler that others thought he might win; second, it diminished the British people's liberty; and third, preparations for combat increased the probability of war. Conscription of British youth had the additional disadvantage that the English could falsely imagine their country well protected and, in consequence, relax their diligence. Simone Pétrement wrote of her friend's objection to war preparations: "Simone believed that preparation increased the probability of war, both by accustoming people to the idea of war and by making civilians hope that in case of conflict they would be safe, unlike the soldiers who would be exposed to death."9

Weil had an inordinate admiration of the English indomitable sense of self-esteem, a trait she considered to be a well-earned part of their national heritage. She stated that liberty had grown there like a plant, eluding all attempts to blight it. The very existence of such a liberty-loving nation added to the worth of the world. But mobilization was, in contrast, a form of oppression that chipped away the dignity of every citizen; the overconfident Nazis would know they had inspired fear. Weil may well have been weighing in too heavily on the effectiveness of psychological states of mind, but her goal was to stress the major role psychology played in international relations both for and against going to war. She also wanted to make the point that an exemplary model of freedom-loving people inspired others with courage and the desire to emulate it.

Wanting to explore a third state of affairs between peace and the "state of the danger of war," she speculated on the unrealized potential of this intermediate stage. An interim, cautiously prolonged between threatening words and actualization of the threat, could provide a hiatus during which stalling allowed other elements to play a part. Tyrannical rule had innate frailties: an autocratic regime had to cleverly manipulate between inspiring fear of external adversaries and winning confidence in its own internal struggle for power. Overplaying either one was a temptation inherent in despotism. This vulnerable aspect of dictatorial powers gave the statesmen of threatened nations an opportunity to parry diplomatically the thrusts of the adversary, staving off the start of war. The negotiators could pull back or move forward, deploying myriad stances—neither too rigid nor too pliant. Such a stand-off could gain additional time during which inner rifts in the aggressor states could widen and lessen chances for unity within the repressive regime. Weil believed that every situation had its weak points, and she wanted to open new paths for negotiation between the pitfalls.

In tightly controlled totalitarian states, the population eventually wearied from the unremitting efforts required of them. Weil cited Russia in 1932 as a prime example of a regime in which popular enthusiasm for world revolution, stretched to the maximum, had long since given way to sullenness. Germany's state of mobilization was only six years old, but signs that the German transport workers had started to buckle under the rigid control were visible in the decline of rail transportation efficiency. But, she wondered, could parry-and-thrust diplomacy be effective enough to outlast the time needed for Germany to wear out from the inside? Weil suggested that although this technique had never been experienced in a peaceful way, there was no proof that it would not work. It offered favorable psychological possibilities.

Weil argued that such a style of negotiations could gain positive advantages when transacted by diplomats representing nations that were generally admired for their ideals of liberty and their support of the value of the individual. In Weil's mind, England, because of its eminent political theorists, had historically earned that reputation. By the same token, France's history had given it the reputation of loving liberty and independence, stemming primarily from the people's uprising against the monarchy in 1789. Tragically, conditions in the French colonial empire had tarnished that distinction. To once again be considered the champion of liberty, human rights, and civilization, France had only to generously give up its tight control over the colonies. Transforming the empire into a body of citizens rather than masters and slaves could offer a precedent of sacrifice, motivation, and homage to higher principles that would rally freedom-loving people throughout the world. Weil trusted that France's virtuous example could inspire other countries to undertake difficult but valid steps toward ethical behavior and thereby bolster the ability to resist Nazi fascism. For Weil, keeping sight of one's moral integrity and maintaining an unshakable faith in individual liberty played a crucial role in decreasing the possibilities of war.

Moral integrity implied encouraging citizens in virtuous actions and, above all, never supporting the abuse of power in other nations. By this criterion, Weil argued, France should stop pretending that certain de facto tyrannies were democracies. France had made diplomatic approaches toward Stalin's dictatorship in Russia in the hope of creating a mutual defense pact against German aggression. Encouraging virtuous actions for one's nation and for one's people might seem idealistic, but experience had shown that when a nation taught its people to kill or to abuse others, this behavior did not stop at the battlefield. Just actions had a way of radiating outward to prompt others to behave in an ethical way, despite formidable resistance. Weil believed that her country did have the potential for representing what was good and right. But double standards in morality made a country's reputation for integrity a source of mockery.

Weil concluded her assessment with a rallying appeal to her readers: "France must appear to its citizens and to the world as a perpetually flowing source of liberty. There must not be anywhere in the world a single person, sincerely loving liberty, who has legitimate reasons to hate France; all serious persons who love liberty must be happy that France exists."[10] Her call applies to all countries that traditionally support human rights, imploring them to continue that support well beyond situations that simply serve their self-interest.

Weil never submitted this long article for publication, perhaps because of the chaotic conditions in Europe, but perhaps also because she sensed that the failed Munich concessions had come as close to her third alternative as she could have realistically expected. Her parry-and-thrust diplomacy had serious limitations—the need for unanimity among defending nations, inordinately skillful diplomats, and steadfast, confident followers—but variations of this stalling technique have worked in the past, primarily because of inherent flaws in despotic governments. Despite the dangers inherent in nations' perpetual striving for prestige through displays of strength, Weil believed that a nation and its people could indeed act with moral integrity, as an entity and as a group of individuals. She remained consistent in encouraging actions that would preserve the dignity, self-respect, and liberty of all individuals, stressing that violence destroyed far more than the material aspect of lives. Brute force, no matter who wielded it, eroded spiritual values beyond the point of recovery. Humankind's natural love of liberty could act as a counterforce to this drive toward domination. The commitment, however, had to be pure and unremitting.

THE EMPIRE OF FORCE HAS SEDUCTIVE CHARMS

The man who is not protected by the shield of lies cannot suffer force
without being pierced to the soul. Grace can block the corruption
from this gash, but it cannot prevent the wound.

Weil, "The *Iliad*, or the Poem of Force"

After Weil's painful concession that force held center stage throughout human history and that no one could confront it with impunity, she explored its psychological effects on the individual. Although she saw war as a glorified human-destroying force, she recognized that humankind had full responsibility for starting and perpetuating the violence. In her consuming desire to alert her readers to the hidden dangers of any resort to violence, she composed "The *Iliad*, or the Poem of Force," a literary piece that was simultaneously a political essay. By framing her ideas within this ancient Greek epic, in which Homer portrayed the mechanism of self-perpetuating force, she created an aura of timelessness. She admired the bard's skill in accentuating the preciousness of all that was lost in war by juxtaposing scenes of the purest human love with descriptions of barbaric acts. The essay focuses on war's transformation of the human psyche, the role of grace, and the courageous choices individuals must make.

Weil's teaching and writing style, characterized by precise wording and the deft use of rhetorical devices, used great literature from the past as a means of illustrating her subject. Her master professor, Alain, had often cited literary texts in his classes and essays to provoke deeper thought on the human condition and to express his own conclusions. The passages that Weil extracted from the *Iliad* made especially vivid her contention that human beings, even when they knew the risk, initiated the use of force, which then proceeded autonomously beyond anyone's control. Like Alain, Weil oriented her commentary on the *Iliad* to the issues that most deeply concerned her; we will see her do the same later on with the Bhagavad-Gita.

Although she did not even mention war until midway into the essay, the relevance of Weil's analysis to the threat of chaos on the European continent was patent to her French readers. The initial readers of "The *Iliad*, or the Poem of Force" would have had the calamities of World War I and the Spanish Civil War still fresh in their minds, and they would have seen the psychological changes a combatant went through, from initial enthusiasm to the despair of interminable killing. The reference to a legendary tragedy implicitly opened a second level of consciousness for her contemporaries caught in the paroxysm of fear. The mercurial volatility of unleashed force in the *Iliad* kept up a relentless movement, shifting back and forth between antagonists, rendering it difficult if not impossible for them to make morally good decisions. Force on the move inescapably punished the perpetrator as well as the sufferer with a mathematical rigor. Once launched into existence, force eventually would play itself out, leaving only a trail of utter despair. Weil wanted her readers to be fully aware of the foreseeable consequences of the coming violence and to remain steadfast in maintaining their dignity, self-respect, and commitment to long-term human values.

In her essay, Weil evoked the image of fresh recruits going off to battle with a light heart, thinking that force was on their side, since they could not imagine the real threat of an enemy who was not yet visible.[11] Once subdued by war, however, their souls cried out for deliverance. But such deliverance became impossible, for "the possibility of such a violent situation is inconceivable before one is in it; but ending it is inconceivable once one is enmeshed in it."[12] The terror, the pain, the exhaustion, the massacres, the dead companions weighed heavily on the combatants, but these same memories created an obstacle to envisioning a reasonable termination. She explained: "The thought that an unlimited effort could have brought little or no gain causes too much pain."[13]

Weil had read Homer's epic in Greek, making meticulous translations of preferred lines, occasionally in three or four rewordings, striving for exactitude and beauty in rhythms and making the placement, number of words, and run-on lines in French correspond to those in the original. Simone Pétrement, her friend and biographer, wrote that Weil might wrestle a half hour with the same line to set the right word in the right spot, particularly at the end of a line.[14] Weil had talked to Pétrement about the importance of exactness in translation for replicating the emotional intensity of the original. Her letters to Jean Posternak, a medical student whom she had met in a mountain sanatorium in Switzerland, contained long translations of Homer's verses. Their correspondence portrays Weil's enthusiasm for the task she had undertaken: she told Posternak to wait for her choice of a translation because "never has anyone created anything so beautiful as the *Iliad;* it is a reading that should not be bungled."[15] Weil admired the ancient poem's complete lack of declamation, whether aimed at evoking admiration for heroism or horror. This, she claimed, was quite rare.

Weil saw depicted in the *Iliad* war's transformation of the psyche; once one submitted to the horror of killing, only the imagination offered a means of escape. Consequently, lies, willingly believed, obscured the reality of force and its consequences because "the man who is not protected by the shield of lies cannot suffer force without being pierced to the soul. Grace can block the corruption from this gash, but it cannot prevent the wound."[16] Although lucidity could mitigate the effects, it could never eliminate them. Eventually, one became as indifferent to the lives destroyed as if they were mere broken toys. Heroism degenerated to grandstanding, sullied with boasting, and a depraved love of violence itself. Homer depicted the warriors as blind, uncontrollable scourges of disaster: blasting fire, flood, whirlwinds, and man-eating lions, everything that violent external forces could propel. Their massacres made up a uniform tableau of horror in this empire of force, which a warrior could escape only by a miracle. As the soul suffered under the yoke of daily violence, living became unendurable. "As soon as the practice of war makes palpable the possibility of death at any moment, the mind becomes incapable of passing from one day to the next without meeting the image of death." Thus the thought of imminent death wiped out the concept of goals or even the aims of the conflict, dissipating the energies needed even to picture putting an end to the fighting.[17]

Weil admired how Homer displayed justice by favoring neither Trojans nor Greeks; his poem gave no indication whether he himself was Trojan or Greek. Warriors on both sides suffered the malignant effects of violence, which transformed men into "things." Their souls twisted under this imposition, but they could not avoid the fate of being reduced to matter in one way or another, whether by death or by fear so numbing that it took over their whole being. Force "petrifies differently, but equally, the souls of those who endure it and those who handle it," leaving them alive but less than human.[18] In emphasizing that in the *Iliad* no one was sheltered from fate, Weil reminded her readers that in war everyone loses. The lamentable fate of the individual soul had never been imagined in the celebration of mass bravura that drove young fighters to war. Neither civilization nor the illusion of progress protected anyone from the defilement that resulted from the necessity to submit to the empire of force.

During this period, when the shadow of censorship hovered over every communication, any serious critique of events required subterfuge. The editor of *La Nouvelle Revue Française* in Paris would not print Weil's essay without major changes, which she refused to make. The essay finally appeared in another important literary review: *Cahiers du Sud*, based in the French nonoccupied zone.[19] The director, Jean Ballard, welcomed Jewish writers and others known for their hostility to the Vichy regime. Weil chose to use a pseudonym, Emile Novis, a sort of anagram, to avoid the Jewish-sounding name of Weil. Her piece had an effect on readers internationally. An Italian refugee, Nicola Chiaromonte, fleeing to the United States from Mussolini's fascism, read it in 1940 in Marseilles and introduced it to Dwight Macdonald, a New York editor-owner of a small-circulation journal called *politics*. Macdonald had the essay translated into English and published in 1945 as a protest over the dropping of atomic bombs on Hiroshima and Nagasaki. Chiaromonte's arrival in America with Weil's essay in his baggage played a crucial part in introducing American activists to the power of Weil's call to say "no" to violence.

Weil wanted all to remain aware of their choices when faced with brute domination: they could respond with acts of violence or they could counter with acts of generosity. The human beings who set violent force into motion longed for life but dealt in death. These same persons, however, could also perform acts of courage, kindness, and love, inspired by supernatural grace. Weil divided readers of the *Iliad* into two groups: those who imagined that progress in human civilization had relegated force to the past and those who realistically discerned force at the center of all human history. The former considered this poem as a document, but the latter found it "the most beautiful, the purest of mirrors."[20]

Weil described the unfolding of the Trojan War as a game of seesaw between victors and vanquished; the conqueror of the moment felt invincible, forgetting his prior narrow defeat and the fragility of his present victory. The victors continued the fighting to totally humiliate the losing army, even knowing that they risked losing everything they held dear. Weil pointed out that at the end of the first day narrated in the poem the Greeks had every likelihood of regaining Helen, along with her riches, and returning home. But that was not to be; at this point in defending their power and prestige, they wanted nothing less than all of Troy as booty. Though the cost was enormous, warriors on both sides clamorously decided to keep on fighting for honor, for prizes, or for vengeance. Consequently, the war lurched on with death after harrowing death, as violence mangled all it touched. When the fighting ended, everyone had lost piteously.

From the start of the narration of the *Iliad*, the Greek audience knew the poignant ending. Weil noted that "all of the *Iliad* takes place under the shadow of the greatest affliction possible for humankind: the destruction of a city."[21] The sadness intensified with the felling of handsome warriors in the flower of their manhood. Weil wrote, "Homer's listeners knew that the death of Hector could give only brief joy to Achilles, the death of Achilles a brief joy to the Trojans, and the annihilation of Troy a brief joy to the Achaeans."[22]

In Weil's analysis, the seductive charms of the empire of force held sway over the bodies and minds of the warriors, whether they were winners or losers. The powerful loved force ignobly, not perceiving its limits, and victims became more vulnerable to others' domination because they could not impose on their conquerors that moment of hesitation from which alone came consideration for fellow creatures in perilous times. But Weil wanted to give prominence to other effects of force, those that stopped short of making men corpses. When force was suspended over a being that it could kill at any moment but did not, it paralyzed him; Homer described men subjected to that force as "crushed," "blinded," or "dragged along." The most severely afflicted of them were mutilated and reduced to matter, altered for life, their souls so severely rent that they were reduced to things, transformed into beings that were neither dead nor alive.

Weil set the stage for this other aspect of force with an opening sentence: "The true hero, the true subject, the center of the *Iliad* is force, force that is manipulated by men, force that subdues men, and force that makes human flesh shrink. . . . Force is what makes whoever is subjected to it a thing."[23] For Weil, force, the main protagonist in Homer's narrative, was autonomous, unrelenting, and coldly indifferent to the havoc it wreaked on the human psyche. Though the behavior lacked the label of physical and mental torture, the psychological effects that Weil attributed to humiliating and degrading treatment were the same as torture. A disarmed and cornered man who saw a deadly weapon directed toward him died in part of his soul before he was even touched. Weil wrote: "The human soul, dragged and blinded by the very force it thought to control, is ceaselessly modified by this relationship. The soul bows under the constraint of force, to which it is subjected."[24] For Weil, the *Iliad* expressed the ultimate secret of war: force was the hero; force sought the souls of the combatants, both victor and vanquished, and spiraled ruinously beyond control until its energies were spent.

Weil held up the illustrious Achilles as a mirror of our human condition, showing him exposed to the necessities of destiny and force. Achilles personified the death-dealing entity that modified the souls of the living. For all his physical prowess and beauty, his human emotions and failings held him in thrall. With arrogant indifference he slew the young, defenseless Lycaon and the princely Hector, both of whom had pleaded piteously, though in vain, for their lives. For the funeral pyre of his dear friend Patrocles, he cut the throats of twelve Greek adolescents as easily as cutting flowers. Achilles knew he would die in the carnage of the war.

> I am destined to die here, far from my dear father,
> far from mother. But all the same I will never stop
> till I drive the Trojans to their bloody fill of war!
>
> (*Iliad* 19.499–501)[25]

In her essay, Weil noted bitterly several times that it was impossible for a person to respect the lives of others when he had extinguished within himself the aspiration to live.[26]

A vulnerable person who begs another not to kill him knows all the same that a moment of impatience on the part of the armed man can end his life. Weil pointed out that some, once their plea for mercy had been granted, could become whole again but that for others "this death stretches out for a lifetime, a life that death has petrified well before having extinguished it."[27] Ten years after Weil wrote this essay, the writers of the Third Geneva Convention, aware of this painful human vulnerability, were moved to proscribe the degrading physical and mental torture of prisoners of war.

For Weil, Homer's characterization of Achilles, the embodiment of terrifying force, showed that in the vicissitudes of war all endured the same fate indiscriminately. Indifferent to his own forewarned death, Achilles persisted in his pursuit of Patrocles' slayer, knowing that his turn would come soon, since fate fell indifferently on man and hero alike. As blind destiny shifted sides from day to day, Achilles reminded his captive enemy, the majestic Priam, of an essential verity portrayed by Zeus's jars that held human miseries and blessings:

> There are two great jars that stand on the floor of Zeus's halls
> and hold his gifts, our miseries one, the other blessings.
> When Zeus who loves lightning mixes gifts for a man,
> now he meets with misfortune, now good times in turn.
>
> (*Iliad* 24.615–62)

This struck Weil as the profound truth in the *Iliad:* "Nothing disguises the cold brutality of the facts of war because neither the conquerors nor the conquered are admired, scorned, or hated."[28] Everyone suffered, no one possessed force, and no man escaped its brutal necessity. She wrote, "Men are not divided into the conquered, with enslaved and supplicants on one side and conquerors and commanders on the other. There is not a single man who must not at some time bend under the constraint of force," and again, "Valor contributes less to determine victory than blind destiny."[29]

Nor was a single combatant spared the shame of fear. Lordly Agamemnon, fearful of defeat, lowered himself to beg the brooding Achilles to return to the battle, but in vain. Achilles refused to forgive the humiliation he had suffered at the hands of the Achaean chief, even though he knew that the war would probably be lost without his fighting prowess. The shame of fear freely passed from one to another in the Trojan and in the Greek camps: no one was untouched. Hector terrified the Achaeans, but later Ajax made the Trojans tremble as he entered the fray. Then Ajax, spirits dashed, was forced to retreat like a trapped beast.[30] Even Achilles trembled and groaned, though caught by an element of nature, the churning, surging rapids of the River Scamander, until the god Hephaestus saved him from drowning. Zeus held the sacred scales of blind destiny, but even he did not control them. Homer recounts:

Then Father Zeus held out his sacred golden scales:
in them he placed two fates of death that lays men low—
one for the Trojan horsemen, one for Argives armed in bronze—
And gripping the beam mid-haft the Father raised it high
And down went Achaea's day of doom.

(*Iliad* 8.81–85)

Homer's depiction of the god's capriciousness deciding the warriors' fate underlined for Weil that "the strong person is never absolutely strong, nor the weak absolutely weak, but neither of them knows it."[31] Thus the stronger was encouraged to act as if no obstacle created the necessity for him to pause and think about the consequences before he acted. Weil continued: "Where thought has no place neither do justice nor prudence."[32] Everything that was destroyed was regretted; no one was spared from being captive to force, and each soul bore it differently depending on the degree of virtue sustained. Weil admired Homer's skill in transcribing the pathos through the choice of a word, a break in the verse, or a run-on line; no comforting fiction, no consoling thought of immortality or vapid patriotic glory alleviated the suffering. Each butchery and agony, described in vivid detail with bones hacked and entrails ruptured, had its antithesis in an evocation of a precarious world of peace, family, and physical well-being. No poetic devices veiled the austere reality that force, once set in motion, razed everything in its path. Weil reflected that if all persons were destined by birth to suffer violence, somehow circumstances had closed their minds to this reality.

Weil chose incidents from the *Iliad* to support her idea that the dominion of force made persons into things by reducing them to a form of servitude. Other than what the victor tolerated, the subjugated had no rights to either mind or body. Briseis, captive of Achilles, wept on the death of Patrocles because a slave was permitted an expression of grief only for the master for whom she had to feign love. Achilles and Priam, master and mastered, were ever mindful of the relationship of strength to weakness. A terrified Priam, braving Achilles, who with a slight gesture could destroy him at any moment, understood that his very existence depended on his enemy's whim, and Achilles himself was afraid that in a moment of impatience he would slay his kingly visitor. He warned Priam:

> So don't anger me now. Don't stir my raging heart still more.
> Or under my own roof I may not spare your life, old man—
> suppliant that you are—may break the laws of Zeus.
> *(Iliad* 24.667–69)

The noble Trojan, humbled before the killer of his royal sons, had become a thing, debased, humiliated, and inextricably caught in the empire of force.

Homer had Achilles, despite his absolute power over the Trojan suppliant, convince the afflicted Priam to share food with him by alluding to Niobe, who

saw a dozen children killed in her own halls,
six daughters and six sons in the pride and prime of youth.

. . . .

And Niobe, gaunt, worn to the bone with weeping,
turned her thoughts to food.

(*Iliad* 24.708–9, 721–22)

Priam, despite his broken heart, did eat a meal with his sons' killer. Weil often referred to grieving Niobe's thoughts of food to show that the physical empire of nature equaled that of force in strength. The ability of physical need to efface emotions as profound as a mother's sorrow reinforced the concept of human subjection to the empire of force.

In Weil's reading of the tragedy, rare moments of grace, when the soul awoke pure and intact, illuminated the dreary monotony of the successive waves of killing. In brief interludes courage and love held prime place, intensified by the juxtaposition of contrasting emotions. The audience, knowing that Hector lay dead outside the walls of Troy, felt the poignancy when Andromaque thought lovingly to prepare a warm bath for her beloved husband's return from battle. Weil remarked wryly that, as in the *Iliad*, almost all of human life took place far from warm baths. "Moments of grace are rare in the *Iliad*, but they suffice to elicit a profound sorrow for all that perishes due to violence."[33]

Human beings safeguarding their soul under terrible conditions through love of others exemplified Weil's contention that love had greater power than force. Individuals coming to grips with the harsh necessity of events could rise to the height of their human potential even while sensing the full extent of what they would lose. Hector courageously faced his destiny alone before the walls of Troy, knowing he would die there. He and Andromaque had just tenderly embraced, fearing they were saying their last goodbyes. Two enemies, Diomedes and Glaucos, with fond memories of former hospitality, declared their friendship and affection. Achilles and Priam marveled at each other's noble bearing, thinking of joys in times of peace. A friendship rising in the hearts of mortal enemies was, in Weil's mind, the greatest triumph of love, for it erased the distance between humble petitioners and the arrogant mighty.

For Weil, Homer's representation of the effects of the empire of force revealed a preformulation of the Gospel message: "Then Jesus said to him, 'Put your sword back into its sheath; for all who live by the sword will perish by the sword.'"[34] She noted that the *Iliad* had expressed the talionic law of exacting compensation well before Christ did. The Greeks had meditated on this fundamental truth and called it Nemesis. The power wielders of the moment believed they could destroy with impunity, but the *Iliad* showed that to be not so: "Ares is equitable, and he kills those who kill."[35] Having to endure human misery with no protective illusions made the mind receptive to justice and love of neighbor. In the *Iliad*, as in the story of the passion of Christ, the souls under constraints imposed by others tasted humiliation that the narrator neither disguised, nor enveloped in facile pity, nor set up for scorn. The poem contains love, humiliation, sadness, arrogance, and debasement, all of which fall without regard for the person. This equal treatment echoes the biblical justice expressed in Christ's evocation of "the rain that falleth on the just and the unjust."

Weil closed her essay, written on the eve of the Second World War, with the reminder that resorting to force had an irresistible appeal to those who believed they could impose their will with impunity. But in Weil's observation, there was no immunity from the terrible consequences, for force engenders force. She feared for her contemporaries who disregarded the warning, as old as the ancient Greeks and renewed by Christ, that those who perpetrated violence would perish by violence, and underscored it by using the fateful events of Homer's narrative. She concluded with the precept: "Do not believe you are sheltered from fate, do not admire force, do not hate your enemies, and do not scorn the less fortunate."[36]

THE HANDMAID OF WAR IS DESPAIR

*Contact with force is hypnotizing: it plunges one
into the world of delusion.*

Weil, Notebooks

The delusion of imagining that force could achieve a worthy goal preoccupied Weil in her exploration of human psychology. Her continued inquiry into the human inclination to deploy force and particularly into war as the archetype of violence is evident in her notebooks. Daily commentaries compacted into densely filled *cahiers* became her medium for exploring both the variants of force in human action and the options for moral behavior available to individuals caught up in a maelstrom of violence. Her thought focused on the conflict between the obligation to use force in rare moments and the aspiration to escape its defiling effects. While conceding that force was a limited tool of last resort, she infused into her assent the idea that forceful actions must be marked by a purity encompassing a sincere love for the other. In her search to identify the counterenergies that could block coercive behavior, she isolated love as having the only potency pure enough to neutralize the inherent contamination in force. The cohesiveness in her ideas came from her belief that obedience to God's love was the aim of all human life. This final section of the chapter traces her progression from pragmatically considering the circumstances under which one should go to war to creating guidelines for the individual and the group confronted with the need to employ forceful aggression.

War and defeat had become a reality: in June 1940 the Germans invaded France, and the Weils immediately headed south for the French Free Zone. During her year and a half in southern France, Simone participated actively in a resistance network and in delivering the *Cahiers du Témoignage Chrétien,* a clandestine paper dedicated to encouraging the French to reject cooperation with the Nazis.[37] Her illegal activity occasioned two or three police interrogations until, through great efforts, her parents got themselves and her passage on a boat leaving for the United States. Four months after her arrival in America to help her parents get settled, Weil returned to Europe and spent the last nine months of her life in England, never relinquishing her ardent desire to reenter France.

Her private observations offer rich insights into her permanent quest to find a unifying truth. In all she numbered eighteen notebooks, now edited and annotated by a team of scholars representing many disciplines and published in four volumes of her *Oeuvres complètes.* During her summer in Marseilles working with the writers associated with the *Cahiers du Sud,* her entries began to take on a succinctness and density, almost as if the intellectual ferment among her friends there, as well as the intensity of the times, had sparked the need to put down all her thoughts on a regular basis in a sort of intellectual biography. In her notes, the reader can detect a newfound rhythmic flow in her daily writing and thought. Florence de Lussy comments, "In her third notebook, Weil's thought has found its points of reference, its principal ideas, and is effortlessly disclosing its riches."[38] It was also a time of severe physical suffering from migraine headaches. Biographer Gabriella Fiori called the contents of Weil's notebooks conversations with herself that recounted the story of her thought and soul.[39]

The first entries from that period were in the yellow-covered exercise books of the École Normale Supérieure; the others were on whatever tablets she could obtain in those difficult times of shortage. Weil rarely dated her entries and pursued several topics simultaneously, so the variations in paper and ink have been the clues for establishing the chronological order of her notations. Writing for her was an essential part of each day. She wrote continuously during the three-month ocean voyage and less frequently during her brief New York stopover; then she started up once again with feverish application during her sojourn in London, never stopping until the last week of her life.[40] The frenetic pace of her writing makes one wonder if she sensed that there would not be time to organize all she had to say. Her notebook entries are elliptical, with multiple topics juxtaposed and many allusions simply noted. She gave a dominant place to meditations on force, revisiting many ideas that she had thought before but underpinning them with Thucydides' "terrible formula": "By a necessity of nature, all beings, whoever they are, exploit to the fullest extent all the power in their command."[41]

This "terrible formula" came from the Greek historian's *History of the Peloponnesian War,* in which he recounted the triumphant Athenian discourse delivered to the conquered people of the island of Melos. Weil referred to the incident five times in her notes, always from a different perspective, seeing in its poignant message an application to themes that she was also pursuing in sacred Indian texts. She transcribed the full incident in the notebook that she took with her on the voyage to America, having given her first eleven notebooks to her admired friend and philosopher Gustave Thibon for safekeeping. The formula reappears in two later essays: "Are We Struggling for Justice?" and "Forms of the Implicit Love of God."

In an earlier unpublished article, Weil had related the Melian incident to support her argument that Hitler, a man of burning ambition, a born gambler, gifted with an imagination that envisioned history on a grandiose scale, sought universal domination. To make her point that he would not voluntarily curb his power, she paralleled his domineering ways with those of the imperious Athenians, who had scorned the claim of the people of Melos that in case of battle the gods would side with their just cause. The Athenians retorted: "We believe with regard to the gods, but we are certain with regard to men, that always, by an absolute necessity of nature, each one commands everywhere he has the power to do so." They then added: "You know as well as we that the human mind is such that what is just is examined only if equal necessity exists on both sides; if one is strong and the other weak, the first accomplishes what is possible and the second accepts it."[42] They confidently asserted that the Melians would follow the same necessity of nature if they were in a position of power.

Weil admired the stark candor, clarity, and acumen of this statement of raw power.[43] The Athenians of Thucydides believed that the gods would exercise power to the extreme limit just as men did. Consequently, the more powerful invaders killed all the men of military age on the island and sold the rest of the population as slaves. Weil couldn't resist inserting an ironic reminder at this point that these people were the creators of Western civilization. She discerned, nevertheless, by the military chronicler's manner of describing their cruel abuses of power, that the Athenians were well aware that other ways of treating the weaker existed.[44] Weil knew that men did abstain, albeit rarely, from commanding wherever they had the power to do so. That was proof enough that the true divine power did not command wherever possible. She tersely proposed: "What is possible for mankind is possible for God."[45] The problem, as she saw it, boiled down to finding ways to establish equity between the weaker and the stronger, giving both entities a level playing field. The Athenians had summed up political reality, but Weil believed alternative resolutions existed.

For Weil, the abuses of war resulted from contempt for limits, a desire to inflate one's own ego, and a country's inexhaustible need for prestige. Indifference to the reality of another people's existence led one to discard any goals that had originally had rational parameters. Base, self-centered attachment to relentless power goaded leaders and followers into excessive violence that, once initiated, ran roughshod over the eternal values of truth, beauty, and goodness. She noted tersely: "Cause of war: each man, each human group feels itself, fairly enough, as the legitimate master and possessor of the universe. But this possession is poorly understood, for lack of understanding that the access—in so far as it is possible for man on earth—passes for each one, through his own body (through the *finite*)."[46]

The finite had strict limitations, but the intoxication of power muddled the distinction between real limitations and unreal illusory limitlessness. Weil noted that one might plan to inflict only limited harm on the enemy but that limiting the devastation was in fact impossible, for "armed weapons imply unlimited powers."[47] The illusionary power that came with arms was the power of destruction, which always met its limit and ricocheted back, bringing the havoc full circle. War had a hypnotizing effect that plunged one into a dreamlike state that hazy thinking could mistake for lucidity.

Weil had her own anxieties over whether she personally could confront force fully alert and not become submerged in a protective fantasy. Her experience in the Spanish militia had revealed the ease with which one succumbed to fear and, worse, to a taste for killing. She stressed that where some had plunged into a dreamlike state over war, others needed to persistently shatter that dream to spur the slumberers' wish to awake, but not so frighteningly as to dispel their desire to regain consciousness. Implicitly referring here to the Germans, she saw them immersed in a nightmare from which they would eventually aspire to wake. To her mind, they would be conquered only when they so desired;[48] and they needed the possibility of waking and seeing the truth of the situation.

Given that certain conditions necessitated war, Weil believed that thought and silence had an essential place in its preparation, just as they played an intrinsic role in the creation of a work of art. Stillness would be critical to the momentous decision of using arms to achieve a higher aim. "As in composing music or poetry one keeps a certain interior silence in the soul and disposes the sound or the words in such a manner as to render perceptible to another this aspiration for quietness, so it is for weapons and the desire for peace." She concluded: "The art of arms is also an art."[49]

Though titles are unusual in Weil's notebooks, she labeled one lengthy entry "War."[50] In it she drew on Carl von Clausewitz's extensive nineteenth-century philosophical and systemic study *On War*. Clausewitz, a Prussian general and influential military theorist, had examined the strategies of war. He insisted that the means used must be commensurate with the goals sought; war must be restricted to being an instrument of policy subordinated to particular objectives. Clausewitz founded his theory on the assertion that violence was the essence of war and that war had no logical "internal" or self-imposed limits on its exploitation of force.[51] From his ideas, Weil selected what was useful to her personal exploration of war. She explicitly referred to this famous treatise only once and even then obliquely by citing without attribution Clausewitz's well-known dictum that "war is the continuation of the politics of peace by other means."

Weil applied her philosophical approach to the three hypothetical aims of waging war that Clausewitz had suggested. One putative goal was to create in the enemy a disposition to obey all the victor's commands. This she deprecated as a war that, in the style of the Roman Empire, crushed the enemy. A second aim was to obtain limited ends that were carefully defined and unobtainable by negotiation. In that case, combat, staying short of provoking terror or inexpiable resentment, was only an extended moment of negotiation that threatened physical harm to the enemy. A third objective was to instill in the enemy the desire for peace—an option she considered preferable, since it was defensive without conquest. For Weil that meant changing the soul of the enemy. It was dangerously easy to slip from the second or third option to the belligerency of the first, for violence appealed to the baser human instincts and fostered the illusion of a quick and easy victory. But this was self-deception since any such triumph would be Pyrrhic. Consequences brought on by the means used must be considered. A victory of the first or second type could not last unless one was ready to dominate the enemy over the long term by enslavement or fear. To arrive at that point was hardly success. For the goal of the third category, peaceful coexistence, one needed strategies and tactics commensurate with the desired end. In all three goals, war must be only one of the means of persuasion, and the method of making war must be adapted to the specified goals. "Copying the enemy is not the way to reach one's goal." She reiterated her essential idea of 1934: "It is not the end that matters as much as the consequences incurred by the mechanisms brought to bear."[52]

Killing might be a means toward a valid goal in a just war, but only if strict restraints were obeyed and as few persons as possible were slain. One had to love life and never inflict death without accepting it for oneself, albeit with great regret. The desire for peace, security, and life, even at the risk of being killed, could not be renounced. The strength to adhere to these goals came from a descent into one's inner depths to connect with true desire. In her anguish over the possibility that there might be an occasion on which she would have to kill another, Weil tried to think out useful guidelines. If in extreme danger the killing of another was called for, it was necessary to (1) keep one's courage devoid of cruelty, (2) retain intact an inner love of life, and (3) not inflict death without accepting it for oneself. She posed the rhetorical question: If the life of another were tied to one's own to the point that the two deaths would be simultaneous, would one still want the other to die? Her response was that if, in that case, both the entire body and soul aspired to live, and if, nevertheless, without lying, one could respond, "Yes," then and only then one had the right to kill the other. Still, she wondered whether that sufficed. She then added: "One must also desire that the other live, no matter that necessity might require the opposite."[53]

Weil's experiences were a source for her empathetic understanding of the will to do violence. Her intense headaches, endured for over a decade, gave credibility to her commentaries on suffering. Apropos the desire to strike out in moments of physical or psychic pain and humiliation, she noted: "Let me not forget that at certain moments of my headaches, when a crisis was building up, but before the highest point, I had an intense desire to make someone else suffer by hitting him precisely on the same spot, his forehead. . . . Many times, in that state,

I gave way, at least, to the temptation to utter wounding words. Obedience to gravity: the greatest, or one of the greatest, sins."[54]

In her reflections on the psychological essence of war and its ability to animate fantasies, she concluded that using force against another was based on an illusion of power, which was the polar opposite of giving sincere and thoughtful attention to the reality of another's existence and needs. Just as moral gravity seduced the powerful into performing low actions, it inspired the victim with an intractable desire for vengeance, causing the spiral of violence to spin out of control. This base seduction of force created a terrible difficulty,[55] for the inherent human tendency was to seek immediate and mean-spirited satisfaction when feeling unfairly wronged. Therefore, clever political leaders, determined to direct their nation toward war, would attempt to manipulate this ignoble desire for power by calling for vengeance, particularly among the disinherited on the lower levels of the social scale. "In those who submit to force, there is an unquenchable thirst to exercise it in their turn."[56] The victimized would feel demeaned if they did not in turn have a chance to exert force, but inevitably this would lead to an endless gyration of blind, savage destruction. The punishing god, Nemesis, always brought retribution to the perpetrators, but unfortunately the vulnerable members of society were also penalized in the outcome.

When a people was wronged, war could seem, in a first reaction, to be an expedient outlet for the irrepressible desire for vengeance; however, once begun, its absurdity was too painful to be faced directly. Despair and disorientation led to erratic acts of malevolence in reaction to the apparently futile sacrifice demanded in war. Weil wanted people to understand the true inescapable costs. "The handmaid of war is despair. Violence must be done to constrain the soul to adapt to a situation where *all* its aspirations are purely and simply denied. . . . The goals of war are forgotten, for one must get to the point of denying all goals. They persist, not although but because they are absurd. This despair exists everywhere man is *sacrificed*."[57]

Killing people and destroying their land was only one of many ways to arrive at a desired end. If the goal of war was to change the thinking of the enemy, carnage could be extremely counterproductive.

For Weil, war, an aberration that fed on fear and a taste for killing, demanded all the personal resistance one could muster. She saw the challenges for everyone involved and warned: "Since war is an action on the imagination, the first difficulty is to withdraw oneself from the effects of the imagination, to have at one's disposal (as for a problem of geometry) the different ways of combining the elements, or the givens, of the situation."[58]

Because of her mystical experiences, Weil's vantage point for reflecting on the human condition had become increasingly transcendent. Empirical evidence showed her that everything social contained force, yet force did not just destroy bodies; it crushed fragile souls and deprived its victims of the ability to turn obediently toward God's love. The thought of the spiritual deprivation suffered by individuals subjected to force was painful for her, and she knew in the depths of her soul the terrible affliction suffered by others who felt abandoned under the yoke of brute force. Since struggle was inherent in the human condition, she subscribed to Heraclites's idea that strife, the essence of life, allowed all things to come to pass. In her view, the struggle when confronted with aggressive behavior was to maintain a level of moral purity, to remember that forceful acts carried their own retribution, and to pause for an objective assessment of the means most likely to achieve one's goal, which had to be infused with love of neighbor. None of these attitudes would come about without a willingness to accept, if necessary, self-sacrifice.

CHAPTER THREE

Love of Neighbor versus Totalitarianism

The Incarnation of Christianity implies a harmonious solution to
the problem of relations between individuals and the collectivity.
Harmony in the Pythagorean sense: a just balance of contraries.
This solution is precisely what men thirst for today.

Weil, "Spiritual Autobiography"

Simone Weil's encounter with Christ in the late 1930s opened new insights for her into the sacredness of the individual but sharpened her
critiques of the Catholic Church and its acceptance of the God of power
as portrayed in the Old Testament. Her experience with Hitler's aggressive actions and propaganda offered proof of the intractability of
raw force. His exploits signaled the dangers that modern totalitarianism held for the freedom of the individual. Each of these circumstances
added new elements to her search for ways that a collectivity could oppose brute force without suffering its contamination. In this chapter,
we look at how the radiance of her supernatural experience led Weil to
a critical reading of Western history, of the Old Testament, and of Hitler's methods as a modern version of those of the Roman Empire.

Weil categorized Hitler as an inevitable product of the cult of grandeur that was part and parcel of the West's glorification of the Roman
Empire. He embodied the delusional striving for personal and national
superiority. She saw the source of his power in the dehumanizing totalitarianism that came with the centralization of state power. For Weil,
the seeds of this totalitarian attitude in the West germinated when the

Christian Church, with its origin within the Roman Empire, took on a reverence for the powerful vengeful God portrayed in the Hebrew Bible. She was deeply critical of the vestiges of authoritarianism that remained in the doctrines and behavior of the institutional Church and of its refusal to censure all past reprehensible acts. Her distress over its lack of honesty regarding present and past wrongful behavior was palpable in her anguished question to her friend Maurice Schumann: "How can one condemn one holocaust when all past holocausts have not been condemned?"[1] She saw that humankind hungered for the harmony promised by Christ but that it was instead being crushed by its own veneration of power. Her search for the protection of the individual from abuses by irresponsible leaders led her to propose a decentralized sharing of governmental responsibilities both within a nation and among nations.

MYSTICAL EXPERIENCE

I felt, without being in any way prepared—never having read
the mystics—a presence more personal, more certain,
more real than that of a human being.

Simone Weil to Joë Bousquet, May 12, 1942

Simone Weil had had a completely secular upbringing in her family. At the Lycée Henri IV, she shared a sympathetic agnosticism with her philosophy professor, Alain. These two contingencies created in her mind a tolerant attitude toward religion, neither hostile nor favorable. Alain, though profoundly anticlerical, found a deep moral sense in what he regarded as the myths of Christianity. Weil, too, considered that religion and morality were closely linked. She wrote Father Perrin that she had never in her life actively sought God and that from adolescence on she had considered the problem of God as one about which there was insufficient information here below. "The only sure way to avoid solving the problem falsely, which would be the worst possible evil, was to not pose it." So she had never posed the question of God, thus neither affirming his existence nor denying it.[2]

In Catholicism, she had sensed the foundational idea of human equality and the powerlessness of God in the face of deep suffering, but prior to her encounters with Christianity she had not reflected on God's relationship to the universe. When she did think about Jesus, for she loved the beauty of the Gospels, she avowed that she never thought about him without simultaneously imagining God. After her experience of being in the real presence of Christ, God became a reality for her, and the passion of Christ became central to her thoughts. She knew with a certainty that Christ was the truth that she had been seeking all her life and that anyone who made a sincere effort of attention could achieve this truth.

Weil's mystical experience of feeling "a presence more personal, more certain, more real that that of a human being" came about in 1938 after a visit to the Benedictine Abbey in Solesmes.[3] Her two prior encounters with Christianity had made a major impact on her. The first had occurred in a Portuguese fishing village in 1935, where she realized that suffering and sorrow were at the heart of Christianity. The second happened in 1937 while she was visiting Santa Maria degli Angeli, a Romanesque chapel in Assisi, where Saint Francis, "God's fool," had often prayed.[4] The first two experiences were more diffuse, giving her an ill-defined yet real sense of a supernatural presence; but what happened a year later while she was reciting George Herbert's poem "Love" as a form of prayer was clear, unmistakable, and totally unanticipated.

Aside from her conversations with a limited number of confidants, Weil kept her mystical experience and her attraction to Christianity very private. After her death, an untitled prose poem narrating her personal and intimate supernatural experience was found among the papers left with Gustave Thibon. Weil had written this poem on the point of leaving France to begin her exile from all that she had known. After arriving in New York, she recopied it from memory and labeled this second version "Prologue."[5] She never specifically mentioned in her essays her meeting with Christ, so its implicit effects of transforming her underlying principles must be discerned from the reorientation of her attention.

Joë Bousquet, a poet and World War I paralytic who endured constant pain from a bullet wound in the spinal cord, was an intimate friend to whom she described the significance that the supernatural presence had for her. Weil, fearing that Joë's affliction, which had embittered him, would keep him from offering his total love to God, shared with him her long years of suffering from racking headaches that had reduced her to the level of slavery. She recounted to Joë that this distress had left no place in her thoughts for the name of God but that everything had suddenly changed when "during a moment of intense physical pain, while I was forcing myself to love, but without believing I had the right to name that love, I felt, without being in any way prepared—never having read the mystics—a presence more personal, more certain, more real than that of a human being. This presence, inaccessible to the senses and the imagination, was analogous to the love that flows through the tender smile of a beloved. Since that instant the name of God and of Christ have been interwoven irresistibly with my thoughts."[6]

Her farewell letter to Bousquet, written on the point of departure for America with her parents in May 1942, gave a preliminary sketch of her spiritual life. She sent a longer elaboration of it two days later to Father Perrin. She had little hope of seeing either Joë or her dear Dominican friend again, but she wanted Perrin as well to know her "spiritual autobiography." Although Perrin had hoped to lead Weil to baptism, she had insistently refused. In her friendship for him, she had considered it necessary to explain why she felt called to stay out of the Church despite her belief that she was Christian in spirit and had been from an early age. The Christian notion of love of neighbor had always informed her thoughts and actions, and since she had been steeped in the spirit of poverty all her life, the purity and poverty of Saint Francis greatly appealed to her. She felt the need to reveal to Perrin that, despite his precious gift of friendship, he could not offer her the inspiration of Christianity because Christ had already come to her in person. Thereupon she described to him her mystical experience.

During her stay in Marseilles and their cherished conversations together, Father Perrin's entreaties for her to join the Church made her analyze critically for the first time the dogma over which the Church exercised its guardianship. Notwithstanding her abiding attraction to the Gospels and Catholic liturgical practices, she applied an intense scrutiny to all that the Church required of anyone wishing to become a member of the Church through baptism. For any doctrine inconsistent with her concept of a God of love she sought clarification, which generally remained insufficient for her single-minded commitment to truth and left her at odds with many members of the clergy.

She found unacceptable and repugnant the Church's refusal to disavow or to be contrite over past actions that had destroyed vulnerable human lives. The pope's thirteenth-century support of the Inquisition and the genocidal crusade against the Albigensians had nurtured the growth of a totalitarianism already present in the institution of the Church. In Weil's opinion, the formula for excommunication, *Anathema sit,* which denied any possibility of truth and its incarnation outside the Church, was proof of the Church's excessive authority. Over many centuries, the Catholic hierarchy had supported the Inquisition's method of using fear and physical torture to ferret out heresies against Christianity. The Albigensian or Cathar Crusade (1209–29), sanctioned by the Church, had employed extreme violence, even by medieval standards, against the Cathars of Languedoc, accused by the Roman Catholic hierarchy of having abandoned their religious faith. The annihilation of the Cathar civilization of Oc in southern France provoked a poignant sorrow in Weil, for she felt that the Albigenses had formed a rare society inspired by true love of neighbor. Not only had they renounced the use of force, but, in order to safeguard the liberty of religious thinking, they had refused to establish religious dogma.

Weil rejected the Church's authority to govern the thinking of individuals and to limit people's thoughts by physical and psychological pressure. Any stricture on the freedom of persons to apply their mental abilities to thorny questions and to come freely to some resolution was diametrically opposed to her philosophy. Maintaining her staunch conviction that where and how to place allegiance required liberty of thought, she insisted that no one should be coerced into accepting either dogma contrary to rational judgments or past behaviors that were incongruous with the "good." Nor should any of the desiring faithful be refused a sacrament. She felt that any sacrament subjected to social conditions was no longer a sacrament; "Priests should not have the power to refuse a sacrament, but simply to warn the faithful that the sacrament is a kind of ordeal and implies a certain risk."[7] She had written to Father Perrin, "Sacraments have a specific value that constitutes a mystery, in so far as they imply a certain type of contact with God, a mysterious but real contact."[8]

Weil wished to witness to the fact that the implications of the incarnation of Christ were universal, not limited to an event or person in time. Persons of goodwill adhering to any faith institution could conceive the "good" in a manner as pure and perfect as Christians. The Incarnation had brought to humankind a necessary and desired message of relationships for its well-being and eternal salvation. "The Incarnation of Christianity implies a harmonious solution to the problem of relations between individuals and the collectivity. Harmony in the Pythagorean sense: a just equilibrium of opposites. This solution is precisely what men hunger for today."[9] Free exercise of the intelligence by the individual was the key to this ability to discern the "good"; the mind must be able to function to its fullest capacity in total liberty. The collectivity's responsibility was to ensure everyone's right of liberty in thought. The Church had undermined its rightful spiritual leadership by excluding nonconforming followers who did indeed love truth.

Weil knew that Father Perrin agreed with her that never in history had souls been in such peril as at the time of her writing and that there was a strict obligation to make known to the public the true meaning of the incarnation of Christ. She insisted that if true friends of God, such as Meister Eckhart, repeated words they had heard in the silence of their hearts in a union of love, and the words appeared to be discordant with the teachings of the Church, it was a question of language, not of contumacy.[10] The Church abused its powers by limiting love and intelligence and by upholding its own sanctioned language as the only norm. This was incipient totalitarianism. Everyone had the duty to recognize and reject imposed subservience to others' authority wherever it became visible. For herself, she preferred to stay "on the side of all that cannot enter the Church,"[11] even though, as she told Father Perrin, "I was born, grew up, and have always lived, so to speak, under the Christian inspiration."[12]

Her mystical experience gave her new insights that redirected her search for truth but left elusive the answers to her deepest concerns for humanity. Her belief that the immaterial force of love, although it appeared weaker, was in truth far stronger than brute force mitigated her despair over the relentless drive for material power overwhelming Europe. This active force of love became foundational for her understanding of the human condition, but she could not yet articulate the means by which love could effectively defy the power to destroy. She wanted to discern fundamental principles in human behavior and then to imagine effective action for safeguarding individual souls. Thought and action were inextricably intertwined in her philosophy.

The goal of understanding the roots and development of abusive power inspired Weil to undertake a study of the origins of Hitlerism, whose growth she suspected flourished in the glorification of power ingrained in Western culture. In her desire to know more about Christianity as embodied in the Roman Catholic Church, she read through the entire Hebrew Bible for the first time, and perhaps the only time. The political events and the explosion of violence taking place in Europe created an atmosphere of urgency both for her study of the rise of Hitler's dictatorship and for the reading of this sacred scripture.

ISRAEL AND THE HEBREW BIBLE

The essential knowledge concerning God is that God is good.
All the rest is secondary.

Weil, *Random Thoughts Concerning the Love of God*

Weil's dogged critiques of Christianity's close association with the Roman Empire stemmed from her conception of the divine and its relationship with the universe and human beings. The inadequate actions taken by the Christian Church to fulfill its full potential for spreading the love of God through love of neighbor deeply dismayed her. Despite her devotion to the New Testament and to liturgical practices, her criticisms often ran counter to Church doctrine, antagonizing many around her. She was hostile to biblical descriptions of inhuman cruelty toward conquered enemies, considering such events influential in the vitiation of the Church's mission. She had come to accept an image of God as pure goodness, a God who loved all universally, not just an elect few. God's providence was to create a universe that followed immutable laws in perfect obedience by withdrawing himself to make a space. He did not enter into the temporal. The image of the divine that humanity should see as a model was an image of love, obedience, and self-emptying. Weil saw the evidence for this image in Christ's passion on the cross and in his question "My God, my God, why have you forsaken me?"

The Hebrew Bible, despite her intense interest in literature of the past, had not previously caught her interest. In her reading of this sacred scripture, aside from admired books, such as Job, the Psalms, the Book of Wisdom, and Isaiah, she focused on the many recountings of the use of force, which she found abhorrent to the kind of Christianity she embraced. Weil read Jehovah as a God who intervened in the world, carried out *anathema* by extermination, and had chosen one people over the universe of peoples as his elect with the assignment to create a nation. All of this went completely opposite to her vision of a God of universal love. In her notebook, she wrote: "Christianity became totalitarian, conquering, exterminating because it did not develop the notion of the absence and the nonaction of God in the world here below. Christianity attached itself as closely to Jehovah as it did to Christ; it conceived providence in the manner of the Old Testament."[13]

Weil brought a historical approach to her initial reading of the Hebrew Bible, reading it entirely from her own perspective, which, at this time, was Christian; she sought no guidance from biblical scholars. This type of direct reading of a text, dependent on one's intelligence and culture to perceive its meaning, was typical of her style. She had read her beloved Greek texts this way and was reading in the same manner ancient Chinese and Persian texts. In many of her studies, however, she had felt the imperative need to know the original language in order to have access to the true meaning contained in the works. For the reading of the Hebrew texts, she made no attempt to learn Hebrew. She procured a two-volume Bible, translated directly from the original text in 1930–31 by members of the French Rabbinical Order. She underlined verses and made multiple marginal notes. The

texts selected for her comments referred to either conquests and de-
filements or dates and chronology.[14] The first category of notation revealed her immediate tendency to see Jehovah as a God who not only
approved of his chosen people using force but also at times even commanded them to do so. The second category underscored her intention
to consider this Hebrew sacred text as a historical account of events.

Jean Riaud, a professor of theology who examined Weil's copy of
the Old Testament, analyzed her interpretation of the Bible and categorized her reading as "naive." According to Old Testament scholar
Etienne Charpentier, "naive" reading applies to the first contact with a
text: the questions raised, the points of agreement or disagreement
with the material read, as well as any pleasure or astonishment incited
in the reader's mind. Charpentier concluded that a "naive" reading informed about the text but just as surely informed about the reader.[15] So
perhaps Weil's rejection of the major part of the Hebrew scripture revealed more about her and her thinking than about the Bible, which
she read during a period when the painful events taking place obsessed her.

One must ask here why Weil was so unwilling to treat the Hebrew
sacred scriptures, in all their complexity, with a fairer, more scholarly
attitude. Many scholars have analyzed Weil's antipathy to the Hebrew
Bible, giving varied psychological reasons for her bias. This study will
refer only briefly to the aspects that involve her attempt to understand
the mechanism of force in order to prevent its harm to human beings.
The full horror of the destructive Nazi juggernaut bearing down on
European nations constituted the backdrop for her initial reading. She
believed that if pure love of the "good" was to be an effective protection
against the contamination of force, every means possible had to be
used to make this evident and realizable. All models using forceful violence had to be honestly portrayed for the reality they embodied.

Of the causes advanced for Weil's animosity toward the Old Testament, most have some substantiation, whether in contingencies of
her childhood, her unique and absolute personality, or her limited exposure to the Hebrew sacred scriptures. Her father, of Alsatian ances-
try, was an adamant agnostic. Except during the visits of her paternal
grandmother, Madame Eugénie Weil, who was of Russian origin and

was a strict observer of the Jewish dietary laws, there was no religious discussion at home. The family was the epitome of successful assimilation into French culture. Weil was formed by her French education to take a place among the finest minds that French culture could produce. She considered herself French, not Jewish, part Alsatian, or part Russian. Her personality was one of consistency, determination, independence, and absoluteness in everything she pursued; she never knowingly became an identifiable member of any group. While no one rationale will serve to fully explain Weil's hostility toward the Hebrew Bible, this study makes an argument for the coherence of her criticisms, however problematic, with relation to her philosophic and religious preoccupations concerning force and the love of God.

In her essay "Israel and the Gentiles," the reader can infer a certain mental groping on Weil's part to find a way to remove any obstacles on the path of seeking a greater good for humankind. She sought to mitigate the effects of what she considered the divorce between the spiritual and profane elements in her contemporary society. For this division to be healed, brute force and cruel indifference to human aspirations, no matter where they were honored and glorified, had to be identified and rooted out. This unfinished essay, found posthumously in her papers, was designed to be part of a more complete work, one that summed up her thoughts on the need to redirect the course of Christianity, purge it of influences that glorified force, power, and prestige, and eliminate the idea of exclusivity.

She opened her essay on Israel and the Gentiles with "The essential knowledge concerning God is that God is the Good. All the rest is secondary."[16] To emphasize that this knowledge was and is accessible to all, she followed with a favorite passage, often repeated, from the Egyptian Book of the Dead in 1242 BCE: "Lord of Truth. I bring you the Truth. . . . I destroyed evil for you. . . . I made no one weep. . . . I caused no one to fear. . . . I did not turn a deaf ear to words that were just and true. . . . I did not advance my name for honors." She wanted to reiterate the point that the obliteration of pre-Christian societies eliminated their ability to bring their perceived truths to bear on the formation of the present-day Church. Weil had come to the firm conviction that the Christian spirituality of love, charity, and faith had to permeate any civilization that wished to counter the force of gravity in human nature that pulled human beings toward the exploitation of their fellow beings. This Christian spirituality was not encompassed in any one structured religion but came from a true belief in God as the source of all good.

In her notebooks compiled between 1941 and 1942, Weil has a terse list covering several pages of the many exterminations listed in the Old Testament. Full of scorn for decimation as a means to suppress supposed idolaters, she grieved over the annihilation of civilizations, which destroyed precious, unique, and irreplaceable insights gleaned over the millennia of their existence. Killing off others who thought differently was the policy being pursued by the Nazis, who had to be stopped before they destroyed European civilization.[17] She deplored the loss of insights into the supernatural garnered by these now defunct ancient societies, whose truths needed to be rediscovered and honored once again. She believed that an atmosphere of glorifying power obscured the image of Christ's humility.[18]

Whether Weil would have arrived at a fairer, more balanced understanding of the Hebrew Bible had she lived longer must be pure conjecture. She read the Old Testament with a certain critical detachment; she did not take the time or evidently have the interest to deepen her knowledge of this complex heritage. At this point in her life, the horrors of violence, both threatened and real, hovered all around her, and she had opted for the Christian message as the truth she had been seeking. Aside from selected books in the Old Testament, she could not accept that the Hebrew Bible, as she read it, furthered God's word. Jewish scholars who admired Weil's life and thought were pained and shocked by her adamant critiques of Israel and Jehovah when *Gravity and Grace* came out in 1949, since her thinking on these matters had been very private.

In 1952, Emmanuel Levinas, a French philosopher of ethics, wrote at length about Weil's objections to the Bible.[19] He praised the manner in which "her writings and grandeur of soul gave witness to her intelligence; she had lived as a saint amidst the world's suffering. Despite all that separated her from 'us,' the love of God remained a common bridge." Levinas put her many criticisms of the Bible in a larger, more revelatory context and reacted to her revulsion at so much cruelty in it with "The extraordinary fact is that we are just as revolted as she." He insisted, however, that another, larger purpose existed for the harsh law of the Bible. "The extermination of evil by violence means that evil is taken seriously and that the possibility of infinite pardon invites infinite evil." He continued, "To admit punishment is to admit respect for the person, even the guilty person. . . . To render to another his due, to love him in justice, . . . that is the essence of a true action." Levinas summed up his response by saying: "The major misunderstanding between Simone Weil and the Bible is not that she ignored the texts of the Talmud, but that she never suspected their true dimension."

Martin Buber, Austrian philosopher and social activist, lamented that Weil had not considered Judaism globally in its itinerary from the Decalogue (the ten commandments given to Moses) to Hasidism, from which emerge small communities founded on fraternal love. Buber's regret was that she and others like her had turned away from a Judaism about which they knew too little.[20]

David Tracy, a professor of theology and the philosophy of religion, regretted that Weil's sense of justice and demand for compassion, which he greatly admired, did not carry over into a more careful evaluation of the Old Testament. She refused "to see how the same prophetic principle, the same liberationist drive for the victims of history that she found in Christianity was central to the Hebrew Bible and to the Christian reading of it as Old Testament." He concluded that this curious anomaly in her makeup stemmed from "psychological and historical reasons beyond our reach" but that we did not need to respect it.[21]

Wladimir Rabi, a French lawyer and magistrate who has written a good deal on Weil, called her a "hot coal in both Jewish and Christian hands" because she had relentlessly criticized the heritage of both religions.[22] But despite his uneasiness regarding some of her texts that rejected Jehovah and Judaism, he extolled her as the only seriously spiritual writer that France had inspired throughout the twentieth century. On a positive note, he found unexpected analogies that evoked the Kabala (a system of Jewish mysticism) in Weil's concept of Creation and in the mystical concept of *Tsimtsum:* the withdrawal by God of a part of himself in order to leave space for the finite universe. Rabi concluded that, despite her rejection of the biblical portrayal of Jeho-

vah, Weil had intuited certain fundamental elements of Jewish mystical knowledge and that her experience of the absolute pursued to its
full extent posed a challenge for us all to dialogue on the authenticity
of our choices within our beliefs.

Weil treated the dogma of the Catholic Church with the same
penetrating criticisms, all of which had some foundation. In her letter
to Father Couturier, written from New York in 1942 on the recommen-
dation of Jacques Maritain, she stated that she wished to present all
her grievances concerning the Catholic Church in order to ask if a person holding those ideas could still be baptized.[23] These concerns,
which she summed up in thirty-four complaints, had dogged her since
her original interest in Christianity. In her eyes, the Church had failed
in its mission because of the unfortunate contingency of coming into
existence within an empire that honored and practiced force. The
Church had embraced the veneration of power and authority; thus it
had wrongly assumed force to be a modus vivendi, internally by imposing excommunication for nonadherence to dogma and externally
by sending missionaries throughout the world to dictate its doctrines.
The missionaries of the Church, in their supposed intent to spread
God's word, had also eradicated spiritual treasures of age-old ethnic
groups all over the world. Weil felt that since the Gospel should not
be imposed on other cultures as dogma, the Church should have
simply presented it as an illumination of valid beliefs those cultures
already held.

Weil believed that "there could be in diverse countries (i.e., India,
Egypt, China, Greece) revealed sacred scriptures of the same quality as
the Judeo-Christian scripture and that certain of the texts that survive
today were perhaps fragments of them or echoes."[24] But the Church's
narrow-mindedness had closed off avenues to any truths that might be
outside its proclaimed domain and that might have been of great value
to forming harmonious relationships within a collectivity. This restriction of thought had created a barrier between the spiritual values of
antiquity and those of Christianity. It had also helped to create the barrier that now existed between the profane and spiritual life. When the
daily life of a society was no longer suffused by a supernatural illumination of love of the truth, there was little hope of blocking the effects

of violence and the ever-increasing expansion of exploitative power. Weil treasured the fragments of sacred scripture from pre-Christian societies that revealed an age-old reverence for ways to carry out love of one's neighbor.

With due humility, Weil had opened her letter to Father Couturier with "The opinions that follow have for me diverse degrees of probability or certainty; but all are accompanied in my mind with a question mark."[25] She felt that it was vital for the Church to live up to its potential and be open to the inspiration of societies past and present that lived in a Christian spirit despite their ignorance of the historic Christ. That spirit meant considering the supernatural as pure good and not as a God of force. If the Church was not truly catholic in the sense of universal, she preferred to remain on the outside, bearing witness to what it could be. For, she stated: "Christ is present on the earth wherever crime and affliction exist—unless men chase him away."[26] For Weil, the real message of Christianity was that all authentic good has a divine and supernatural origin. The good tree that produces only good fruits is God, the distributor of grace. She insisted that anywhere there is good there is a supernatural contact with God, even in an African tribe that worships fetishes. This example echoed her deep concerns about how colonizing nations patronized African peoples and assumed them to be uncivilized savages. She concluded that the objections she had raised to Church doctrine and practice, problems "of capital, urgent, and practical importance," had to be addressed if Christianity was to suffuse the secular life of its adherents.[27]

In her inquiry into whether the Church would openly discuss her criticism of its excessive authority, Weil suggested that Hitler understood very well the power to be gained by emulating Rome's incorporation of Christianity as the official religion in their empire.[28] He planned to do the same by creating his own sanctioned religion based on the superiority of the Aryan race, making the state the source of authority and the exclusive object of devotion. Weil urgently wanted her countrymen to understand the enormous challenge that the forms of totalitarianism, gaining strength in the current chaos, posed to their physical and spiritual well-being. The Church's autocratic ways gave an unfortunate model of inhibiting people's ability to think and inquire freely. For Weil, the Rome that she detested was in many ways Hitler's paradigm for his means to attain worldly conquest. Weil decided that her next study for publication should be a detailed analysis of the origins of Hitler's rise to power.

ORIGINS OF HITLERISM

A power that has no legitimately imposed limit tends
by necessity to increase within and without.

Weil, "Some Reflections on the Origins of Hitlerism"

In her lengthy article "Some Reflections on the Origins of Hitlerism," one senses Weil's increasing urgency to warn her readers that the totalitarian strategies of Hitler's Third Reich paralleled the worst policies of ancient Rome.[29] She believed that the admiration accorded by Western culture to Rome's insolent domination of the Mediterranean countries obscured the misery inflicted on a staggering number of victims. Under Rome's supremacy, "all local and regional life had perished in its immense territory; the best proof was the disappearance of individual languages in the majority of conquered countries."[30] Weil's anxieties that her compatriots would submit to a curtailment of their freedom had validity, since groups in France periodically clamored for a powerful central authority both nationally and internationally. Dissidents admired Franco's authoritarian control in Spain and vociferously criticized the French Republican 1930s left-wing governments. Others willfully turned a blind eye to the full implications of Stalin's rigid dictatorship in Russia. For Weil, the resemblances between Hitler's form of domination and that of Rome were powerful, revealing, and disturbing; the West had ignored important lessons that could be learned from that earlier and horrifying part of history.

In Weil's analysis, "Hitlerism" refers specifically to the National Socialists' form of domination, but Weil was, in fact, seeking fundamental truths, while philosophically investigating the heavy atmosphere of violence threatening Europe. Delving into the psychology that motivated war-mongering, she warned presciently that an initial sign was the increased centralization of power in the bureaucratic state that paved the way for a soul-crushing totalitarianism. She urged clear thinking, confidence in the value of liberty, and, above all, integrity when faced with incipient fascism. We will examine three central ideas in this dense composition: the dangers of stereotyping the character of nations, the stunning effects of Hitler's acts of propaganda, and the oppressive consequences of his tight internal control.

The first of the three parts of Weil's essay, entitled "Hitler and the External Politics of Ancient Rome," dealt with Hitler's psychological warfare: his ability to hit hard where least expected, attracting the maximum amount of awe and prestige. This section, published in the *Nouveaux Cahiers* on January 1, 1940, was the only piece to reach the wartime public. Her next part, "Hitler and the Internal Regime of the Roman Empire," warned against a strong centralized state that constricted thought and creativity, diminished human dignity, and spread spiritual sterility over all it controlled. Although already in printers' proofs, censors forced its withdrawal. The part that she wrote last, "Permanence and Change in National Character," was planned as an introduction to the other two parts. In her introduction, Weil felt the need to highlight the danger of hypocritical assumptions about national character, which obscured the ability to critically evaluate any political situation. In 1960 Albert Camus joined the three parts in their intended order, making a whole article to include in a collection of her historical and political writings.

"L'ÉTERNELLE ALLEMAGNE" AND "LA FRANCE ÉTERNELLE"

The foreign policy of [Louis XIV] rose from the same ruthless
spirit of pride, the same skilful art of humiliation,
the same bad faith as did Hitler's.

Weil, "Some Reflections on the Origins of Hitlerism"

Shallow stereotypes that characterized a nation, one's own or another's, were an additional warning that attentive assessment of the international situation was being deliberately avoided. Weil wanted to alert the French people against deluding themselves with two particularly perfidious clichés that they were bandying about to bolster their own sense of self-righteousness over that of the German people. The view that Germany was an incorrigible menace to the world while France was a bearer of civilized virtues was founded on bad faith. Condemning German transgressions while ennobling similar exploits perpetrated by the French was dishonest and evasive. Characterizing the German aggressor as incorrigibly warlike implied that the French nation was above reproach. The French education system reinforced this egregious misrepresentation of self-glorifying nationalism, which created major obstacles to peaceful coexistence. The opposing country was always in the wrong, allowing the defending country to assume that all virtue was in its camp. Using historical examples, Weil argued that in fact France, by its own past unscrupulous actions, bore equal responsibility with Germany for the present predicament. The French could not make rational choices without recognizing this. National character, judged by whether it fostered war or peace, did not remain constant but took on varied aspects according to conditions. This section will examine Weil's arguments for taking an honest look at both Germany and France, her selection of events to make her logic more persuasive, and her emphasis on the vital role of education in furthering attitudes of either belligerent competition or of generous cooperation.

For Weil, both of the widely circulating clichés, *l'éternelle Allemagne* and *la France éternelle,* simplistically summed up proverbial insights into national character as if they were a priori correct. The first cliché held negative subjective connotations, signifying a Germany that was forever bellicose; the second, in contrast, implied a praiseworthy France that merited eternal gratitude for its gifts of enlightenment and civilization. (In French, the placement of the adjective before or after the noun alters the meaning.) *La France éternelle* betokened a confident superiority on the part of that country's citizens, requiring no further explanation, while *l'éternelle Allemagne* signified a permanent menace to the world. Carried to the logical conclusion, only the annihilation of Germany would end its persistent threat to peace, whereas France merited protection at all cost, since her existence was an eternal blessing to humankind. These clichés inhibited the possibility for a just resolution of political conflicts and boded ill for how

Germany would be treated after an Allied victory. The time for foster-
ing any chance of future peaceful relationships was the present.

For Weil, "Hitlerian Germany" was not *l'éternelle Allemagne,* either
figuratively or literally; it was a recent phenomenon that had little resemblance to the society of the ancient warrior tribe of Germans as described by Tacitus and Caesar. The early tribal Germans, despite their
penchant for battle, loved liberty and did not subjugate the peoples
they conquered. Rather, Hitler's model was ancient Rome, which had
disarmed and enslaved its neighbors. The Führer and his followers
craved domination, not war, she claimed: they dreamed of a peace
where all were subservient to their will. "If someone resembled Hitler,
in barbaric behavior, premeditated treachery, the art of provocation,
the efficacy of ruse, it was Caesar."[31] We see Weil here selectively using
historical happenings to make her point.

For the French people to be fair rather than vengeful in their eventual treatment of postwar Germany, they needed to picture themselves
in the same situation. Weil reminded her countrymen that, of the four
past major threats to civilization from countries pursuing universal
domination, the first came from Spain and the second two from France.
Germany's more recent qualification for this dubious honor came
from emulating their example. Prior to Hitler, she remarked sardonically, Frederick II had taken Richelieu and Louis XIV as his models
and had gotten his outsized reputation of glory from illustrious French
writers of the time, who, by implication, were flattering him to seek his
favor. Hitler, having gained power domestically, had profited from lessons given four hundred years ago by Charles V and his son Philip II
in sixteenth-century Spain and by Napoleon, who had continued the
policies set up first by Cardinal Richelieu and refined by Louis XIV. Although some preferred to believe that Napoleon had spread the ideas
of liberty and equality following the French Revolution, he had instead
intensified the centralization of power into a unique source of authority and an object of veneration.

The central bureaucratic state, with no sense of morality, sacrificed everything to "prestige," violating treaties and inciting wars under
the cover of dissembling pretexts. Weil punctuated her argument with
a pithy observation that is unfortunately still valid today: "States advocating war claim, rightly or wrongly, that they are making war in order

to avoid it."[32] Thus Germany had no greater claim to the titles of persistent aggressor than did France. If the French were less attached to a sense of national superiority, perhaps they could imagine ways to stabilize international interaction without resorting to violence.

HITLER, ROME'S REMARKABLE EMULATOR

[Only] those conquests horrify which one has to endure; those that one achieves [even vicariously] are always commendable.

Weil, "Some Reflections on the Origins of Hitlerism"

In "Hitler and the External Politics of Ancient Rome," Weil reinforced her warnings about Hitler's insights into the psychology of waging war. His methods, updated versions of those used effectively by ancient Roman conquerors, inspired fear by deploying massive force in imaginative ways and by disseminating subtle threats of violence, which were then carried out capriciously. These techniques destabilized the intended victims, sapping their will to revolt by interspersing deceitful moments of hope with terrifying displays of force. Hitler's intent was to increase Germany's national prestige by creating the illusion of invincibility, luring the vulnerable to capitulate. For Weil, this was a replay of Rome's method of expanding and maintaining its huge territory. Roman discipline and organization handily supplemented the conviction that the Romans, as a superior race, were born to command. This sense of entitlement allowed them to treat others with cold-hearted cruelty, duplicity, and indifference to any respect due to human beings. Their disingenuous propaganda sacrificed people and morality to prestige.

Weil considered the comparison between Hitler and ancient Rome striking, but she understood that her countrymen were hard put to recognize it because France, in its literature and educational system, had persistently extolled the achievement of this Mediterranean empire. Western civilization had associated itself with Roman glory and with Rome's domination by martial behavior devoid of compassion. She underscored the fact that ancient Rome's history was known through the eyes of the Romans themselves or penned by their Greek subjects who had to flatter their masters. No opposing versions written by the conquered Carthaginians and Gauls or the subdued Spanish, German, and Breton tribes existed. The triumphant satisfaction that emanated from descriptions of the victories distracted modern readers from thinking that they too could be susceptible to colonization. She noted that only "those conquests horrify which one has to endure; those that one achieves [even vicariously] are always commendable." By refusing to analyze with lucidity and honesty the reality facing them, the French could succumb to the dire threat posed by the Third Reich: the loss of their cultural heritage through a form of colonization.

In Weil's analysis, a nation seeking power over other nations had to believe that its destiny for all eternity was to be master over others. The Romans had the ingenuity to manipulate at will others' emotions of fear, terror, anger, indignation, hope, tranquillity, and torpor. Carrying out such manipulation required a savagery without limits or hesitation. The Romans' confidence and self-satisfaction permitted them to keep a clear conscience in the midst of terrible crimes. Even barbarous force needed self-righteous pretexts to cover its base acts, such as believing that one was always right—not just right by being the strongest, but right "pure and simple."

A Roman citizen held Rome in his soul above all else. This idolization, in Weil's eyes, rendered spiritual life there nothing other than an expression of the will to reign over others. To be an enemy of Rome called down the harshest punishment; even failing to promote Rome was culpable. Therefore, one had to outwardly show devotion to Rome; Rome itself had perfected the appearance of feigned friendship. As evidence that Hitler's methods embodied the same perfidy as Rome's, she referred to his calculating precept: "Never treat someone as an enemy until the precise moment when you are able to crush him."[33]

Weil compared Roman cold-blooded treachery with Hitler's policies in his inexorable push for supremacy. Using citations from historians of Roman times—Appian, Polybius, Plutarch, and others—she described the imperturbable ferocity of the Roman soldiers in dealing with other cultures, particularly the Carthaginians, who suffered a long period of deprivation and humiliation before being totally annihilated.

The incident of an impotent Carthaginian delegation pleading futilely for peace before the Roman Senate evoked for her how on March 14, 1939, Hitler had imperiously summoned Emile Hacha, the president of the Czechoslovakian Republic, to Berlin, where he was kept constrained and helpless while the German troops invaded Bohemia.[34] Weil likened Callicrates, the pro-Roman leader of the Achaean League who more than once betrayed Achaea to Rome, to Arthur Seyss-Inquart, the Austrian Nazi who deceitfully facilitated the invasion of Austria on March 11, 1938.[35] The anguish of countries currently trembling under the shadow of Hitler's domination resembled that which had gripped the Greeks after the Romans destroyed Carthage. The tragic Carthaginian annihilation portended the same harrowing fate for the Greeks.

Weil inserted at this point a poignant portrayal of the mental disarray, bordering on derangement, of individuals caught in the throes of terror. The description prefigured future psychological conditions manifesting themselves in sectors of her own country under Nazi despotic rule. She translated from Latin the selection in Polybius's *Histories* where he described the dread felt in Greece as the Romans exacted retribution for the Greeks' ill-fated objections to certain heartless imprisonments: "Struck with terror by what was happening in the cities, some [Greeks] irrationally took their own lives; others fled the towns for impractical places without the slightest idea of where to go. Some denounced one another to their enemies as having been hostile to the Romans; others delivered and accused their neighbors, before anyone even asked for an accounting. Some went to accuse themselves of failings before being charged, imploring punishment. So many threw themselves off precipices and down wells that the stench itself should have elicited pity."[36] Yet neither heroic resistance nor humble submission saved the ancient Greek civilization with all its marvels. Rome, in retribution for Greece's insubordination, reduced it to the level of a colonial regime. Weil feared this same debasement for her country if France were to capitulate to Germany's aura of invincible strength.

The barbarities that Rome inflicted heightened its prestige by inspiring fear and enhancing the impression of impregnability. Weil tried to make her readers critically aware of how artfully Hitler had elevated Germany's international standing. He knew that when leaders could spread terror, only an impulse stronger than fear could hold out against the oppressors, and she understood the challenge of countering fear. As soon as anguish became widespread, passions and not intelligence determined people's attitudes. Each success of the victor augmented the capacity to inspire dread, leading to the day when power would be accompanied by a prestige so formidable that no one dared attack such a strong nation.

Propaganda and force reinforced each other; force rendered the propaganda more effective. With each new Roman conquest, the unnerved peoples and their leaders became more and more accustomed to accepting them as masters, which allowed Rome to obtain diplomatic victories as pitiless as those that could have been won through arms. To make her point, Weil recounted an anecdote, familiar to French lycéens, about a Roman senator who, on arrival at the court of a foreign king, traced a circle around him and ordered him to declare his intentions concerning the demands of Rome before he stepped outside the circle. The king, paralyzed with fear, conceded without delay all points. Weil then queried rhetorically: "Couldn't one take this senator for a minister of foreign affairs of the Third Reich?"[37]

Weil concluded this section with the assurance that Hitler was less formidable to his neighbors than the Romans had been to theirs because he had begun to apply high-handed methods even before conquering his Carthage, that is, England. But although his methods were inferior to those of the Roman regime, she conceded that Rome had never had such a remarkable emulator, if in truth he was emulating and not inventing. His intention of imposing peace on other peoples through servitude and compelling them to conform to a supposedly superior organization and civilization did not differ from Rome's. In her skillful style of drawing her readers into her argument through use of the first-person plural, she exclaimed sardonically that surely "we" would not be such dupes as to take the cult of Wotan, the neo-Wagnerian romanticism, or the religion of Aryanism seriously or to be so gullible as to take Hitler's racist policies as anything other than rampant nationalism. But she wrote the article precisely because she knew that it was human nature to admire the powerful and to want to share in collective glory. Weil blamed the phenomenon of nationalism for permitting the concentration of internal power in the hands of an anonymous bureaucracy, a development that in turn led to re-current cycles of war. A nation inexorably satisfied its unassuageable need for prestige by exhibiting raw power, which in every case sacri-ficed human values.

THE SPIRITUAL STERILITY OF A GLORIFIED STATE

If Germany, thanks to Hitler and his successors, enslaved the
European nations and abolished the greater part of past
cultural treasures, history would certainly
say that Germany had civilized Europe.

Weil, "Some Reflections on the Origins of Hitlerism"

Weil's concluding section of her "Origins of Hitlerism" essay, "Hitler and the Interior Regime of the Roman Empire," stressed that all social structures had a natural tendency to concentrate too much authority in a leader. Democracy was no exception when governed by self-serving politicians. In the Roman Empire, deliberate policies of the state made violence a familiar element of everyday life: the gladiator games fos-tered sadistic pleasure in seeing blood flow; burdensome taxes and usurious loans forced the defenseless into abject poverty and slavery. Writers who portrayed this historic debasement of all levels of society as "civilization" bore a great deal of blame in Weil's eyes. She fore-warned her readers, "If Germany, thanks to Hitler and his successors, enslaved the European nations and abolished the greater part of past cultural treasures, history would certainly say that Germany had civi-lized Europe."[38] The voices of the vanquished from the European cul-tures would disappear, as had those of the Carthaginians.

Weil worried that her readers, in their deep-rooted admiration of ancient Rome, would fail to recognize the perils of a totalitarian state. She insisted that in the Roman Empire "never were human beings more completely bowed down under the power of one man or con-strained more harshly by the cold stranglehold of force."[39] Absolute power rested in the state; one emperor could be replaced by another with no slackening of the constraints that could freeze the souls of men. These conditions dried up creativity in the arts, raised the state to be the unique object of spiritual adoration, and expunged human virtue. The overly glorified state, she continued, subsequently sapped any spiritual presence throughout the Mediterranean basin. No religion was as foreign to the notion of good or the salvation of the soul as that of Rome.

Hitler's massive incarceration of selected victims in concentration camps and his crushing of Bohemia equaled in every way the Roman treatment of slaves and the colonized in their provinces.[40] But again, she offered a faint glimmer of hope for her countrymen: Hitler was prematurely exercising a totalitarian dictatorship before he had become master of the world. His overhasty extension of control beyond his borders endangered his plan for universal domination, since a totalitarian state could crush its own subjects far more easily than it could conquer other countries.

In her concluding remarks, Weil refuted the argument that progress in human moral behavior invalidated the parallel between Roman and modern times. Not so, she insisted. Moral standards existed from time immemorial; as proof she cited once again the four-thousand-year-old utterance of the Egyptian Sun God: "I have made the four winds that every man might breathe thereof like his brother. . . . I have made every man like his brother, and I have forbidden that they do evil, [but] it was their hearts which undid that which I said."[41] She pointed out that 2,500 years earlier the Greeks had "unequivocally denounced the institution of slavery, Aeschylus in 'Agamemnon' [had] explicitly condemned violence and war, [and] Sophocles' Antigone [had] rejected all hatefulness that ever existed."[42] Even the Romans covered their treachery and brutality with a veil of hypocrisy, indicating an awareness of moral behavior. By eliciting admiration for Roman deceitfulness, the French education system was undermining its own efforts to raise peace-loving citizens. She asserted: "If I admire or even excuse in my thoughts today an act of brutality committed two thousand years ago, I fall short in human virtue."[43]

Bringing in a positive model from recent history for generous ways to treat a defeated enemy, Weil evoked the exceptional half century of tranquillity following Napoleon's failed attempt to dominate Europe. She attributed the long period of peace to the fact that France's former adversaries did not extort vengeful retribution. By the same token, if the Allies won, Germany also should be treated in a way that was commensurate with the goal of securing order and should not be punished by a subjugation that required long-term constraints, damaging to both victor and vanquished. She wrote: "A victory is more or less just, not contingently on the cause that sparked the conflict, but according to the order established once arms are laid down."[44] Order, for her, required decentralization of authority, not only within Germany, but also within the victorious nations.

For Weil, the juridical notion of the sovereign state was incompatible with the idea of international order or of respect for the individual. She agreed with those who blamed Germany's national unification as the catalyst for aggression: "All peoples who submit to a centralized bureaucratic military state become a curse for their neighbors and the world."[45] France was no worse; she had simply become a nation earlier. "The state to which Richelieu gave body and soul . . . wasn't the crown, or even the public good; it was the anonymous, blind machine, producing order and power that we know today as the state and that is the object of adoration in certain countries."[46] Over time, this transformation in attitudes had occurred everywhere that sovereign nations had formed. Weil repeated her philosophical conviction: "A power that has no legitimately imposed limit tends by necessity to increase within and without."[47] A state enjoying such power would inevitably become as coercive and absolute as its accessible force would warrant. She lamented that because of the contemporary loss of traditional contexts for one's obedience—the family, the workplace, and the local culture—unconditional allegiance gravitated by default to the state, which in the long run diminished individual freedom.

All legitimate authority imposed conditions on its subjects, even when it committed transgressions in the name of the collectivity. Too often, the measures taken to chastise an offending nation, whether war, the threat of war, or radical economic pressures, unfairly deprived all that nation's people of basic needs. Weil suggested that ways be devised to protect a people from obeying depraved leaders and consequently from sanctions imposed from without. She saw a solution in a federalist order that would share the responsibilities of governmental oversight between nations and within each great nation. But as long as all human ties were mediated by the state, the state would continue its systematic and periodic massacre of its subjects, which meant that no public opinion, no efforts of goodwill, no international maneuvers, at that point, could prevent disaster for the individuals. Harmonious relationships between individuals and collectivities required a delicate balance of obligations and responsibilities. In cases where a strong authority threatened to usurp all power, members of a group needed support from outside the collectivity to reestablish a balance between governmental power and respect for the dignity of the individual. The availability of help from the international community to support the weaker elements in the society merited serious consideration.

Looking ahead to what Europe might be like after World War II, Weil thought that a more durable postwar international order could be founded if Germany were treated fairly rather than subjected to humiliation. Punitive dismemberment of vanquished Germany would require force to maintain it. By forcibly imposing their will on defeated Germany, victors would turn into future dictators, falling into what Weil called the Hitlerian system of total control over others. If partition of the conquered state was decreed, it would be best if the victors in turn decentralized their own legislative, judicial, and administrative jurisdictions, since measures perceived as justly imposed and fairly shared would have the best chance of success.

In this long exploratory piece, Weil wanted to impress upon her countrymen that their unquestioned acceptance of the glories of Rome had blinded them to the oppressive effects of bureaucratic centralization of power in the state. Alternative structures based on the dispersal of centralized authority were feasible, valid, and essential for ensuring human dignity. She blamed the traditional view of history for narrowing the ability of young French minds to imagine alternatives. Worse, the French educational system fed the pervasive cult of grandeur in the study of the past and of literature. She gave as an example the epic *Song of Roland,* the oldest surviving major work of French literature and studied by every French schoolchild, which unequivocally extolled Charlemagne's campaign for universal domination. But Weil deplored the short shrift given humble men of courage who stood up for the "good." These scorned and humiliated heroes, common in Greek literature and central to the Gospels, offered valuable countermodels to the young, who needed to be aware of the havoc left in the wake of opportunistic power-driven leaders.

Weil believed that political centralization was headed toward its own chaotic demise, though at the cost of great suffering, because no entity in nature escaped limits. She felt that human misery and irreparable destruction (material and spiritual) could be diminished if enough responsible persons of goodwill lucidly prepared for a transformation of the nation into smaller political and social units. These guidelines constituted Weil's positive message for the postwar world. She was not alone in advancing them, since others after her have pursued varied forms of regionalization, in France and elsewhere. Nevertheless, the trend has been in the opposite direction, as globalization has been leading to the disappearance, so lamented by Weil, of innumerable ethnic groups, with their languages, cultural treasures, their spiritual insights, and close knowledge of their natural surroundings.

"Some Reflections on the Origins of Hitlerism" included a number of insights into the sources of brute force and preventative means to counter it. In Weil's opinion, the past glorification of force led directly to the present violence beginning in Europe. One can well understand the occupiers' determination to keep her writings unavailable to the public. The seeds of violence she saw in the national drive for unlimited prestige, spurred by misleading slogans, were embedded in Hitler's origins and methods. Her partial solutions to the problem of relations between individuals and their collectivity at this point in her thinking involved developing the ability to read history objectively, seeking ways of decentralizing government, and accepting the importance of obedience—freely chosen. The last idea—the need for obedience, though with the absolute necessity of freedom to choose where to place one's obedience—would become, until the end of her life, a key focus of her reflections on the divine destiny of humankind. She foresaw postwar conditions as a new opportunity for societies to reorient themselves toward seeking ways to provide for greater harmony in human relations. She continued her campaign against centralization within collectivities on the principle that it was lethal to the freedom of individual thought.

CHAPTER FOUR

Values for Reading the Universe

An idolatry without love, what could be more monstrous or more sad?

Weil, *The Need for Roots*

Simone Weil's religious conversion gave her insight into the notion that a positive force had the power to stop the spiraling of violence brought on by the attraction to brute force inherent in human nature. This revelation deepened her understanding of the underlying psychology behind human motivation and led her to imagine just social institutions inspired by the power of divine love. Her close observation of the rhythms of the universe reinforced her view that the cosmos was an example of perfect obedience; in contrast, Hitler's reading of the regular movements within the universe as a model of overwhelming power appalled her. That two readings of the same phenomenon could be so opposed—one beneficial to humankind and the other destructive—showed Weil the necessity of education to guide uncertain minds toward a true reading of the physical world. She believed that the power of divine love, although seemingly weaker, was, in truth, infinitely stronger than Hitler's deployment of unmitigated force. For Weil, "Faith is more real than *realpolitik*."[1] This chapter will juxtapose her interpretation of the movement and structure of the material universe with Hitler's and will explore her proposition for a Corps of Frontline Nurses as a pragmatic contrast to Hitler's brilliant but cruel stunts to stun his intended victims before ruthlessly dominating them.

Wanting to find methods by which persons could be sufficiently enlightened to interpret (or read) phenomena accurately, Weil probed into the psychology behind Hitler's successful appeal to fanaticism. Her goal was to present principles that could operate as criteria for objectively assessing situations and would guard vulnerable minds against false conceptions. She desperately wanted to counter Hitler's aggression, not by imitating his hostile techniques, but by devising corresponding actions whose source lay in pure goodness. She conceded: "Violence is often necessary, but, to my eyes, there is grandeur only in gentleness. (I do not mean by that word anything bland.)"[2] This "gentleness" was available to everyone who willingly embraced God's grace. Weil's determination to uncover "gentle" but potent ways to effectively confront force and her skill in presenting her convictions make her contribution to understanding the human condition uniquely valuable.

HITLER'S READING OF BLIND FORCE

As long as something in our soul is capable of being proud of
[our civilization], we are not innocent of any of Hitler's crimes.

Weil, *The Need for Roots*

In the "Origins of Hitlerism," Weil had portrayed Hitler's success in emulating the methods of the Roman Republic in its domination of the Mediterranean basin and those of the Roman Empire's oppressive internal rule as inevitable outcomes of values that exalted glory and prestige. She also knew that Hitler's interpretation of the universe, described in *Mein Kampf* as a model of force that indifferently crushed all in its path, was a misinterpretation. Weil's hope was for people to resist with all their strength burgeoning despotic force before it became overpowering and never to admire sheer force. Her conviction of the absolute necessity to rebut Hitler's materialist conception of human relations becomes evident in her letters, notebooks, and fragments of essays. In her last work, *The Need for Roots (L'enracinement),* she fully discredited his interpretation and presented a theoretical structure of a new form of civilization that instead of relying on force had work as its spiritual center.

For Weil, the Third Reich was a paradigm of the disastrous results of making force the rule of behavior and of believing that one's control over others had no limits. Since the rise of Hitler had its origins in Western civilization, other tyrants would periodically emerge if no efforts were made to activate an opposing force that was grounded in pure "good." Hitler symbolized much that had taken a wrong turn in the West, and no one could pretend to be innocent of any of his crimes, above all not "those who were able to wield a pen."[3] Typically, she included herself, as a writer and thinker, among those responsible for serious failures in the task of guiding their compatriots toward good actions that relied on honesty and truth. Everyone, intellectuals, educators, and political leaders, had a share of the blame. Weil intended to expose the mores that led to the disaster of World War II and to find ways to reorient humankind toward eternal values.

Contrary to Hitler, Weil believed profoundly that the "good," situated outside the material universe, served as the wellspring of all goodness that occurred in "the world here below." She called the impartial force that ruled over the material universe "necessity," but that "necessity" was not the reign of naked force, such as despots impose. For Weil, "God has written his signature in the laws of necessity. . . . This universe is a machine to fabricate the salvation of those who consent to it." According to this interpretation, "The soul ceases to be crushed by a continuous reading of force in matter."[4] Hitler's enormous misjudgment was to think that the "good" lodged in a material thing: hereditary Aryan blood.[5] He had trusted in the mechanism of "the notion of an elected race, a race destined to subdue all others and then to establish among his drudges a kind of justice suitable for slaves."[6] Because he had confounded the "good" with a material force, Weil knew he could be checkmated by the immaterial force of love, seemingly weak but paradoxically stronger than physical force.[7]

For Weil, Hitler was neither a mediocre intellectual crazed by megalomania nor a derisible primitive tribal chieftain, as many of her fellow Frenchmen charged. To properly assess the threat he posed, they had to acknowledge his considerable talents, one of which was his clear vision of the political means to increase Germany's power. Weil saw Hitler's genius in his exploitation of the economic situation to gain the support of millions of uprooted disconsolate Germans suffering from the humiliation of 1918. She believed that "one who is uprooted uproots; one who feels rooted does not uproot."[8] Hitler's view of the human condition led to nightmarish behavior and suffering for the rest of the world because he knew how to combine technology with a manipulation of the contemporary distress from uprootedness.[9] His rise to power had its source in the acute moral malaise caused by inflation and widespread unemployment following increasing industrialization due to modern technological advances. These combined factors had immensely amplified Hitler's potential for exerting unfettered authority in domestic and foreign affairs.

Weil's primary interest was not to dissect Hitler's character or to assign culpability; rather, she wanted to identify underlying principles that would establish future hindrances to exploitative power. To start, the West had to admit that its own conception of grandeur had grave consequences. Those with the authority to write, teach history, and generate propaganda had to remain alert to the influence they had over young unformed minds avid for renown. In Hitler's biography she saw a miserable, uprooted adolescent wandering the streets of Vienna, thirsting for the type of renown he read about in accounts of Sylla, the vainglorious, deceitful, and cruel Roman consul. That legendary figure, however despicable, fed the young Adolf's outsized craving, and the future Führer set out to attain a similar notoriety. Weil ironically complimented his boldness, saying that at least he recognized something as a "good" and went out to grab it; not to do so would be cowardice.[10] In his desire to win a place in the annals of history, he would stop at nothing.

Thinking ahead to Hitler's defeat, already foreseen early in the war, Weil questioned what possible punishment of this idolater of powerful personalities could check the contamination he had unleashed. Since he wanted to be honored in the chronicles of history, "the only punishment capable of both penalizing him and of diverting young ambitious adolescents from following his example was to so totally transform the traditional sense of grandeur that he would be excluded."[11] Weil knew this would be a major task and would even be foolish to consider if each person did not accomplish the change of attitude within himself. One could, to this end, honor other historic leaders who had not aspired to superficial grandeur, such as the Roman emperor Marcus Aurelius. Weil admired this stoic philosopher and his refusal to emulate unjust leaders. He had declared, "Alexander and Caesar were not just; nothing forces me to imitate them." By the same token, Weil insisted, "Nothing forces us to admire them either."[12]

Also, omnipresent and unflagging propaganda had to be frankly assessed for its role in obscuring questionable motives. A skillful master of such propaganda, Hitler had made a new contribution to mob psychology by masterminding showy displays to manipulate public opinion. Weil saw the brilliance of "his ingenious observation that brute force cannot triumph alone, but it can easily succeed by making use of a few ideas, as base as could be imagined."[13] To enhance the effects of his flow of words, Hitler had devised spectacles that captured the imagination of the German people and overwhelmed them emotionally. Rome too had used this brazen stratagem with astounding success. For Weil, using propaganda that did not stir the emotions was as futile as pumping the accelerator in a car whose gas tank is empty.

Weil concluded, however, that no one must be fooled that artful propaganda could ever lead people to the "good" because "propaganda does not aim to inspire, it closes and seals all openings through which inspiration might pass; it swells the entire soul with fanaticism." It could not serve a positive purpose; for that one must resort to education.[14] Her own country was not above using propaganda basely. Weil accused France of having profited too often in the past from guilefully disseminating biased information that enhanced its own self-image while it was oppressing manual laborers, the population of Brittany, and the millions of subjects in its colonies. Education had never been a high priority in France's treatment of the marginalized.

Education, for Weil, meant learning from past humble models whose principal aim was to discover the truth, as well as honoring contemporary leaders who furthered positive human relationships. She devised a practical application of her belief in the value of offering warm, caring attention at life-threatening moments with her project to put women, well trained in first-aid methods, among the wounded on the battlefields to give them on-the-spot attention. Her goal was to convince onlookers that selfless attention had far more worth for humankind than ruthless force.

SIMONE WEIL'S PROJECT FOR THE FORMATION OF A CORPS OF FRONTLINE NURSES

Grace alone can give courage, while leaving one's tenderness intact,
or can give tenderness while leaving one's courage intact.

Weil, Notebooks

While composing "Origins of Hitlerism," Weil began to formulate a plan to ensure her participation in the defense of occupied France and, more importantly, to offer a strategy that would oppose Hitler and inspire her compatriots with courage. Her project entailed creating a special formation of mobile frontline nurses who would bring "first aid" (she used the English term) directly to soldiers in the most perilous areas of fighting. A small unit of women would be prepared to perform rudimentary but urgent tasks of bandaging, applying tourniquets, and giving injections. Weil believed that their presence and words would bring inestimable moral comfort to the wounded and dying men by offering human warmth, promising to deliver messages to the families at home, and remaining close to the traumatized soldiers during their agonizing wait for the stretcher bearers. The humanitarian aspect of the project sufficiently justified her proposal, but Weil argued that the execution of such a project carried an even higher value, in that its essential moral qualities would be particularly suitable for countering Hitler's awe-inspiring psychological warfare.

The Corps of Frontline Nurses remained Weil's major preoccupation from its first conception in the early 1940s to her death, which may have been hastened from grief over never receiving official permission to enact her plan in France. In 1942, just before leaving Marseilles for America, she confided the full details of her strategy to Joë Bousquet, her friend and a paralyzed veteran of "the Great War." Bousquet responded with two pages of his reflections, generally laudatory.

In a moving letter, he supported the need for immediate aid on the battlefield by recounting how the men in the World War I infantry had been formally forbidden to stop in the midst of the fray to help the wounded. He remembered how his lieutenant, an admired Jesuit, had warned him not to weaken his vulnerable determination to fight by exposing himself to visions of others' agony. The officer said it was impossible to maintain the two competing emotions of courage for war and instinctive compassion for the wounded, and he described how a sensitive person could keep up his courage to fight only by hardening his heart to the suffering around him. As Joë recounted the officer's advice: "The soldier who attacks belongs to his mission, to his duty, and to the great battle gathering momentum as he watches in awe; he does not belong to himself, he is prey to his imagination and his duty. But a moment with a dying fellow soldier brings back his awareness, undoes the firm will formed for the event, and leaves him unfit for the clash. Pity and fear give him a tender conscience that becomes all pain and suffering."[15]

Bousquet told Weil of another stirring memory, this time of feminine valor on a battlefield being readied for attack. Young women, American, English, and French, were driving automobiles laden with the wounded, picking up traumatized men, and taking them to a makeshift field hospital. The tenacity and loving compassion shown by the women for these bloodied companions bolstered the soldiers going into battle with visions of promised care in their own time of need.[16] Weil anticipated that the compassionate presence of nurses in the combat zone could harmonize the conflicting emotions within a combatant. She believed that the source of the women's strength in such a dangerous situation would be a supernatural virtue informed by grace. Weil's exploration of contradictory emotions, such as courage and tenderness, led her to note that an infusion of grace would permit both to exist together. Grace could engender courage, leaving tenderness intact, or it could do the reverse, inspiring tenderness but leaving one's courage steadfast.[17] She added later, "God is present, Christ is present, everywhere that man offers man an act of supernatural virtue."[18]

Deeply grateful for Bousquet's testimony, Weil meticulously drafted, during her stay in New York, the full version of her Nurses

Project, in which she used all the rhetorical skills at her command. She
sent the plan of action to her friend Maurice Schumann, a spokesman
for General Charles de Gaulle in London, and implored him to do
everything in his power to obtain official permission to enact it. In
Weil's thinking, the Nurses Project was a valuable political strategy
that could inspire people fighting for their survival. She wrote Schumann, "We can and we must show that we have a different kind of
courage, more challenging and rare."[19]

To emphasize Hitler's skill in dazzling his own military, the
enemy, and the international observers, Weil cited two of his most
loathsome successes: (1) the stunning strike by the first squadrons of
German parachutists who invaded the island of Crete by air and (2) the
special formation of SS troops, known for extreme brutality against
civilians and prisoners of war. In the awe-inspiring May 1941 invasion
of Crete, 3,500 men of the elite Seventh Parachute Division, borne
by brightly colored parachutes, dropped from the sky. The Cretans
watched, temporarily aghast at an apparition they had never before
imagined. The islanders heroically rallied to defend their land by foil-
ing the aggressors for an astonishing ten days, wielding only makeshift knives, pitchforks, and sickles against the well-armed German
parachutists. Through sheer brutality, the Nazis won the battle for
Crete. But the decimation of their troops and the time needed to beat
down their victims threw the later German military campaigns devas-
tatingly off schedule.

All the same, Hitler had gained a huge victory in terms of prestige
and power. His "live airborne weapon" was a first, but his henchmen,
the ruthless SS troops, also won him valuable but despicable prestige.
The SS, who sowed an atmosphere of paralyzing terror wherever they
appeared, carried the euphemistic German title of *Schutzstaffel*, or
"protective squadrons." Their black uniforms with skull-trimmed caps
set them apart as an elite and fearsome group who had been selected
for their "racial purity" and their unconditional loyalty to Hitler and his
Nazi party. One of their divisions became the Gestapo or secret police,
and they all operated de facto above the law. Weil was sensitive to the
psychological impact of Hitler's feats that incurred either grudging admiration or pure terrorizing dread. The innovations corresponded to

the black-hearted spirit of the regime and the ominous designs of its leader. In her view, Hitler had generated an ersatz religion, for which its members—his loyal followers—offered to sacrifice everything, even their lives. Therein lay one of the principal sources of his power.

Just as idolatry reinforced the savagery of the Nazis, an analogous inspiration could elevate the aspirations of the French, not a mirror image but something fresh and equivalent: a sign of moral vitality. Weil believed that her Project for a Corps of Frontline Nurses offered an example of actions that stemmed from an authentic and pure source, the ethical opposite of what gave rise to the desire to kill. Sending a unit of unarmed nurses into situations of great peril would illustrate a moral resource of ineffable quality. Giving close attention to extreme affliction would require fortitude on the part of these women, for nothing was as hard as looking directly and attentively at pure suffering. In Weil's thinking, their principled strength would be contagious. Theirs would be a duty chosen from love for their fellow man, not from constraint. The servicemen in the defending army, who had been torn away from their homes and loved ones, would find in the women a powerful reminder of why they were fighting.

While she pushed this plan for a novel deployment of women on the battlefield to the full extent of her persuasive powers, Weil kept in mind that her audience was composed of skeptical military male leaders with ingrained habits and ideas of their own. Her rhetorical skills were perhaps never so desperately employed. She took great pains to stress that the candidates would be carefully selected for their probity, cold resolution, and tenderness—a rare combination, she conceded, but such a fusion existed. Their willingness to sacrifice their lives for this authentic and pure cause would contrast starkly and positively to the SS troops' sacrifice for the evil cause of terrifying and trampling down others. She specified strict expectations for the morality of the women, who would live in close proximity to the men.

To appeal to de Gaulle's sense of military tradition, she described a custom of ancient nomadic German tribes, known for their prowess in war and for their notable distinction of never having been subjugated by the Romans. The ancient German tribes had understood the exalting character that feminine presence brought to the toughest of combats. When heading into battle, their fighters would place a young girl surrounded by elite youthful warriors in the front lines to inspire all their compatriots with the courage to persevere for what they held dearest.

The Corps of Frontline Nurses held great personal importance for Weil. She considered its strategic value essential for inspiring confidence in the rightness of the Allied cause and in the possibility of confronting force without perpetuating a spiral of violence. At full risk to their own well-being, the nurses would offer human warmth and attention to men in intense suffering. Their act of pure goodness would help diminish evil, creating a glaring contrast to base acts that simply transformed the evil without lessening it. In her notebook entries from 1941 to 1942, a reader can perceive her preoccupation with finding ways to lay the foundation for a moral order that would keep evil reduced to a minimum. "To change something (suppress an evil) in the moral order, within one's self or in society, one needs an action that corresponds to the desired effect. Without that, the evil remains under another aspect, but equivalent."[20] How to imagine and put into effect such an action had paramount significance for her.

To reinforce her argument to de Gaulle, Weil included in her project description Joë Bousquet's detailed recommendations, along with an addendum from the *American College of Surgeons Bulletin* that lauded the therapeutic value of on-site treatment for wounds to prevent shock.[21] Hoping that medical authentication and a World War I veteran's knowledge of the battlefield would supply convincing support, she pressed on until the very end of her life to have the project accepted. When it was ignored, she blamed Maurice Schumann with deep bitterness for not sufficiently pleading her case with de Gaulle. One can imagine many reasons why permission was refused. None of them, however, diminished her belief in the moral significance of witnessing with all one's being to a higher value than that of brute force. One of the last items in her notebooks just before her death was the isolated word "—Nurses."[22]

This project articulated the essence of Weil's political and mystical goal: to inspire her people to act according to eternal values that had their source outside this world. She had confidence that such behavior could thwart the evil effects of brute force. Her critical examination of the contemporary violence that was putting the very survival of civilization at risk made her realize that the grave social failings were not just in one man or one group but rather in Western society as a whole. Defeating the Nazis by their own methods of cruelty not only would fail to prevent future disasters but would sow the seeds for later conflicts. New attitudes had to be imagined, and untried methods given a chance. Too many people, admiring power and its superficial grandeur, would read humanity's role in the universe as perversely as Hitler did and mold their behavior toward the futile goal of dominating others. Weil knew that such readings produced only an endless cycle of wars and heartache.

TWO CONTRARY READINGS OF THE UNIVERSE: HITLER'S VERSUS SIMONE WEIL'S

[Man] is certainly not the lord and master of nature, and Hitler was right when he said that man was mistaken in believing so.

Weil, *The Need for Roots*

Weil was appalled by Hitler's "profession of faith" in pure materialism and his claim that brute force governed the universe and men's actions.[23] Twice in her final work she cited with scorn a key offending passage from *Mein Kampf:* "Man must never fall into the error of believing that he is lord and master of nature. . . . Then he will realize that in a world where planets and suns follow their circular orbits, where moons circle planets, where force alone reigns everywhere as mistress over weakness, which she constrains to serve her docilely or be broken, man cannot lay claim to any special laws."[24] She dismissed Hitler's self-serving interpretation of natural law by saying that if force reigned alone and supreme in the universe, as Hitler and others claimed, there would be no place for justice, and justice would consequently be unreal. But, she asserted, justice was not unreal. The proof of its existence endured in human hearts, and "the structure of the human heart is a reality among the realities of this universe, just as is the trajectory of a celestial body."[25] For Weil, justice—the equivalent of truth—provided a counterbalance to exploitative elements in society; it allowed weaker parties to defend themselves against the crushing will of those who would dominate them. She lamented, however, that a growing lack of respect for justice was blocking the reestablishment of a viable and equitable civilization.

Although Weil believed that an indomitable force existed in the cosmos, she knew that life in surroundings where limitless force reigned alone and supreme, coldly smashing anything fragile, was untenable. Her fundamental belief was that Divine Wisdom had created the universe. The regulated interacting elements in the cosmos, following unwavering patterns, constituted, for her, "necessity": the "network of limitations imposed on man by the physical laws of the created world and by the forces, equally restrictive, of human nature and of society."[26] Human beings could work within those constraints, making their surroundings more or less habitable, but they could not alter the laws that regulated the universe. The limits had to be obeyed.[27] Traces of the limitations imposed on physical matter were evident in the world around us, and they attested to similar unbreachable boundaries imposed on man's conduct that he could ignore only at his peril. While these restraints imposed hardships on humankind, they also offered magnanimous beauty.

For Weil, the universe had symbols woven throughout its texture that revealed to human senses its rigorous submission to necessity and exemplified its limitations—but its very order inspired human beings to hope.[28] For example, a wave in the sea "rises, rises, rises; but at a point, where there is only emptiness, it stops and must fold down;"[29] a marble flicked up an incline ascends just so far before it must redescend. She cited God's reassuring promise in Psalm 104 that no matter how terrifying events on earth after a flood could become, he had "set a boundary that [the waters] may not pass, so that they might never again cover the earth."[30] She also treasured the ancient Greek philosophers' observation that while the cosmos was subject to limits, man too had limits of which he had to be ever mindful. Attempts to exceed or ignore these boundaries inevitably brought on some form of Nemesis: a downfall in the form of a penalty or price. For Weil, Hitler's attempts to exceed his limits had already begun to foreshadow his downfall, but his hubris had blinded him to the reality of his eventual ruin.

Although Hitler was right in recognizing that man was not a master over nature and did not follow different laws, she knew that man as a thinking creature held a privileged status: the status of being particularly loved. To explain her divergence from Hitler, she wrote: "[Man] is certainly not lord and master of nature, and Hitler was right to say that in thinking so, man was mistaken, but Man is the son of the master of the house, the fair-haired child. . . . A very young child in a rich house is subject, in many things, to the servants; but when he is on the knees of his father and identical to him through love, he shares in the authority."[31] And that authority had its source in self-denying love, as evidenced by God's creation of the material world, which modeled, in perfect form, mankind's ethical relationship with others.

Weil regarded Hitler's reading of the universe and of man's place in it as deviant. She faulted him for imagining that brute force could make the celestial objects go in circular patterns. For her, circular constraints, inducing motions of pure beauty and unwavering obedience, had to stem from a generosity of love, which was Divine Wisdom. Obedience to a greater truth underlay the model that the universe exemplified for humankind, and it led to social institutions inspired by justice. To the contrary, his reading of human relationships meant applying cold, ruthless force that imposed an opportunistic and false concept of justice on enslaved populations. The members of Hitler's Aryan race were to coerce everyone else to their will, establishing among them an arbitrary justice that claimed to be a beneficially imposed order.[32]

SLAVERY: THE EPITOME OF INJUSTICE

A thousand signs show that men of our era have
hungered for obedience. But others have profited
from this need to put them in bondage.

Weil, *The Need for Roots*

For Weil, slavery was the most horrific form of force that could be imposed on an individual. She had explored the psychological causes and

effects of enslavement earlier when reflecting on the oppressive working conditions that could destroy the essence of humanness. The critical factor in the relationship between the possessor of human flesh
and the possessed was the inherent arbitrariness capriciously imposed
by the master and suffered by the subjugated. She wondered, "What
makes subordination to capriciousness an enslavement?" Her answer
was: "The ultimate cause resides in the relationship between the soul
and time. Persons subjected to the arbitrary are suspended in the passage of time; they await—the most demeaning of situations—the vicissitudes of the next instant; they passively submit to the present. They
do not dispose of their moments; they do not have a lever to affect the
future."[33]

Individuals subjected to the arbitrary eventually become dehu-
manized and are no longer able to use their energies for freely chosen
positive goals. She commented in her sardonic style on the crushing of
souls in this fashion: "What refinement—to force the mind to continually taste the enslavement of the body! To bear this, one must mutilate
the soul. Not doing so would create the sense of being freshly offered
alive every day to be mortified."[34] The sense of humiliation in the person who could not bear to think of either the past or the future shriv-
eled his body and soul, leaving mere matter in place of the human
being. Force thus made a living person into a thing.[35] That slavery
makes a person lose half his soul was sufficient justification for using
strong-armed force to stop Hitler's drive to dominate and enslave as
many European populations as he could.[36] His evil intention and capacity to achieve his goals determined that a just cause existed for
using force to defeat him and his military.

The empirical evidence of Hitler's intention to hold in thralldom
all under his command had made clear to Weil that there were situations and persons for whom only a solid display of force created an
impediment. Without any reference to a just-war theory or to those
who had carefully considered the question before her, she accepted the
necessity to block certain inherently evil actions with the just means
available. Hitler's intended victims risked losing their souls under his
domination; the Allies, therefore, had righteous cause to employ aggressive self-defense as their last resort, but always while keeping the

means commensurate with the goal. Had Weil lived longer, it would have been quite consistent of her to sharply question the proportionality of many of the Allies' offensive tactics, such as the obliteration bombing of Dresden, the firebombing of over fifty Japanese cities, and the atomic bombing of Hiroshima and Nagasaki. These strategies, which were clearly designed to destroy in the most terrifying manner huge numbers of noncombatants and their means of survival, perverted to the greatest degree humanity's obligation to live with an awareness of others' essential needs and with care for everyone's physical surroundings.

As a philosopher concerned about people living in harmonious relationships, Weil was obsessed with the potential for divergent readings of the cosmos and of human relationships. She felt the need to explore the human psychology that underlay such diametrically opposed readings. Given her mystical framework, she believed that only a reading enlightened by love, which gave a central place to the concept of justice, led to the true interpretation (or reading) of any situation. In Weil's philosophy, justice equaled truth, which in turn equaled love. Consequently, hers was no idle dream that people could live together in a just society. True justice rectified the imbalance created by oppressive social conditions and never reinforced inequity. Justice could thwart an impending use of force that threatened disorder and discord. Seeing to just conditions for everyone did not mean creating a stasis; on the contrary, it implied a constant rearranging of the balance of power to restrict those who had exceeded their limits and become coercive.

Hitler's distorted inference from manifestations of force in the physical universe was unquestionably wrong, and the fruits of his attempt to dominate the world and enslave the non-Aryan populations verified the perversity of his reading. Weil believed, quite to the contrary, that the universe was the language of God, a network of metaphors communicating a variety of meanings but never perversions. One could distinguish the true from the false by measuring the means and outcomes against the eternal criteria of beauty and goodness, which led, not to chaos and disorder, but to greater order.

THE PHYSICAL UNIVERSE AS METAPHOR

*The world is God's language to us; the universe
is the Word of God, the Logos.*

Weil, Notebooks

Weil hoped that empirical studies of the operating laws of the universe would help clarify practical criteria for judging the true value of attitudes and goals in living and thus diminish the worst effects of force in daily life. She perceived the universe as a paradigm for human behavior, displaying obedience, respect for limits, and equilibrium after ruptures and compensations. Laws underlying the movement of the cosmos, in her opinion, indicated correlative social mechanisms in human interactions. Her thoughts on the relationship between the cosmos and the human condition appear in her notebooks as notations on the physical properties of gravity, energy, entropy, inertia, and other quantitative elements. Her inquiries into the laws of the physical universe took the form of questions, citations, and diagrams, revealing her desire to find analogies for human motivations that renewed and raised or exhausted and lowered the stamina and courage of people who were confronted with arduous dilemmas.

She believed that what furnished more or less energy to meet difficult challenges depended on how individuals read their place within the universe and in relation to others. Their readings could replenish their motivating energies or, on the contrary, deplete them. One's place, due to accidental circumstances for the most part, imposed obligations both toward oneself and toward one's fellow human beings. She believed that the choices made in reading relationships within one's natural surroundings obeyed laws similar to those of gravity.[37] But just as the sun transmitted energy to plants, allowing them to defy gravity and grow upwards by means of chlorophyll, a spiritual force existed that enabled individuals to defy moral gravity and strive toward justice.

She noted in capital letters: "There is good reason for the effort to formulate in psychology and in sociology analogous principles to the conservation of energy and to entropy, which have limits. . . . Their principles have never been clearly stated."[38] She sought to understand the mechanism by which the valuable human energy contained in desires was expended, degraded, or reinvigorated: "All desire is precious, for all desire contains energy."[39] The transformation of the quality of energy toward a higher value was of major importance. She believed that unfulfilled desires created a void that had to be filled in one way or another. If that void were filled by imaginary solutions, the available energy would be squandered, or, worse, the situation could lead one to lose contact with reality. "Energy liberated by the disappearance of certain motivational goals tends to descend to a lower level," as if pulled by gravity.[40]

Gravity became her metaphor for human beings' tendency to exert undue force in interpersonal relationships and to behave in immoral ways. Moral gravity signified thinking primarily of oneself and of one's need for comfort and protection while neglecting to consider another person's perspective. She wrote, "Gravity in the physical universe is the force par excellence," and stated that it was in fact the sole measure of force.[41] But this natural downward force could be countered because in the universe, where all things took place in conformity with its laws, chlorophyll allowed plants to obtain energy from light and to grow upwards.[42] She wondered what aspect of human nature weighed down human behavior, just as gravity made unsupported material objects fall to the ground, and, analogously, what force could counter the downward pull. In a preliminary reflection, she had noted: "Gravity. What one expects from others is determined by the effects of gravity in oneself; what one receives from others is determined in a general sense by the effects of gravity in them."[43] Nevertheless, humankind enjoyed a privileged exception: the intervention of supernatural grace. Grace exerted an uplifting counterforce against base tendencies: "Grace is our chlorophyll."[44] But grace, the mediation of the divine, came only to the person who desired its gifts and consented to the obedience it required.

To illustrate human behavior, she used her own spiteful reactions in moments of subsiding energies. From early adolescence on, she had been subject to tormenting migraines, apparently due to a sinus infection that had no known cure at the time. She described how, as the agony approached its pinnacle, she generally lacked the energy to care about reacting in any way. The pain would dissipate her energies, leaving a small empty space in her mind. But as the throbbing increased to a paroxysm of pain, the expanding void was filled by low-grade energies that brought on a mean-spirited wish to inflict suffering on others.

In Weil's language, the energy degraded by the utter inability to end the pain degenerated into the sordid desire to harm others. She commented that this was why frustrated, marginalized members of society struck out first against those who were weaker or equal. She observed: "This phenomenon responds to the need to transfer suffering. *Gravity*—the effect of one's situation in the social hierarchy on the imagination—is *almost* without exception . . . as irresistible as [physical] gravity."[45] In later notebooks, she continued discussing the human need to transfer suffering to another within one's power, giving the example of "the rebuked captain who broods over the reprimand from the colonel until he can relieve his frustration by punishing the lieutenant."[46] Recurring ruptures in social harmony and its misplaced compensation installed an uneasy truce among men until the increasing exasperation of those who felt abused led them to take out their desire for vengeance in one way or another against the authorities. The ensuing upheaval created an even greater rent in the social fabric, which intensified the challenge of restoring equilibrium.[47]

There was also a form of inertia in human behavior by which the humiliated, induced to accept their belittlement, preferred the existing state of affairs to gathering energies for revolt. Weil explained: "There is a disposition to persist in the same pattern [inertia]: for the evildoer to exploit even further, for the humiliated to continue submitting to the debasing treatment."[48] But if the persons involved never stopped to take stock of the situation and to revitalize their positive energies, the cycle of suffering and vengeance would spiral relentlessly downward.

In her stints in three metallurgy factories (1934–35), where she was subjected to poorly maintained, dangerous machinery and patronizing, capricious supervisors, Weil encountered the full impact of dehumanizing conditions. She had voluntarily placed herself in these situations to know the factory workplace firsthand. The actuality had reinforced her sensitivity to the vulnerability of the human psyche, which affected both those who commanded and those who obeyed. In her mind, the conditions she found were akin to enslavement. The higher social position of the authorities fed their inner illusions of superiority, so they exploited their subordinates. The chain of events leading to this outcome, she claimed, operated like the pull of gravity,[49] although, paradoxically, it theoretically elevated some above others by giving them the false sense of having greater importance. She saw little evidence that the oppressed workers tried to change their onerous situation.

She speculated on the best course of action when gravity—moral or physical—created, in a real or figurative sense, a problem by placing an apparently insurmountable obstacle in one's way. Where could one find the strength to effectively pit one's weaker strength against a much stronger force? Looking for an image to serve persons who found themselves confronted with seemingly insurmountable obstacles, she chose the lever. Just as a lever could multiply the mechanical force applied to another object maintained in place by gravity, a psychological disposition, conjured up through reflection, could exert intangible force against ostensible barriers.

Philosophically, Weil sketched out three alternatives for dealing with daunting obstructions: (1) brute force, (2) fantasy, or (3) reflection and assessment. In her mind, the third choice was the only one that had the potential of enhancing human dignity, even if the impediments remained blocking the way.

A stone is found blocking the path down which one is hurrying. Not wanting it there, or accepting its presence, one rushes to shove it out of the way. Optionally, one could exhaust energy by creating the fiction that the stone isn't there. Or one could contemplate the stone, oneself, and the desire to pass, recognizing that the stone is there but is not the end of everything. A pause, at this point, permits an indirect action, such as the use of a lever. The one who impulsively pushes often succeeds, but if he doesn't succeed, the stone becomes an absolute, impossible to remove. For the one, however, who manages the lever, even if he doesn't succeed, the stone does not become an absolute. He thinks he could have succeeded if . . .⁵⁰

If the obstacle were accepted as immovable, paralysis of the mental process would set in; but, if, on the contrary, the solution were left open, individuals might persist in seeking desirable resolution, feeding the capacity for mental reflection. This last option enabled the perplexed to maintain more positive energy in reserve. She understood that the situation could well remain the same but that the reading of the mix of elements in a situation could vary, invigorating powerful sources of energy for the individuals involved or, in contrast, diminishing their vitality to nothing. A good deal depended on whether the desire was of a higher quality (i.e., in view of the supreme "good") or of a lower quality (i.e., oriented toward one's personal attainments). Desire was a twofold motivation for human actions; it could drag people into endless infernal disputes, or it could be a springboard toward their salvation. The values one honored at the time of decision had essential importance for the outcome.

Despite its lack of precision, Weil's model of gravity offers practical insights into the moral significance of human behavior toward others. Pirruccello, in her excellent study "'Gravity' in the Thought of Simone Weil," concluded that Weil's notions of degraded energy and its contrasting higher type of energy related to two incompatible ways of life: "One is a way of life lived in self-aggrandizing, illusion-fostering patterns without concern for a view of things untainted by personal interests. The other is a life lived in the spirit of impartiality and aversion to illusion. The latter seeks to attain a view of things that is not simply a reflection of what one happens to desire."⁵¹

Weil wanted to make these two contrasting ways of life vividly evident to her readers and to convince them that the second pattern enriched their most human attribute: the ability to think. Her examples from nature were chosen to corroborate her arguments for man's strongest assets: knowledge, apprenticeship, and the true assessment of hurdles in any situation. Careful reflection could lead one to expend energies toward honoring ever-higher values, whose source was in the supreme "good." In her philosophy, the thinking, well-disciplined mind, directed by a desire for truth, constituted humankind's unique safeguard against depravity brought on by violence and exploitation. The concept of a lever exerting force against gravity illustrated the principle that weaker forces could be used effectively to confront and stymie stronger forces. Marginalized persons could marshal the power to insist on just policies, showing that apparent weakness, if morally grounded and intelligently employed, could counter pitiless strength.

However, believing that the full extent of the principles governing humankind's nature and relationships remained undiscovered and misunderstood, Weil appropriated for her use Francis Bacon's formula: "Man commands nature by obeying it." In her 1934 essay entitled "Reflections on the Causes of Liberty and Social Oppression," she wrote that Bacon had defined "the true work that makes men free, so long as it is an act of conscious submission to necessity."[52] She stated that "the notion of work considered as a human value is without doubt the unique spiritual conquest that human thought has made since the Greek miracle."[53] Work brought one into direct confrontation with the limitations imposed by the material universe as one attempted to achieve one's goals. In work, methods chosen through careful reflective thought had to adapt to the fixed laws of the material universe. Similarly, social power pushing up against limitations had to eventually result in a readjustment of the distribution of power within the society and compensation for those who had sought change. Unfortunately, too often this readjustment occurred only after great harm had been done to many innocent victims.

Weil understood that desires were unlimited, while their satisfaction or frustration took place within stringent limits. When ambitions were fulfilled, the achiever gained the sense of having merited the outcome. This success supplied renewed vigor and incentives to attain still higher goals. On the opposite end of the spectrum, the thwarting of wants left a residue of discontent that pressed for compensation— usually in a destructive way. The energy in frustrated aspirations became, as Weil expressed it, degraded through a process analogous to that of entropy: diminished and less available for achieving higher goals. Weil wanted to learn how to marshal and expend the energy contained in desires toward good ends.

In a comment on entropy, she noted that since the energy in all closed systems had the tendency to degrade, the energy that made them ascend came from outside the system—that is, radiant energy from the sun.[54] For humankind, supernatural grace was the radiant energy that permitted ascent to higher virtuous actions, despite the occasional intrusion of mean-spirited desires to inflict harm, inspired by hate, bitterness, and rancor. She believed that grace—or "supernatural bread"—sufficient to overcome the pull of moral gravity was available to anyone who sincerely yearned for it. She wrote: "All energy on this earth comes from the sun, except gravity. Everything is a combination of solar energy and of gravity (apart from supernatural bread)."[55] In her conception of human psychology, solar energy took on a symbolic character, as did "supernatural bread," which was the spiritual sustenance enabling one to operate in daily affairs on a level above the psychical pull of moral gravity, or egocentrism.

Weil juxtaposed entries on entropy with comments on the irreversible passage, or descent, from good to evil;[56] entropy, she noted, was tied to the degradation of energy and had as its principle that "the world descends from order to disorder."[57] Consequently, entropy measured energies that were no longer available for good purposes. They became "'low' or 'base' energies incapable of producing love or of discerning balance and harmony in human relationships."[58] Instead, they lent themselves to disruptive actions that destroyed harmonious relationships. The metaphors—up and down, ascent and descent, entropy and energy—run through her reflections.[59] She stated, "The fundamental analogy between the mind and the world is the relationship of high and low, which depends on gravity. Gravity is the force par excellence. Is there, strictly speaking, any other force? That which suggests ascent suggests an increase in value."[60]

According to Pirruccello's study of Weil's use of the term *gravity*, "Weil makes it clear throughout her writings that 'upward' is the figurative direction of the Good, which is the highest value and reality."[61] Weil wrote, "Force is naturally on a lower level; it pulls toward the bottom; gravity."[62] On the other hand, pure attention had a power making it possible for one to reject acts of moral gravity against one's neighbor. All the same, attention could not be fully actualized without having a spiritual dimension, according to Weil. In the graceful essay she wrote for Father Perrin's lycée students, "Reflections on the Right Use of School Studies with a View to the Love of God," she emphasized that "all attention oriented toward God has the same substance as prayer; . . . every time one truly pays full attention, some evil in oneself is destroyed."[63] The essence of attention was not just love of God, but more importantly love of neighbor, which could not be separated from the love of God.

To illustrate the plenitude of love shown by attention, Weil alluded to the Arthurian legend of the Holy Grail, in which the king who guarded the Grail suffered from an excruciatingly painful wound that paralyzed three-quarters of his body. The holy relic represented the consecrated host. The legend held that whoever gave full attention to the king's terrible affliction, asking, not "Where is the Grail?" but "What ails thee?"—or as Weil rephrased it, "What are you suffering from?"—would merit the Holy Cup that miraculously satisfied all hungers.[64] Giving full attention to persons in affliction and considering them as equal in importance to oneself was never easy; pure attention required a denial of one's personal gratifications and limitless desires and an openness to receive God's grace. Weil believed that the energy thus acquired was available to accomplish other actions toward a higher "good" and did not devolve into low or base energy.

Identifying potential sources of energy of the highest sort and setting them in motion against oppressive actions had preoccupied Weil from the beginning of her struggle for social justice. In her notebooks, she had speculated on what could reestablish a balance between man and the universe when the forces of nature and society risked overwhelming and immobilizing him. After making a brief parenthetical allusion to the cross of Christ, she evoked the image of a sailor in his boat equaling the infinite forces of the ocean. She drew a parallel between the boat and a lever. "At each instant, the pilot, guiding—with his weaker muscles—the rudder and the oars, balances that enormous mass of air and water. Nothing is more beautiful than a boat."[65] She had confidence that humankind, through skill, knowledge, and tenacity, could reduce its vulnerability to exterior forces imposed by both society and nature. To do so, however, would take determination and the ability to read the world from a perspective other than one's own and to overcome the natural impulse to place oneself at the center of the universe.

The images of the lever and the skillful boat pilot thread their way through Weil's reflections on the human condition. The lever, adroitly employed to act against gravity, and the experienced navigator, who propels his boat through the turbulent waters, accomplished their tasks because such actions were taken in obedience to nature's laws. The ship's pilot represented humankind intelligently and skillfully steering its course through tempestuous elements after an apprenticeship in assessing a situation accurately, making experienced judgments, and keeping energies in reserve to maintain equilibrium in unstable situations. These skills were the result of trial, error, and experience. Weil saw, in addition, the need for an apprenticeship in virtue, particularly with an eye to situations in which unconstrained force threatened to dominate. The formulation of such training became a principal focus for Weil's efforts to encourage moral behavior.

Weil's scientific analogy depicting her notion of moral gravity has its inadequacies. Pirruccello has sorted out with clarity where Weil's parallel functioned well and where it unjustifiably "obliterated distinctions between phenomena connected with human agents and those not so linked."[66] We have already glimpsed this conflation in Weil's description of the movements of the universe performing in "perfect obedience," one of several circumstances in which she attributed moral characteristics to material forces and transformations. Blind forces of the universe were "just" or "unjust," they could be "punished," and they "disobeyed," terms that appeared to classify transformations according to a hierarchy of values. This is a language she had taken from the ancient Greek Anaximander.[67] Pirruccello argues that Weil's attempts to "combine scientific description and moral value created confusion," since Weil considered, on the basis of her philosophy, that even the most morally degraded people made *choices* that resulted in a qualitative transformation of their energies. Such persons were not acting by necessity in their insistent push to extend their limits; their energy was degraded quantitatively and qualitatively. In contrast, blind matter could not choose: losing usable energy through entropy, it did not choose either to do so or not to do so.

Pirruccello's analysis coincides with that of other readers of Weil who agree that the value in Weil's model of gravity does not come from its being a theoretical scientific model. Despite that, it can still contribute to linguistic and imaginative resources as a way of referencing the moral significance of our desires and actions. By using Weil's scientific metaphors, Pirruccello concludes, "we could articulate the significance of our desires in light of the kind of quality of life they express. And this would allow us to evaluate the worth of our desires such that they strike us as noble or base or depraved or lofty and so on."[68]

The value of this effort is evident in the reactions of a multitude of readers who have had little difficulty relating to the moral significance of Weil's notion of gravity as portrayed in *Gravity and Grace,* a collection of aphorisms culled from her notebooks by her trusted friend Gustave Thibon. Weil has, in fact, opened new avenues for looking at human desires and motivations and for evaluating their means to help or hinder the ability to lead a meaningful life in a harmonious, yet dynamic, interaction between egoism and altruism. Pirruccello insists, all the same, that had Weil lived longer and pursued the scientific model that she apparently had in mind, a more careful framework for her comparisons would have become necessary.

Weil felt that if the mystery of transferring energy toward good ends could be clarified, other mysteries in human lives could also be fathomed, such as the wellsprings of positive energy, the persistence of damaging emotions, the divergent interpretations of sensory perceptions, and the intermediary role our energies play in gaining knowledge of the world. The following excerpt on energy from her notebooks exemplifies her telegraphic style by which she put down for future reflection as many aspects of an idea as possible. These notebook entries formed the bases for her further exploration of the notion of energy as applied to human choices.

There are efforts that exhaust and others that give new energies: where is the source of the former?
The mechanism by which a too difficult situation debases is that the energy furnished by elevated feelings is—generally—limited.

If the situation demands that one go further than that limit, it is necessary to have recourse to the baser emotions (fear, envy, desire to excel or coveting exterior honors) richer in energy (why?).
This limitation holds the key to many reversals.
Infinite fecundity of the notion of energy applied to human life: unexplored source.
Emotion. Relationship between the world and the mind: emotion comes directly from the world through sensations, but it varies according to the direction of energy within the person.
Let this energy become a way of exploring the world—a blind man's stick.[69]

Weil's profound love of neighbor and her unwillingness to see others diminished in any way animated an unending desire to understand the human condition and to incorporate respect for human dignity as fully as possible into social institutions based on justice. By calling upon a good force infused with God's grace, one could check irresponsible leaders who aimed to shackle others in mind and body. Her Project for a Corps of Frontline Nurses was a practical application of her conviction that actions stemming from pure motives radiated goodness and bit by bit destroyed evil. She found analogies in the physical universe for her message on ways to strive for justice and social harmony. But her mystical view of the divine end of every individual led her to formulate the inalienable obligation of every human being to nurture the ability of others to surmount the powerful effects of moral gravity.

CHAPTER FIVE
Reading and Justice

*The world is a text of many meanings, and one passes
from one meaning to another by work, work in which the body
always plays a role. . . . Without that, any change in the
manner of thinking is illusory.*

Weil, Notebooks

Observing the movements of the universe had led Hitler and Simone
Weil to diametrically opposed meanings. Hitler's reading translated
into chaos and terrible consequences for millions of vulnerable souls,
whereas Weil's reading signified a social order based on obedience to
God's love and shown through love of neighbor. The values that people
used as criteria to determine their reactions to the sensations they received from the material world were a matter of great concern for Weil.
She explored this phenomenon in two expository essays, one on the
notion of reading and the other on the notion of values, and embodied
it in two historical recountings, one about a religious group in the thir-
teenth century and another about an island republic in the sixteenth
century. The devout Cathar sect exemplified for her a society whose
criteria for reading the universe were based on the values of pure
love of neighbor and disdain for violence. These people of Languedoc,
whose values brought them into harmony with each other and with the
natural world, had thrived in southern France seven centuries ago, but
unfortunately, exterior forces, exploiting their vulnerability and their
adamant refusal to use force, destroyed them and their culture. To il-

lustrate a different result, Weil composed a play, *Venise sauvée*, about a society that was saved from subjugation by a moment of grace brought on by the contemplation of beauty. The sight of the beautiful city shimmering in the moonlight had altered the resolve of the man charged with Venice's destruction.

Weil wanted to discern by what process a person passed from a first reading of a situation—too often weighed down by moral gravity—to a second, higher-level reading. This transformation was surely governed by laws that one could learn, thereby increasing the quantity of "good" in social interaction. Her written notes give examples of this conversion from one reading to another that make clear its eminent value to daily life. In her mystical philosophy, beauty and supernatural grace played an essential role in modifying a gravity-laden judgment to conform to higher values. This pivotal chapter examines four compositions in which Weil explored influences on people's interpretations of situations that led to a wide range of reactions. Increasingly, we see the importance she gave to being open to God's grace.

AN ESSAY ON THE NOTION OF READING

The true goal is not to see God in all things, but that
God through us sees the things that we see.

Weil, Notebooks

Weil's interest in human consciousness had intensified at the École Normale Supérieure while she was writing her dissertation for the *diplôme d'études supérieures* on Descartes' insights into perception. In Weil's thinking, Descartes' theory of a blind man's dependence on his stick as an extension of his body made a striking analogy for the role the body played in first receiving the sense impressions and then making judgments about them. She called the process "reading," that is, the translation of sensations into meaning. She chose a familiar word to define this critical notion because "at each instant of our lives we are struck, as if from the outside, by meanings that we ourselves read into appearances."[1] Weil believed that there was one true universal reading at the heart of every situation, a reading that furthered positive relationships in a just social environment.

Her particular notion of reading as the direct interpretation of sensations became more clearly defined in her later spiritual period. From the time of her dissertation, Weil repeatedly referred to Descartes' example of a blind man exploring and building up his sense perceptions by successive probes with his stick as a means for sense impressions to reach the mind. The blind man's stick became an intermediary limb that permitted him to be in contact with obstacles before him. With practice, he no longer felt the pressures of the stick on his hand; rather, "he taps the things directly with his stick as if his stick had feeling and was part of his body."[2]

Weil admired this Cartesian theory, saying, "The human body is like pincers for the mind to comprehend and probe the world."[3] She mused over the mystery that sensory objects, almost indifferent in themselves, could affect us through their significance as violently as a blow to the stomach.[4] Human beings feel the emotional impact of their sensory perceptions without necessarily registering the physical attributes of the vehicle that carries the message. To illustrate her point, she gave the poignant example of two women who receive letters announcing, "Your son is dead"; one faints, while the other does not react. The first mother, immediately struck with grief, has grasped the full significance of the message, for she is literate; the second, in contrast, is illiterate and sees only the letters formed on paper. She does not comprehend the heartbreaking message; nevertheless, a terrible reality corresponds to the news. The paper, the ink, and the letters are neutral, only their meaning has an importance, but knowing their significance requires apprenticeship and effort.

Weil settled on the word *reading (lecture)*, which, though serviceable, was not entirely satisfactory for her purpose.[5] She had dismissed the word *imagination* as less suitable, since emotional effects are produced by appearances of objects that scarcely register on the mental screen, such as the form of the letters or the color of the paper on which a painful or joyous message is conveyed. Nevertheless, she chose *reading* to signify the emotions or illusions that are stirred within an individual by external sensory perceptions. These internal effects, such as fear or sadness, are modifiable, for the emotions are not in the visible appearances but in the interpretation or reading. Throughout life, the appearances that reach the sight are interpreted, not as the simple bare objects they might be, but by the meaning one perceives in them. She sought to determine the training that could enable a reshaping of first impressions.

Indications in her notebooks reveal Weil's intention to dedicate a small book to the concept of reading or interpretation. But with only two short years left for writing, the book remained in the planning stage. Her "Essai sur la notion de lecture," published posthumously in 1946, was constructed from her notebook entries on reading.[6] For the English-speaking public, this concise essay, though key to her thought, remains relatively unknown. Drafts containing some of its ideas and phrasing are scattered throughout the first eight notebooks, along with reflections on potential guidelines for obtaining true readings. Weil was convinced that not striving to achieve true readings would entail continual suffering for all persons caught in the clutches of ambitious leaders who sought unlimited power. Her final notes written in New York and London have few entries on reading, but her writings from that time reveal how deeply she had considered the practical and theoretical aspects of the complex process of reading one's relationships with others and with the universe.

Despite Weil's initial admiration for Descartes and his *cogito ergo sum,* in which the thinking being knew himself in the act of thinking, her mystical experiences had since redirected her mind toward knowledge of the self considered in relation to God.[7] Her own internal orientation toward mystical obedience had taken precedence over Descartes' moral doctrine of imperturbable practical resolution.[8] Indeed, Weil believed that one had to forsake one's personal self, with all its attributes, to approach the impersonal realm of the supernatural. This relinquishment resulted in a suspension of judgment and one's usual mode of interpreting in order to be open to the true reading, which, for Weil, implied a form of nonreading.[9] This form of nonreading—a paradox that became central in her theory—came from eliminating the interference of all personal desires and leaving the mind open to receive universal truths.

To illustrate how two persons with widely different experience could make opposing readings of the same situation, she used once again the example of a navigator at sea, this time evoking a captain and his passenger caught in the throes of a violent storm. The captain's experience and skill, which would allow him to use his boat as an instrument by which to read the elements, would enable him to assess the situation more accurately than the inexperienced passenger, whose sensation of limitless danger and fear might weaken his will to stand fast. From the same phenomena, the captain would read necessity, limited danger, means of survival, and an obligation to be courageous and honorable, all of which would stimulate the necessary energies for him to perform his duty. But the frightened passenger, with his lack of navigational expertise, might read a wildly different scenario with disastrous results. In this case, the ultimate proof of having made a right choice of reading would come from surviving the ordeal. On moral questions, however, bad readings due to an egoistic set of values would bring profound destruction and suffering.

For Weil, the human tendency to place oneself at the center of space and time and the base desire to protect and enlarge one's power and importance was the major stumbling block to cultivating an ethical sensitivity. She foresaw great difficulties in getting individuals to reduce self-centered illusions that sapped available energies for pursuing higher goals. In a world that held many meanings, each meaning had to be considered and weighed against a hierarchy of values that could situate its relative importance according to variable contingencies in the situation. In her essay on the notion of reading, she offered parameters for a true reading or interpretation of one's role in the world. Silence was essential for reflection, as was an orientation toward the supernatural and a detachment from one's egoistic desires. Any reorientation had to include both mind and body; persons gleaned knowledge from the sensations felt through their material bodies, but the mind had the critical function of honing and testing the accuracy of the received knowledge.

Deeply engaged in trying to discern by what criteria certain readings were preferred over others, Weil began with the thought that the simple existence of a diversity of readings did not automatically create a hierarchy of values by which to judge them. She believed that all persons chose according to their perceived sense of goodness, but she wanted to ferret out the process by which one opted among readings for the choice that appeared to promise a greater satisfaction of desires. Some alternatives available to certain persons spelled disaster for others. Why did one person, faced with the option to appropriate an object of value left in his trust, steal it, whereas another did not? Weil noted that everyone had been, at one time or another, in a situation in which the desire to commit a breach of trust was blocked by an inner refusal to do so, or the reverse situation in which the desire to do the right thing was blocked. Weil explored the underlying questions concerning the criteria that permitted persons to decide between varying options and the hierarchy of values that led them to read the situation in one way rather than another. She concluded that only detachment from self-aggrandizing desires opened the possibility of seeing a true order of values, the eternal order whose source was outside this world.

She stated that there was no easy answer to resolving right and wrong readings but that "the problem, thus set out, merits meditation, for it unites and makes concrete the question of an order among values."[10] All readings did not have equal claims, though each might be valid from particular perspectives. She explained: "I know very well that my friend who is in my bedroom has a different view of my room than I. Both readings are true [but incomplete]. The unity of the truths is found in God," since God has no point of view.[11]

The justness in reading that Weil so wished to inspire in her readers could be approached by making an effort to feel the attitudes and emotions of another person caught in the same situation: that is, to regard one's own perspective and that of others as having equal value. The master-slave relationship represented the polar opposite. Slavery meant forcing another to read himself as you read him; conquest meant forcing the other to read you as you read yourself. She described an extreme scenario of contrasting perspectives, in which Roman conquerors triumphantly paraded a defeated king in chains with his enslaved people tied behind him. While the Romans scorned the king as a vanquished slave, his followers still revered him as king and leader. The interference between readings rendered dialogue for the most part futile, since force played a major role. Weil recognized that no effort could bring the imperial Romans to read their place in the world in the same fashion as did their subjugated peoples. But she did stress that "an effort could lead them all to a third reading, the same for all."[12] She believed that there was for each situation a universal reading that encompassed all perspectives. In her essay, she concluded that the universal reading had a relationship to truth, beauty, and goodness, difficult to think of simultaneously but impossible to separate.

JUSTICE AND THE GIFT OF READING

The gift of reading is truly supernatural;
without that gift, there is no justice.

Weil, Notebooks

According to Weil, justice depended on charitable respect for another, a prerequisite to any attempt to approach successfully a "third reading" or unity of readings. Justice meant being continually ready to admit that another person was other than what one read him to be. One had to be continually aware that one's self-image was very different from what others perceived. In citing once again the passage from the Book of the Dead, "I never closed my ears to true and just words," she added: "Every being cries out in silence to be read otherwise. One must not be deaf to these cries."[13] She became convinced that the choice of charitable or unjust actions depended on one's reading of the situation. The Gospels, a continual source of beauty and truth for her, furnished supporting examples for her premise. "The miracle of the good thief was not that he thought of God but that he recognized God in his neighbor. Peter, before the cock crew, no longer recognized God in Christ, or he would not have denied him."[14]

Bad readings of justice belonged to the realm of an unreality that obliterated goodness in something that was good. Bad readings amounted to the consummate evil.

Evil is always the destruction of tangible things where there is a real presence of good. Evil is done by those who have no knowledge of the real presence of the good. It is true that in this sense no one is voluntarily evil. The relationships of force give ignorance the power to destroy the good that is present. . . .

One can hardly contemplate without terror the extent of evil that man can do and undergo.[15]

Absent a certain quality of attention, the reading of people and events obeyed the pull of gravity, which led to injustice. Despite this natural tendency to form petty, self-aggrandizing opinions, a high quality of attention could allow one instead to objectively appraise moral gravity's seductive pull toward uncharitable behavior and to imagine diverse ways to reorder the relationships in a situation.[16] For her own reflection, Weil proposed two alternative causes of unjust behavior: "One can be unjust by a willful desire to offend justice or simply by a bad reading of justice." The first merited corrective punishment, the second, understanding and an attempt to reorient the reading toward more elevated motives. She considered the second to be more common: "It is almost always (or always?) the second case."[17]

Weil suggested some ways that one might prepare oneself for a universal reading or nonreading: one could try to read, from outward appearances, what another, situated differently and impelled by other motives, could read through the same effort. Or one could purposefully regard both one's own perspective and that of another as equally worthy of attention. To succeed with either of the above, one needed to practice detachment (nonreading) by giving silent attention entirely to the person or situation, with willful suppression of one's own personal desires and attachments. This was what Weil called a decreation of self—not a destruction of self but a clearing away of what the imagination had deemed important to the self. Decreation was indispensable for giving pure and full attention to another, particularly to one in affliction. Only by this unique emptying of self could the soul unite itself to God, and only by opening oneself in silence to God could one access a universal reading of one's fellow human being.

Accurately perceiving the truth in a situation required an apprenticeship, just as learning to read one's maternal language or a foreign tongue demanded a long and guided education. The goal of apprenticeship was to develop new habits in reading the external world and to sharpen the ability to modify initial responses. Weil believed that such an apprenticeship could generate an internal aptitude that would allow the reader to intuit the reality behind the material sensations and to forestall the instinctive drag of egocentric interpretations. Where no elevating force countervailed, gravity prevailed, creating situations full of injustice. Directing one's actions toward the "good" required authentic readings that reinforced the impetus to love one's neighbor. The malleability of an individual's ability to read significance in material phenomena implied a caveat: the mind could be shaped just as easily toward performing evil deeds. According to Weil, this foundational idea needed more serious attention.

Each apprentice needed to keep in mind the final goal, for each apprenticeship aimed toward a certain reading. Apprenticeship could be slanted toward a good or a blatantly false reading because objects or persons were neutral. The significance inferred was crucial. Weil believed that the sky, the sea, the sun, the stars, human beings—in short, everything that surrounded human existence—was something that was read. The elements in the universe were mediators between the human and the divine, just as the blind man's stick was a mediator between the mind and the object.

The phenomenon of reading also involved successive interpretations made by the same person. Later readings eliminated former readings, making it difficult even to conjure up the first impressions again. The first reading had to be considered as one of multiple possible interpretations. The second reading, in which personal considerations had little or preferably no impact, could then become a form of non-reading, the universal or true reading that was as close to God's reading as could occur here on earth. To clarify her point, Weil sketched another image, in which an ominous shadow glimpsed ahead on a somber path immediately struck fear in the heart of a solitary stroller. But once the dark shape had been identified as shrubbery and not a lurking man, the panic disappeared, along with the prior image, making it difficult to re-evoke either the crouching assailant or the terror that had gripped heart and soul.

She wrote: "All our lives are woven of the same cloth: of meanings imposing themselves successively; each one, when it appears and enters us through the senses, reduces to phantoms any opposing ideas."[18] Transforming the significance human beings gathered from their sensory perceptions was the underlying pragmatic structure of war, politics, eloquence, art, education, and all such actions affecting others' behavior. Fully understanding this notion of reading could lead to amassing energies into counterforces for warding off potential acts of violence.

How subjects responded to Hitler's chimerical claim of bringing greater civilization and order to "inferior peoples" depended on their reading of the circumstances. Hitler was exploiting all the force at his command to superimpose his readings of the world on fellow human beings,[19] but his goals were delusive. For the victims to maintain their dignity as humans, they had to keep in sight the ultimate end: one in line with the eternal "good." The use of evil means would destroy positive relationships and perpetuate the spiral of violence. Acceptable methods could employ measured force and be just, but only if force were considered as the last resort and kept within stringent limitations. In Weil's view, the importance of thwarting Hitler's determination to impose his delusions on others justified using measured force against him. Better yet would be to inspire in the Nazi aggressors a new mental state that could lead them to a different, truer reading of their situation.

That the passage from one mental state to another was rapid, had the appearance of reality, and reduced former beliefs to the level of the imaginary was vividly illustrated by Weil's examples of friendly attitudes of peace suddenly being turned inside out after an enemy attack or a declaration of war. A state of war reoriented priorities and criteria. The surging desire to kill fellow human beings could come from factors within a nation, such as a civil war that pitted neighbor against neighbor, or from external threats, which made foreign-looking persons the feared enemy. Intentionally reorganized concepts could arouse the desire to annihilate persons officially categorized as vile. In contrast, in times of peace, the idea of killing another human being did not spring from differing internal ideologies or someone's external appearance. Rather, the prohibition against killing remained the dominant reading. One's reading affected first one's mental attitude and then one's actions. Weil noted, "I believe what I read, my judgments are what I read, I act according to what I read, how can I do otherwise?"[20] She was convinced, however, that the future of civilization depended on clarifying the process by which one reading metamorphosed into another.

Hitler understood that authorities could purposefully transform the significance read into events and consequently the actions people would most likely take. Bodies reacted to the significance contained in the reading. Weil pointed out that a military commander used strategy, surprise, and new weapons to inspire fear in the hearts of the enemy so that they would flee and not hold their ground. At the same time, he had to inspire in his own men the desire to stand their ground and kill on sight. If one read honor, one rushed forward; if one read shame, the opposite direction was taken posthaste. Weil admired the Führer's skill in simultaneously manipulating the imaginations of his people, his enemies, and his spectators. He had taken seriously the necessity to strike the imagination of his men by creating new impulses to advance and the imagination of the enemy and of his observers by fomenting maximum confusion and astonishment.

The interpretations that Hitler intended were in no way arbitrary. He began with carefully structured conditioning so that he would get the reactions he sought. Those who could not detach themselves to see what he was doing were caught in his web of evil intentions. They could resist the pressure and not absorb the imposed meaning, but the effort required was arduous. Weil claimed, "I possess the power to change the meanings that I read in the appearances that impose themselves on me; but this power is limited, indirect, and exerts itself through work."[21]

JOAN OF ARC: FORCEFUL HEROINE OR TREMBLING SOUL

One reads in Joan of Arc's story what contemporary public opinion dictates. But she herself was uncertain.

Weil, Notebooks

Weil's varied commentaries on Joan of Arc illustrate the theory of different readings that derive from different perspectives. She referred to two contrasting readings of the legendary Joan of Arc: as the forceful heroine designated by God to lead his chosen nation, France, to victory and, alternatively, as a humble, uncertain soul tremblingly in love with

God. Weil preferred the latter reading and spoke of her personal admiration of Joan's persistent obedience to God's will despite feeling forsaken.[22] This devoted girl turned warrior intuitively followed God's instructions, with no guarantee of any specified outcome. Just as with Job, her task was to be steadfast in her love for God.

Joan loved France with a selflessness that encompassed all her country's weaknesses. She had assumed the thankless task of ridding her nation of usurpers. She loved France, not as a powerful nation, but as her home, whose existence was under dire threat. Over the centuries, the exploitation of Joan's military accomplishments for propaganda purposes exemplified the human tendency to be swayed by impassioned public opinion, which hindered the ability to read clearly. The real criterion by which to measure Joan's actions, in Weil's mind, lay in her fragility, selflessness, and uncertainty. Her unquestioning obedience showed the "purity" of her love for God.

Consequently, Weil considered Joan's own reading of the situation as universal and true. Weil saw a corollary between Joan's uncertainty that God was with her and Christ's cry from the cross: "My God, my God, why have you forsaken me?" For Weil, Joan's and Christ's uncertainty (and the public's too frequent failure to perceive it truly in either case) illustrated the enormous difficulty of accepting the true order of values, one that commended humility and obedience over power. Weighed down naturally by moral gravity, no one automatically preferred to be on the weaker side of a conflict; the prestigious glories of victory in the eyes of the world were far too enticing. Yet Joan's unaffected love of God and the universe and her demanding life as a peasant had prepared her to take on the task of protecting her homeland.

Weil's concept of apprenticeship in reading had as its final goal a fine-tuned relationship between the universe and the mind that involved the discipline of the body. She wanted her own body to be trained and hardened for whatever challenges the future might bring. As an adolescent she had diligently participated, albeit awkwardly, in athletic contests with her peers. She had confessed to friends her worry over not being able to resist bodily pain if pressed to do wrong, and she imposed stringent practices on herself to be reassured that she could resist pressure should the necessity arise. Consistent with her conviction that knowledge came through the senses and that the body mediated between the universe and the mind, Weil believed that one could gain the power to resist the pull of moral gravity in reading situations but that such power involved bodily discipline, learned from work that inculcated good habits.[23]

Ultimately, Weil's endeavor to specify practices that would allow a person to read accurately the truth in situations remained sketchy, with only glimmers of directions she found potentially effective. Her overall philosophy integrated the value of suffering, work, beauty, and the need to give full attention to the afflicted. Suffering, accepted patiently, allowed the universe with its immutable laws, movements, and rhythms to be at one with the body. Work, using tools that can shape and refine raw materials, forced the body to conform to the reality of the material world and to experience its limitations. Contemplation of beauty created a bridge between the material and the divine, for one could admire but never possess beauty. Complete attention given persons suffering from affliction meant trying to perceive the world from their perspective.

Scenes of natural beauty, such as a sunset or the countryside, satisfied a deep inner need for Weil, as did the repetition, with full concentration, of the beautiful words of the "Our Father" recited in Greek, or the mystical poem "Love," by George Herbert. In the Benedictine Abbey at Solesmes, she had listened with total attention to the reverent, monochromatic tones of Gregorian chant as a means of focusing on something perfectly pure. The beauty of the music had a relationship to her mystical experience. She cited liturgy, prayer, and contemplation as forms of a blind man's stick reaching out to God and believed that contemplation of things perfectly pure could destroy evil, slowly but efficaciously. But one had to discern the purity in situations by reading the signs accurately.

In her notebooks, she posed the question "Who can flatter himself that he will read justly?" which she then answered: "That is why one must implore the truth [from God]."[24] Beseeching God was a far cry from beseeching another human being. "Imploring a man is simply a desperate attempt to imprint with forceful intensity one's own system of values on the mind of the other. Imploring God, on the contrary, is an attempt to imprint divine values on one's own soul."[25] Sincerely imploring the truth from God was a great assurance of reading justly. She reminded Father Perrin's young scholars that "the best support of faith is the guarantee that if one asks the Father for bread, he does not give stones."[26]

REFLECTIONS CONCERNING THE NOTION OF VALUES

The notion of value is always present in the mind of man;
every man orients his thought and actions toward some good;
he cannot do otherwise.

Weil, "Some Reflections on the Idea of Value"

In her exploration of the ways individuals read situations, Weil gave primacy to the notion that values come into play at all points of human decisions. Different sets of values compete for dominance in every decisive situation, just as multiple readings of a situation vie simultaneously for acceptance. As with reading, she believed that an individual's grasp of the hierarchy of values can be molded and transformed. Educating people to judge their actions by a criterion of values that led toward an outcome that took into account the ultimate good of mankind was essential. Her deepest concern over the uprooting of values during times of upheaval was that the reign of violence diminished possibilities for either the perpetrator or the victim to freely orient his soul toward the highest good: love of neighbor, which was equivalent to love of God. By delineating the necessary conditions for reexamining one's values, Weil wanted her readers to understand the importance of pausing to reflect on the ultimate ends one desired before choosing violent means to obtain them.

She began to sketch out her thoughts on the reality that the reflective mind was always in some tension over values. Distinguishing between values required detachment from all values, an almost impossible feat. Only the intervention of grace allowed some resolution. No words adequately expressed the eternal goals toward which one needed to orient one's life. Her quest to discover and reveal the means of discerning an eternal hierarchy of values challenged her at a time when an apparent indifference to values seemed to her to be the public consensus. Weil argued for philosophy as a means to discern a hierarchy among all values of this world and to use this hierarchy as a criterion for making decisions.

While in Marseilles, she planned her essay on values, which opened with "The notion of value is at the heart of philosophy."[27] She explained that one had to study truth first and then live, because the choice of actions that decided life or death in any determined situation implied a comparison and ultimate ordering of values. This essay, entitled "Some Reflections on the Notion of Values," was probably begun early in 1941 but was left unfinished and was not published until 1999, when it appeared in *Oeuvres / Simone Weil*, edited by Florence de Lussy. De Lussy considers this piece a key text in Weil's thought and describes it as "a covenant for a new art of thinking in troubled times in which all values are disparaged."[28]

This unpolished piece, along with Weil's notebook commentaries, reveals the evolution of her thinking on the essential role of values in human lives. Weil argued that to properly discern and judge values, one needed to know their source, be detached from personal desires, have time for quiet reflection, and be open to the necessary grace. Making decisions in accord with true values required contemplation reinforced by courage and strength. Their indefinability did not facilitate the undertaking. Means taken as goals such as money or power were easily defined and offered self-gratification, so they were too often considered desirable ends. But by exuding a dangerous aura of limitlessness, they encouraged ambitious climbers to overreach their capabilities, fall, and leave a legacy of suffering for others. "The reversal of means and ends, which is the very essence of all social evil, is inevitable, for the good reason that there is no end. Thus the means is taken as an end. . . . Only the one who loves God with a supernatural love can regard means simply as means."[29]

Even in its unfinished form, this piece is a fine illustration of Weil's habitual thinking as a philosopher. In it she defended the premise that philosophy was a means by which one arrives at truth. Truth dwelt in the domain of the eternal, she argued, so philosophy provided access to the divine. Philosophy required careful, uncoerced reflection: humankind's most precious attribute. Values had to be weighed by one's conscience so that one might distinguish between false, seductive, and easily propagandized objectives and true, eternal, and ineffable ends. Because persons might not be consciously aware of their values even while applying them as criteria for actions, an objective comparison between values became crucial. "The notion of value is always present in the mind of man; every man always orients his thoughts and his actions toward some good; he cannot do otherwise."[30] An authentic comparison of values needed an impartial, philosophical thought process.

Weil firmly believed that everyone had access to knowing the true criteria for action and decision making, namely those values whose eternal source was outside this world: "The sole good not subject to chance is the one outside this world."[31] The reality of a "good" situated outside this world was absolute and corresponded to an imperative desire in the heart of every human being, whose constant desire for the absolute "good" set the immutable foundation for the obligation to respect every other person's dignity. She opened her "Draft for a Declaration of Obligations toward the Human Person" with "There is a reality situated outside this world, that is to say, outside space and time, outside the mental universe of man, outside the entire domain that the human faculties can attain. To this reality corresponds, in the center of the human heart, that demand for absolute good which is always present there and can never be satisfied by any object in this world."[32]

In contrast, violent times led people to soothe their deep anxieties by creating illusory fantasies. In so doing, they repressed the images of reality around them and took out their frustrations on others, intensifying the spiral of violence. In Weil's mind, this act of repression, which inhibited the possibilities of ending the cycle of suffering, was too often committed through ignorance or error. She noted down the following question: "Isn't evil analogous to illusion? Illusion, when one is caught up in it, is not felt as illusion but as fact. . . . Evil, when one commits it, is not felt as evil but as necessity or even obligation." She cited Plato once more: "No one does evil voluntarily,"[33] a concept from which she inferred that knowledge of "good" was the best path to virtuous actions. She ardently believed that a greater awareness of values whose source was absolute goodness, as opposed to values whose root was evil, would reduce the amount of violence in the world. This knowledge, she knew, would allow more souls to seek the highest good, although she never suggested that the path would be smooth.

For Weil, as we have seen, the true measure of virtue was love: love of God joined with love of neighbor. As she was gathering her thoughts for her essay on the notion of values, she was concluding a different essay, "Reflections Related to Quantum Theory," critiquing the effects of modern science and its applications with the following assessment of the place given to values. "The tempest that surrounds us has uprooted all values, dismantled their hierarchy, tossed them up for question, and left them to be weighed on the false balance of force. Each one of us, at this time, can also call them into question in order to weigh them in silent attention within ourselves in the desire that our conscience become a true scale of values."[34]

Weil blamed contemporary writers for the collapse of values that had led to one of the worst disasters of all times: war. In her letter/essay entitled "Responsibilities of Literature," published in the *Cahiers du Sud,* the influential literary review in the Free Zone, she railed against a current of indifference to right and wrong among authors: "Writers don't have to be professors of morality, but they do have to express the human condition. Now, nothing is so essential to human life, for all men, at all instants in time, as good and evil."[35]

Weil wanted her readers to clearly distinguish between perceiving an order of values and gaining human factual knowledge. The latter came through the senses and dovetailed with other known facts, leading to hypothetical conjectures, requiring experience and constant questioning. The elusiveness of the former, with its need for silence, detachment, and intense desire, complicated the search; success could come only through the miracle of grace. Consequently, upholding a value meant orienting one's mind and soul toward it; the process was recurrent and in constant need of renewal. When two values conflicted there could be a wrenching distress. After reflection, the value given primacy would receive the mind's full attention and cause a reorientation of the soul. Without this continual process, there would be intellectual decline.

The fact that the criterion of good values escaped definition added a note of anxiety to most struggles where persons sought to achieve something higher, yet could not specify what it was. As evidence that an order of values existed, Weil offered the example of an artist seeking to create something beautiful without an explicit measure for beauty. Artists acknowledged that no specific criteria prevailed for judging one work to be aesthetically superior to another; nevertheless, every artist knew that such a hierarchy existed. Some creations were beautiful while others were not, and certain works were more beautiful than others. If this were not the case, artists would not strive so hard to create a beauty whose existence they intuited but could not describe in advance.

Weil prized the contradiction between the impossibility of clearly defining values and the reality that every person's life was oriented by them. She argued that this contradiction, far from negating the validity of values, served to strengthen the necessity of a constant reflective search (not without anguish) to ascertain how values were to be applied at a given moment. That there was a set of values she did not doubt, despite the impossibility of precise definition. She believed that the set of values could be discerned by reflection and were a source for greater goodness in society. "The notion of value is always present in the mind of every human being. All persons always orient their thoughts and actions toward some good; they cannot do otherwise. . . . It is true that individuals almost never reflect on the values that give direction to their efforts, but this is because they believe they have sufficient motives to adopt them."[36] Contradictions, she maintained, were essential to thought; they needed to be exposed honestly, not hidden or smoothed over, for all philosophical thought contained contradictions, since they were the material for serious reflection and the means of grasping a higher truth.[37]

Discerning by reflection a hierarchy of values, which could never be imposed by external forces, required an unending process of personal detachment from all predecided aims. Weil's concept of detachment, as we saw earlier, was paradoxical and unique, for she believed that without being detached from egotistical aims one could neither discern the universal reading nor objectively apply the value criteria that went with truth. The engaged intellect, however, by whatever manner it chose, always maintained in tension its stance toward its values, both directing its actions by them and practicing detachment from them.[38] Even seeking a scale of values paradoxically implied a value.[39] This value, although very real, most often remained implicit and abstract because of the linguistic inadequacy of expressing eternal values in words. Renouncing all values, yet holding detachment as the supreme value, was a contradiction, but this contradiction had its resolution in grace. Detachment did not mean a disregard for our physical milieu, which Weil referred to as the "world here below." Instead, it meant diminishing one's ego to let the true interpretation come by intuition. Thus a true reading of values became a nonreading that was inspired by values coming from a supernatural source.

Although the essay on values remained unfinished, we can see expressed in it a summation of Weil's thought on the motivations that activated human decisions and on the importance of reflecting philosophically on the true hierarchy that ordered the values of this world. The criterion of values coming from outside this world applied to the world here below, which must be loved, and the source of this love was supernatural. "To believe in the reality of the external world and to love it is one and the same thing. After all, the medium of belief is supernatural love, even in regard to things here below."[40] The work of learning to detach oneself from the ego and from preconceived values was essential because positing a value and orienting one's soul toward it were inseparable. One learned to orient one's soul in the direction of an eternal "good" by recognizing that careful, quiet, attentive reflection would lead to the truth because truth was a value of thought.[41]

THE CATHAR CIVILIZATION

*Each civilization, like each person, has at its disposal the
entire range of moral concepts from which to choose.*

Weil, "Agony of a Civilization Seen through an Epic Poem"

Weil believed that the Cathar religious sect had oriented its society toward the eternal "good"—love. Seeking models of individuals or groups who, recognizing the double contamination of force, adamantly resisted it, she chose the thirteenth-century Cathars. Their members, also known by the geographic name of Albigensians, had formed the *civilisation d'Oc* in southern France. This culture of "gentle folk" developed their belief and culture around the ruling principle of love of God through love of their neighbor.[42] In her studies of the Cathars (a word that comes from the Greek term for "pure"), Weil admired most of all their rejection of violence, their focus on love as a primary value, and their attempt to live peacefully in full awareness of the powerful domain of force. Unfortunately, from 1209 through 1229, the Albigensian Crusade instigated by the papacy brutally exterminated this religious group because of their opposition to the authority of the Church.

Weil contributed two articles by invitation to a special series entitled "Le génie d'Oc et l'homme méditerranéen" ("The Genius of Oc and Mediterranean Man"), sponsored by the *Cahiers du Sud* in Marseilles. Her essay "Of What Does the Occitanian Inspiration Consist?" recapitulates her thoughts on the self-perpetuating aspects of force, which this culture had recognized and refused to admire. She explained that the inspiration for the Occitanian culture, similar to that of the Greeks, arose from a constitutive knowledge of force. The Cathars had rejected participation in any form of violence and had instead based their society on compassion. What she knew of the Cathars corroborated her own belief that societies could be organized around true love of neighbor even through all the vicissitudes of the human condition. She wrote, "To know force is to recognize it as being almost absolute in this world and to refuse it with disgust and scorn. This scorn is the other side of compassion for all that is exposed to the wounds of force."[43]

In Weil's perception, this long-since-vanquished society had lived integrally with the idea that love in its fullness was love of God lived through the love of neighbor. Like the Greeks, the Cathars saw human love as one of the bridges between the human being and God. Weil poignantly summed up her admiration of their manner of life and her hopes for her contemporaries in the closing sentence: "To the extent that we contemplate the beauty of this [Cathar] era with attention and love, to that extent will its inspiration descend on us and render impossible little by little some part at least of the baseness that constitutes the air we breathe."[44] Several of her contemporaries marveled at her innovative perspective on the Cathar civilization. George Grant, a preeminent twentieth-century Canadian philosopher, has judged Weil's two essays on the Cathars as her "noblest."[45]

The Cathar civilization of the "good people" in southern France did not survive the massive exterminating force used against them during the twenty-year crusade; refusing to respond with force did not save their civilization. Even knowledge of their positive influence has been largely effaced. But just as she had often found inspiring examples from the past, Weil saw the Cathar form of love as pertinent to the salvation of humankind in her time. Remembering that these people had existed and contemplating their finest qualities could elevate thoughts and desires and mitigate some of the evil that the contemporary admiration of force was perpetrating.

The dominant conviction that everything subjected to the contact of force was debased, whatever form the contact took, was woven through all of Weil's writings. To strike or be struck was all the same defilement. She became more and more confident, however, that supernatural love could allow the soul to escape this defilement. Her own people were in harm's way, and she did not want them to lose the irreplaceable heritage in which they had their roots, nor, above all else, to lose their souls. For her, the traces remaining from the Cathar civilization shed additional light on the question of how her people could confront the force that was overrunning all of Europe while still avoiding its debasement. She addressed this same concern in her poetic drama, *Venise sauvée* (Venice Saved).

SIMONE WEIL'S *VENICE SAVED*

Jaffier's moment of meditation at the end of the second act is the moment when reality enters into him, because he gave his full attention. . . . To believe in the reality of the exterior world and love it is one and the same thing.

Weil, *Poèmes*

In June 1940, Weil, hoping eventually to reach a port from which she could embark for England to continue the struggle against France's occupiers, took an unfinished play script on her long trek south.[46] She and her parents left Paris abruptly for Marseilles but stopped for two months in Vichy, where a lingering leg infection limited her activities. So she spent her time stretched out on a sleeping bag in the kitchen of a tiny rented apartment, recomposing a drama in poetry and prose that she had started in Paris.[47] The plot of her play, from a work by the seventeenth-century French historian Saint Réal, focused on a civilization in peril, whose situation was not unlike that of wartime Europe in the twentieth century and of the Cathars seven centuries before.

The critical point in Weil's play takes place during a moment of suspension when Captain Jaffier, contemplating a scene of beauty, abandons his goal of conquering Venice and resolves instead to protect it. A moment of grace has brought the mercenary face to face with the reality of what he was about to destroy, and his reading of the situation changes. Weil constructed her intrigue from the point of view of the conspirators, all of whom, exiled and uprooted from their own countries, lacked intimate connections to a vital human milieu.

The drama revolved around a failed conspiracy instigated in 1618 by a Spanish monarch who decided to usurp the Republic of Venice by suborning its mercenary soldiers, mostly foreigners quartered in the city. In Weil's version of the incident, the uprising fails because the captain of the venture, Jaffier, heartened by the unique beauty of the city and by memories of Violetta, the innocent and trusting daughter of the sovereign, recants and betrays his accomplices. Contrary to a promise of amnesty exacted from the Council of Ten in return for the revelation, all his companions die horribly.

Weil wanted the play to portray the varied ways persons could read a situation and then decide whether to enforce their will on others. She noted cryptically: "The destructive affliction of 'I' [or ego] destroys reality, removes reality from the world. Plunges [one] into a nightmare," transmuting real life into a dream.[48] Her depiction of the "I" wreaking havoc is epitomized in the role of the French lord, Renaud, hired by the Spanish king, who seeks to expand his empire even at the expense of destroying what he has conquered. Renaud plots the surprise attack for the dead of night: the renegades will simultaneously set fires in key parts of the city and kill any resisters on sight. This exiled nobleman masterminding the expedition nourishes the illusion that his destiny is to be a powerful dominator governing the world, and all his hired men, equally deluded, believe that by possessing this rich city by force they will gain limitless honor, prestige, and power over others.

After his capture, as the Venetian loyalists lead Renaud off in chains, he cries out in disbelief: "Who are they who have stolen my destiny, my rightful share of power and glory? I whose intelligence has raised me higher than an eagle over these troops of men made to serve me. I intended to become the favorite of the King of Spain, in whose name I would become the master of Christianity, conqueror of the East and commander of the whole world."[49] Renaud, even at death's door, refuses to accept his degraded status or give up his illusory reading of a universe where he, all-powerful, is destined to reign over others.

Had he succeeded, the conquered Venetians would have been enslaved in their occupied city, but the perpetrators' lives would have also been sullied by their evil actions. Through the character of Captain Jaffier, Weil explored the idea of ethical criteria conflicting with the desire to live as if only one's self mattered. She asked: "Is there a law of similarity between the two extremities of an evil act that applies an analogous evil to both the one who accomplishes it and to the one who undergoes it?" Then she asked an even more pressing question for her: "Would it be the same for a good action?"[50] Her query concerning whether goodness can imbue others with love for humankind became a constant underlying theme for Weil. She wanted others to know and love the "good" and thereby to forego the use of force, despite the sacrifice that such a renunciation demanded.

In her dramatization, Weil gave the key role to Venice's savior Jaffier, who begins as a leader of thugs who want to possess the wealth and power of a living community of people but do not recognize the impossibility of doing so. His sudden awareness of the illusory quality of his dream of domination comes in a climactic reverie as he contemplates Venice on the eve of the assault. At first, however, he proudly imagines how this peaceful city, ignorant of its fate, will become his when his hand crushes it, transforming it into a cadaver that no morning sun can wake. Any person left alive will hasten to do his bidding after suffering the trauma of witnessing the murder of loved ones. His reveries acknowledge his covetousness: "When I see that city so beautiful, so powerful, and so peaceful, and when I think that in one night, we, a few obscure men, will become its masters, I believe I'm dreaming."[51]

Yet while his behavior exemplifies the lure of natural moral gravity, Jaffier is a person in love with the delicate beauty of everyday life. Before his eyes, the city assumes a tender fragility, and his reflections subtly change in tone, pace, and meter as this captain of mercenaries visualizes the surviving Venetians wandering in dazed disarray, looking in vain for familiar palaces, houses, and churches. He poignantly imagines the songs and voices of the Venetians all silenced; even the sea will become mute as day after day the enslaved hear nothing but orders to obey.

Following this doleful vision in which he sees Venice through the perspective of the subjugated Venetians, Jaffier reassumes his arrogant tone and rhythm. Nevertheless, his words transmit a nuance fraught with significance. Concluding his monologue (which occurs just before his decision to reveal the plot to the Venetian Council), he considers the setting sun over Venice, la Serenissima, and muses poignantly over whether he has the right to be indifferent to this magnificent city in all its natural beauty. The critical point of his meditative discourse begins with:

> The city is still happy in its splendor;
> For yet another evening its people remain intact and proud.
> This last sun alone covers it with rays;
> If it knew, it would doubtlessly halt its path in pity.
> But the sun has no pity for Venice, alas, neither do I.

Then the critical moment comes as he pauses to ask:

> Am I allowed to be as indifferent as the sun,
> I, whose eyes see the real city that must perish?[52]

At this mysterious moment, the reality of Venice's fragile beauty jolts Jaffier into a stark awareness of the terrible fate awaiting the city under his command. Because of this awakening, his cold-hearted intention to brutally crush a living community is transformed into a tender desire to ensure the safety of its people. In his inner self, he knows that Venice must be spared, no matter the cost. By a mad gesture of love, Jaffier thus converts his drive to control others into a different kind of energy that is invigorated by the need to preserve what is good, even if it means personal sacrifice. Unlike the intractable outlook of Renaud, Jaffier's viewpoint has shifted from seeing himself as the focal point in the universe to perceiving the world from the Venetians' perspective. In Weil's vision, the salvation of Venice comes about through an intervention that takes place in the heart of a person originally bent on evil. This outcome illustrates, in Weil's thinking, the descent of grace into an individual during a moment of quiet, concentrated attention on a fragile object of beauty.

"The vulnerability of precious things is beautiful because it is a sign of their existence. Blossoms of fruit trees. It is the same for the vulnerability of the soul to cold and to hunger."[53] Violetta's happy innocence is also analogous to the blossoms of fruit trees: precious, fragile, and exposed. As the beautiful young daughter of the Venetian Council's secretary, she is particularly vulnerable to the proposed desecration.

Weil composed her play with an eye for the perceptive function of the theater: "Theater must render evident both external and internal necessity. On the scene—the slow maturation of an act with the universe around it—then the act precipitated into the world."[54] Jaffier's love of beauty prepares him to receive the grace that gives him the courage to protect a community of human beings from enslavement, but his action thrusts him into the world of men, where he must betray his friends. The social necessity in the web of human relationships prohibits the simultaneous attainment of his two conflicting goals, the safety of Venice and amnesty for his companions in crime.

In the aftermath, the Council of Ten dares not keep its word and free the leading conspirators, especially since pardons could suggest weakness on the council's part. Disregarding their sworn oath to Jaffier, they dispense orders for the torture and death of his friends and then try to buy him off with gold and forced exile. Jaffier, humiliated with shame and anguish over his part in the death of his fellow plotters, including his best and only true friend, rejects their blood money, preferring death. The taunt of cowardice defiles his self-image as a proud man who values honor. This unexpected outcome afflicts his mind, body, and soul.

The play enacted Weil's belief that the pull of moral gravity in human relations could be countered by infinitely small but luminous moments of grace. In her article "Morality and Literature," Weil wrote: "A necessity as strong as gravity condemns man to evil, keeping all good from him except in limited quantities, painfully acquired, all mixed and soiled with evil, except for the appearance here below of the supernatural that suspends the effects of earthly necessity."[55] Good acts perpetuated further good acts; all the same, the doer of good deeds seldom escaped ensnarement in the mechanism of social forces, while the full effects of either good or bad acts remained unknown for the most part for the persons who performed them.

Weil concluded her drama on a note of hope: Jaffier's gesture, although severely punished, creates positive ripples. The lovely, pure, and innocent Violetta offers the valedictory in a moving poetic form when she sings a paean of praise to the new day. She has come out to enjoy the beautiful promise of the sun's rays as the city prepares for rejoicing on the Feast of the Pentecost, in remembrance of when the Holy Spirit came in fulfillment of Christ's promise of a new beginning and his challenge to spread the Good News. Although she has no knowledge of the harrowing events of the prior night or of Jaffier's sacrifice, Weil's audience would be simultaneously aware of the narrow escape of the "City of Light" and of the dangers surrounding France.

Weil had written earlier: "The triumph of art is in leading to something other than itself; to life functioning in the full knowledge of the pact that ties the mind to the world. A fugue of Bach, a painting of da Vinci, a poem, denote, but silently. . . . Art is knowledge. Or rather, art is exploration."[56] And that is what she tried to do with her art forms, a fine example of which is Violetta's hymn of joy concluding *Venise sauvée*, in which she extols the beauties of nature, the city, and a liturgical celebration of faith. In Weil's philosophy, these were God's traps, meant to entice humankind to love and thus to choose good over evil. Jaffier, beguiled by the beauty of Venice and by the pure innocence of Violetta, must follow a tortuous path, one that entails personal sufferings. The two beauties—the young woman and the beautiful community—bring him to the realization that beauty is ephemeral and once shattered cannot be restored. He does not get to see Violetta rejoicing on the Feast of Pentecost, but he knows that his action protects her continued joy in being surrounded by her countrymen. Weil composed Violetta's final song to remind the audience of the positive role of beauty, as well as its evanescence.

> Beautiful dawn that appears suddenly like a smile
> Hovering in the air over my city and its thousand canals.
> Those who dwell in your peace
>   See how sweet the day is.
>
> This night has satisfied my thirsty heart
> More than sleep ever had before.
> Yet the gentle day has come and filled my eyes
>   Even more than sleep.
>
> And so, the dawning of this day so anticipated
> Caresses the stone and water of the city.
> In the air still mute everywhere,
>   A quivering has surged forth.
>
> Your happiness is there my city, come and see.
> Spouse of the seas, see far, see near
> So many waves swelled with happy murmurs
>   Blessing your wakening.
>
> The limpid light spreads slowly on the sea.
> The celebration will soon fulfill our desires.
> The calm sea waits. Oh! beautiful the rays of daylight
>   Shimmering on the sea.[57]

Violetta (and the author) sing the praises of beauty that could be easily sullied by brute force. Poetry, Weil wrote in a later notebook, expresses a combination of impossible joy and pain.[58] Violetta's poem in its rhyme, meter, and odd number of syllables to a line—a rare phenomenon in French poetry—eschews any idea of closure, but words referring to light *(daylight, clarity, reflections on water)* are juxtaposed to words suggesting sight *(see* and *eyes)*. These words allude to God's grace, which comes to one who waits with attention, open to his illumination. That morning, pious Violetta sings the liturgy of Pentecost where the Holy Spirit is addressed: "O blessed light fill the hearts of your servants; without your help there is nothing in man that is innocent." Her simple trust in Jaffier as mediator counters the destructive force of the conspirators and symbolizes the minimal quantity of good that can overwhelm the criminal forces of defilement, though at great cost: Jaffier's life.

For Weil, truth was inseparable from human tragedy. In her very last days, she wrote: "There is a natural alliance between truth and affliction because one and the other are silent suppliants, eternally condemned to remain voiceless before us."[59] In this drama, her portrayal of the fragility of a civilization has timeless validity, particularly today as modern technology perfects its power to annihilate communities in which people have put down their roots through land, language, and culture. Weil's play is a reflection on ruthless power and its potential to annihilate communities that have evolved through generations of loving care. Venice's peril in 1618 was not unlike Europe's precarious situation in 1940. Weil reconstructed a situation in which a person inspired by love of beauty and of his fellow human beings welcomes God's grace, which gives him the courage to prevent a terrible action that has been conceived in an illusion of power. She correlated the vulnerable beauty of human beings with that of their communities: precious distillates of time and human genius.

Believing that her contemporaries faced a terrible evil that risked destroying everything of value, Weil wondered if the hope for moments of grace could be instilled in persons facing impossible choices and whether a reliance on such moments of grace would be enough. The open-ended drama she was writing provided no final answers, but it did stress the need for constant struggle and vigilance and offered the pointed reminder that personal sacrifice could not be avoided. In her notebooks, Weil had scattered the name "Jaffier" amid her other thoughts as if it were a periodic reminder to herself of the efficacy of good acts. Even a minuscule quantity of good had the potential to obstruct or burn away evil.

Simone Weil and her parents finally arrived in Marseilles in mid-September 1940, three months after their precipitous departure from

Paris. They had left Vichy before she finished her play.[60] Later in London, she still considered her unfinished play important enough to request that friends send her the manuscript and notes so she could complete *Venise sauvée* there. But death intervened before its completion.

The influence of Weil's religious conversion has now become fully evident in her writings. Her acceptance of humankind's divine end colored her political goals, placing her in the rare category of mystical political philosophers. She saw the vital need for social institutions that honored the obligation to protect the secret space within each individual that was reserved for the loving, obedient reception of the divine. She set about outlining the obligations for everyone to live in the world in such a way that not only would his or her sacred impersonal space be open to supernatural grace, but the physical and spiritual needs of all other persons would also be met so that everyone could freely make the decision to accept in perfect obedience God's love.

By struggling against Hitler's justifications for using force in human relationships, Weil pointed to new directions that her contemporaries could take. She wanted to convince them that their present habit of returning violence for violence was a path toward personal destruction and the implosion of civilization. Actions motivated by purity of ends and means had to be imagined and undertaken. Not only was it morally right to do so, but actions guided by eternal goals were the only way to escape from spiraling brutality. She believed in the efficacy of supernatural love and in its ability to permeate human relations if individuals would open their minds and hearts to divine grace. Being open to supernatural love was the first step in reading the truth underlying each situation and in applying values as criteria for actions that would serve the world and mankind's long-term divine purpose. She was convinced that reading situations in the light of supernatural love and evaluating actions by the hierarchy of values whose source was in the eternal and accessible to everyone would reduce the mindless violence that destroyed human aspirations.

CHAPTER SIX
Simone Weil and the Bhagavad-Gita

*It was while reading the marvelous words
[of the Bhagavad-Gita], so Christian in tone,
placed in the mouth of an incarnation of God,
that I felt forcefully that we owe to religious truth
an adherence of an entirely different category
from the respect accorded to a beautiful poem.*

Weil, "Spiritual Autobiography"

Simone Weil sought religious truths about the human condition in millennia-old sacred texts. Wisdom flowing from the East had nourished the West and then flowed back to the East in a mutually enriching cycle, with the Mediterranean, in her view, destined throughout history to be the crucible for this fusion of Occidental and Oriental traditions. The backdrop of occupied France added pertinence and poignancy to her quest for answers to the spiritual and practical knot she wanted to untangle. Her studies in Hindu philosophy brought to the forefront religious concepts that supported her conjectures about ways to mount an effective counterpoise to brute force. By this point, her mystical experience had infused her political philosophy, affecting her lifelong social preoccupation with the means to achieve a just society. She wanted to share with her French compatriots gripped in an oppressive vise her ideas about how to check the contamination of force. At this critical point in our study of Weil's trajectory from integral pacifism toward an acceptance of the reality that a limited use of force had its place, we look at the illumination Indian philosophy gave to her understanding of humankind's persistent reliance on force and on the spirit necessary for using force in a noncontaminating way.

The Bhagavad-Gita indicated a spiritual resolution for the dilemma of how to participate in forceful action while avoiding its contagion. Already discernible in Weil's philosophy were certain nascent concepts: recognizing obligations, accepting the responsibility to fulfill them, stopping for a reflective pause before carrying out an action, and embracing the ruling principle of love. Their significance was heightened by the study of this mystical text. In addition, the Hindu precept of renouncing the fruits of one's actions resonated with her unique theory of "detachment" and "decreation."

Early in 1941, arriving in Marseilles, she encountered René Daumal, a former classmate from the Lycée Henri IV, who had become a scholar of Oriental religions and a writer steeped in metaphysics. Daumal loaned Weil his copy of the Bhagavad-Gita, handwritten in Devanagari script, along with his notes on Sanskrit grammar.[1] Under his guidance, she read the Vedic texts in their original script. The mystical allure of this encyclopedia of ancient sacred lore enriched her understanding of the intimate relationship between God and his creation and of the obedience humankind owed the supernatural. Those themes had become dominant for her since her three mystical contacts with Christianity.

Before arriving in southern France, Simone knew of her brother André's appreciation of the Gita, which he had read in a French translation. In Marseilles under the guidance of Daumal, she learned to read and draw the Devanagari letters and became enthralled with the language, the script, and the philosophy imparted in the Gita. Within the next year and a half, she acquired sufficient knowledge of the language to make her own judgments on which French words best transmitted those ambivalent connotations in Sanskrit that were unfamiliar to Western thought. Convinced that beautiful ideas merited the discipline of a beautiful script, she studiously traced over and over the Devanagari letters with close attention to their appearance. Returning Daumal's grammar and Gita manuscript, she thanked him for having offered her the "precious stimulant" of Sanskrit and confessed that she had a keen appreciation of this language and the wisdom it disclosed.

She wrote: "I hope that I shall never cease loving these sacred characters that have, perhaps, never conveyed anything base."[2]

Her notebook entries on the Gita begin with selected verses copied out first in Devanagari and then in French, including commentaries and translations by Orientalist scholars. From her more discretionary study of the Upanishads, she gained valuable insights into the question of how to maintain a desire for the "good" when one is caught in situations where elements of good and evil intermingle. The greater part of her reflections on Hindu thought specifically concerned the Bhagavad-Gita.

Assimilating concepts from other cultures to harmonize with her deepest personal concerns was what Weil did with everything she read and learned. The philosopher Marie-Magdeleine Davy described Weil's unique method, which involved both faith and knowledge, of searching for truth in the venerated texts of ancient cultures:

Simone Weil sought out exclusively fragments of the truth [in ancient sacred writings]. She desired not simply to regroup them but to set them apart and to find in them the power of genesis that has animated the universe from its very beginning to its fulfillment in the incarnation of Christ. In her research, she was attentive to that impulsion born of the primordial source, which, like a river, runs through history to finally arrive at Christ, that is to say, at God's active emergence into history.[3]

To help Weil's readers understand her process in studying this mystical poem, Gérard Colas, a specialist in Sanskrit texts, assembled and organized all the verses she had copied from the Bhagavad-Gita, both in Devanagari and in French, over nearly two years of intense study of Sanskrit and Hindu literature. As an anthropologist and scholar of Hinduism, Colas discerned through Weil's original translations the key insight she drew from the Gita: "the tie of love existing between God and the faithful believer."[4] This love demanded total abandon to the Absolute Being.

Weil's citations of the Gita became more numerous in her notebooks right up to her departure for the United States. There was a temporary hiatus during her stay in America, when finding passage back to Europe preoccupied her thoughts. On her arrival in London, however, her writings once again clearly reveal threads of Indian philosophy integrally woven into her own. The Sanskrit scholar Alyette Degrâces observed: "Indian thought takes on for Simone Weil the force of an edification; Weil seems to consider the instruction received by the hero Arjuna as if it were for her."[5]

WEIL'S READING OF THE GITA

To think of God, to love God, is nothing other than
a certain way of thinking of the world.

Weil, Notebooks

The Bhagavad-Gita narrates the struggle of the warrior prince Arjuna, whose duty obliges him to fight but whose sense of humanity makes him rebel against killing his cousins, who have usurped his kingdom. During a pause before the terrible battle for justice begins, the reluctant warrior carries on a long philosophical dialogue with Krishna (an incarnation of the supernatural), who enlightens the young man on the necessity of assuming his obligations. Love, the reciprocal love between the divine and humankind, influences his decision to perform his duties and fight. The lessons Krishna gives to Arjuna in this philosophical meditation profoundly affected Weil's own reflections on war.

Weil perceived in the Gita's message a mystical antidote for the contagious evil inherent in force, a validation of the message she had perceived both in the Gospels and in the *Iliad*. All three texts engaged violence, but each portrayed critical moments when the temptation to deploy brute force could have been deflected. Once these fleeting possibilities passed, ramping down the violence became close to impossible, for everyone got caught up in the spiraling chaos. Pressures of war prioritized self-centered motivations and swept aside Christ's timeless exhortation: "Blessed are the peacemakers." The irrepressible drive for glory blinded the maddened warriors to the terrible price they and everyone else had to pay. "Once arms are unsheathed, the ascendancy of prestige is installed; nonresistance is not a way out of the situation.

Even Christ himself was deprived of God for a short time. Contact with force, from whichever position one grapples with it—the hilt or the point of the sword—deprives one of God at that moment. From there, to the Bhagavad-Gita. The Bhagavad-Gita and the Gospels complement each other."[6]

This Hindu poem solidified Weil's conception that only the "good," whose source was Krishna, or God, could purify the evil spread by force. Although she had always firmly advocated keeping in mind an ultimate good as the goal, the Gita expanded her notion of the role of supernatural grace. Ancient Indian philosophy broadened her perception of how to extinguish the spark that inflamed the vicious, self-perpetuating spiral of force, and Krishna's dialectic with Arjuna gave her fresh inspiration in her quest for purity in the use of force.

Created several centuries before the Christian era, the Gita, or Song of the Blessed One, was inserted into an already existing legendary Indian war epic, the Mahabharata, whose origins stem from the same Vedic period as the mystical Upanishads. The more ancient Upanishadic literature promoted meditation and withdrawal from active life, but the Gita blends idealism with practical wisdom, which integrally suited Weil's conviction that relevant action always had to accompany philosophical thought. The lessons that Krishna, God incarnate, gives to Arjuna, a warrior prince, valorize the necessity to act in the world, but only with action inspired by loving obedience to the divine and renunciation of personal gain. Krishna tells Arjuna that discipline surpasses renunciation of action in bringing about good action.

> Renunciation and discipline in action
> both effect good beyond measure;
> but of the two, discipline in action
> surpasses renunciation of action.
> (Gita 5.2)[7]

The metaphysical significance of the Gita and the language of the Upanishads addressed Weil's quest for ways to express the relationship between the individual and the divine. As Degrâces (now

Degrâces-Fahd) has noted, "Weil finds in the Upanishads a new language that allows her thought to advance still further. She extricates notions, not only from the desire to understand, but because she wants to live them, that is, to pit them against her own questions, to push them to the extreme limit wherever rigor and authenticity lead."[8]

Precise wording held supreme importance for Weil. Her purposeful decision to retain the Sanskrit words *dharma, atman,* and the three *guna* (*rajas, tamas,* and *sattva*) served their many-layered meanings and revealed the extent of her immersion into ancient sacred thought. This refusal to translate key words and her choice of favorite verses to render into French highlighted her perception of the human condition, according to the truths that she believed were being passed down through this ancient lore. The Indian vocabulary served her effort to clarify humankind's relationship with the divine, given humankind's penchant for exploiting force. This study uses the Sanskrit words where feasible; their English translations function merely as indicators pointing the reader's mind toward the wider significance of the terms in Sanskrit.

THE GITA'S MYSTICAL SONG

Necessity. Accept submission to necessity:
only act by uniting with it. War. Gita.

Weil, Notebooks

The mystical song of the Gita, widely recognized for its poetic beauty, opens with a full array of battle lines ready to attack. In this narration framed by war, Weil found consolation for the heartrending dilemma of a peace-loving person confronted with the obligation to do violence to others. The context of the conflict concerns a quarrel between two branches of the same royal family: the Pandavas and the Kauravas. The Kauravas have fraudulently seized the kingdom after winning a wager in a game with loaded dice. After thirteen years of exile in the forest, the disenfranchised cousins, Arjuna and his five Pandava brothers, return to reclaim their native land. In defiance, the Kaurava warlord, Duryodhana, refuses to share power or even the smallest parcel of territory. As the Gita opens, the opposing troops are waiting for the signal to start.

Before this point of no return, Arjuna's older brother Yudhushthira, also pacifically inclined, downgraded his family's demands to the modest request of only five villages. On Duryodhana's refusal, Yudhushthira sends his friend Krishna to negotiate a final bid for peace. Everyone knows that Krishna's role is to appear on earth periodically to reorient men toward the paths of virtue in a world gone awry.9 In the Gita, Krishna explains the purposes of his recurrent appearances:

> To protect men of virtue
> and destroy men who do evil,
> to set the standard of sacred duty,
> I appear in age after age.
>
> (Gita 4.8)

Though he recognizes Krishna as an avatar of the great god Vishnu, Duryodhana obstinately rejects Yudhushthira's offer, thereby defying God himself. The stage is set for violence.

Before this climactic moment, the princely leaders have the opportunity to ask help from Krishna, who responds with an equitable offer of support to each chieftain: they can choose either Krishna's immense army or Krishna by himself without arms. Duryodhana, partisan of force, chooses the powerful army. Arjuna, leader of the Pandavas, having confidence in the wisdom of Krishna, rejoices to have Krishna on his side.10 Consequently, the field of battle, considered "the field of justice," becomes the setting for a confrontation between power and wisdom, evil and good.11 On the verge of initiating the battle, however, Arjuna's nerve fails him, and he tells Krishna,

> I do not want to kill them
> Even if I am killed, Krishna;
> Not for kingship of all three worlds,
> Much less for the earth!
>
> (Gita 1.35)

R. C. Zaehner, professor of Eastern religions and ethics, writes that in order to convince Arjuna that he must obey the divine command, "Krishna is not content merely to use arguments already familiar to him—his caste-duty as a warrior for instance; he sees fit rather to reveal to him the structure of the universe as it really is and in which Arjuna is merely a pawn moved by the hand of an all powerful God whose will no man or god can resist or thwart."[12]

Weil saw in Arjuna a struggling soul seeking salutary truth. He represents the soul aspiring toward perfection, while confronting a painful duty. Krishna spurs his faltering indecisive pupil to have confidence in him as master. The young initiate, as a warrior for justice, must carry out his personal duty and defeat the traitorous members of his clan. Though Arjuna sees only evil omens in his obligation to fight family members, Krishna instructs him unequivocally that he is duty-bound to accomplish his assigned task (or *dharma*) and that he must never to try to avoid it nor seek to do another's:

> Your own duty done imperfectly
> is better than another man's done well.
> It is better to die in one's own duty;
> another man's duty is perilous.
> > (Gita 3.35)

and again,

> You are bound by your own action,
> intrinsic to your being, Arjuna;
> even against your will you must do
> what delusion now makes you refuse.
> > (Gita 18.60)

Imagining the *dharma* as a balance with unequal arms, whereby "a weaker balances a stronger by the *dharma* [the law]," Weil considered its inherent equilibrium analogous to Zeus's golden scale as depicted in the *Iliad*.[13] Zeus had shown both justice and obedience to blind necessity in his dropping of weights onto the scale pans. She jotted down in her notebook: "The golden balance of Zeus, [a] symbol with two purposes. Symbol of blind necessity and symbol of a decision by the just. Union of these two symbols, mystery."[14]

In the social realm, seeking justice implied a constant struggle for stability in the need to add more importance to the lighter pan of the metaphorical scale: that is, to the weaker and more disadvantaged in society. Weil wrote: "For that which is higher to weigh as much as that which is lower, one needs a scale with unequal arms, the *dharma* (in the social sense). Society tends ceaselessly to sink by persistently bestowing power on baseness. . . . [A] natural relationship [exists] between power and baseness; on the other hand, there is the law; an unstable equilibrium is a positive image of good in a society and in a soul."[15]

Weil commiserated with Arjuna's despair over the collision of baseness and goodness enacted in the Gita, but she took solace in Krishna's repeated reassurance that Arjuna's salvation was still possible despite the violence, though within strict parameters. She understood that once the armies were face to face the warrior prince's responsibility did not allow him to abandon his people. Nevertheless, she asserted: "[The Gita] teaches that, even in such a situation, if, in action one rejects actions that are beneath one, and if one loves Krishna, salvation is there."[16] "Actions that are beneath one," in Weil's eyes, were unworthy actions that harmed others. To avoid such demeaning actions, one had to remain detached from any personal or selfish gain that could result.[17]

Her contemporaries, like Arjuna, faced the dire predicament of being uncertain where virtue lay: required actions would involve a varying mix of good and bad with positive and negative ramifications. Weil had entered in an early notebook: "Virtue consists in keeping within oneself the evil that one suffers, not liberating oneself from it or spreading it about through acts or imagination."[18] Although he is unwilling to fight, Arjuna, as a member of the warrior elite, is duty-bound to drive out fomenters of chaos in his kingdom. But he suffers physically and mentally from the thought of harming his kinsmen and former tutor, saying to his charioteer, Krishna:

I see omens of chaos,
Krishna; I see no good
In killing my kinsmen
In battle.

(Gita 1.31)

For Arjuna to accomplish his obligations without committing evil or further damage to his kingdom, he has to perform his duty or *dharma* as an act of obedience to Krishna. To reinstall harmony and justice in his kingdom, he has to suppress his own will, be disciplined in his love for Krishna, disassociate himself from any fruits of his actions, and perform the task ordained by his *dharma,* not *for* God, but *through* God. Yet pity suffuses his spirit, and in his torment he asks Krishna:

What joy is there for us, Krishna,
In killing Dhritarashtra's sons?
Evil will haunt us if we kill them,
though their bows are drawn to kill.

(Gita 1.36)

He describes his bodily aversion to the thought of the evil he must do:

Krishna, I see my kinsmen
gathered here, wanting war.

My limbs sink,
my mouth is parched,
my body trembles,
the hair bristles on my flesh.

The magic bow slips
from my hand, my skin burns,
I cannot stand still,
my mind reels.

(Gita 1.28–30)

Throughout the dialogue, Krishna, Arjuna's charioteer and spiritual mentor, insists that Arjuna's *dharma,* or sacred role as protector of
justice, imposes the obligation to forcibly restore order by repulsing
usurpers who perpetuate injustice. He has no choice but to fight. He
could accomplish his task well by submitting his will to Krishna, allowing the divine to act through him, or he could perform poorly by letting
the circumstances embodied in his "nature" rule his actions. Faced
with Arjuna's despair, Krishna encourages his disciple:

> If you are killed, you win heaven;
> If you triumph, you enjoy the earth;
> Therefore, Arjuna, stand up
> and resolve to fight the battle!
>
> (Gita 2.37)

To conclude his many persuasive arguments, Krishna insists that
the situation, as it has evolved up to that point, leaves no alternatives.
By the very nature of his role as royal defender, Arjuna must take to
the field and fight for justice. Krishna admonishes his pupil:

> Your resolve is futile
> if a sense of individuality
> makes you think, "I shall not fight"—
> Nature will compel you to.
>
> (Gita 18.59)

In Hindu belief, *nature* (or *prakrti*) refers to three strands of primordial matter *(guna)* that are interwoven in varying proportions
to compose individual patterns of behavior. Weil called them "inertia," "passion," and "harmony or life." In reference to Krishna telling Arjuna that his "nature" would make him fight undeterred by his
despair, she wrote: "*Prakrti* with its *guna* does everything—even the
good—even the evil—the evil and the good, everything."[19] Weil identified Arjuna's debilitating emotion at this crucial point as caused by
the basest qualities of life: darkness, inertia, and mediocrity, which
lead persons to follow their inclinations and to neglect their responsibilities. Krishna explains,

When dark inertia increases,
obscurity and inactivity,
negligence
and delusion, arise.

(Gita 14.13)

If Arjuna refuses to fight, the enemy representing the forces of chaos will take over his kingdom. If he fights without submitting his will to that of Krishna, he will incite the self-perpetuating chaos of violence. In either case, he will be the victim of delusion.

THE EXTREME SCENARIO OF WAR

The Gita teaches that even in such a situation salvation is present, if, while acting, one rejects actions beneath one, and if one loves Krishna.

Weil, Notebooks

That the Gita describes Arjuna's education in relation to his going to war is puzzling for many readers. Weil considered several reasons for his fighting: obligation, social mores, and obedience. She highlighted the paradox faced by Arjuna: he wishes *not* to fight, but he *has* to fight; he prefers *not* to kill, but he *has* to kill. Many Gita readers agree with her assessment that "in the Gita a scandalous example of the duty of *charité* was purposely chosen."[20] The author's most likely intention, she suggested, might have been to underline the primacy of obligations in paradoxical situations where duty and love of neighbor appear to clash. Everyone had obligations toward his fellow man, which had to be performed through loving obedience to the supernatural, but the exigencies of the provocation that Arjuna faced seemed to violate that responsibility. Weil treasured contradictions for the learning opportunities they offered, for she believed that contemplation of equally valid opposing ideas was a means of arriving at a higher truth.

According to a major theory concerning Arjuna's required participation in violence, Arjuna, as a member of the warrior class, was expected by his society to fight for the protection of others and could not cause a scandal by avoiding his responsibilities. Mores and customs preordained his *dharma*.[21] One's duties were determined by the social expectations of the collectivity, within which a person not only had a role but had already made deliberate decisions. What's more, Weil indicated, the arena of war in the Bhagavad-Gita highlighted unequivocally that the struggle for a greater good required obedience to the supernatural and suppression of self-centeredness even in the most harrowing, ambiguous, and uncertain of circumstances. All these varied suppositions for the Gita's setting in the "battlefield of justice" were pertinent to Weil's thought, for they echoed the reality of a society involved in a war, just like the one she and her countrymen were facing.

A LOTUS LEAF UNSTAINED BY WATER

A man who relinquishes attachment and dedicates actions to the
infinite spirit is not stained by evil, like a lotus leaf unstained by water.

Gita 5.10

In the Gita, Krishna comforts his follower by explaining that a man's way of obedience in this case means that he has to fight but that he can surrender to God/Krishna the dire consequences of his action. Arjuna needs to reflect on the task at hand and to relinquish all personal desire for gain. These guidelines, Krishna instructs, lead to a form of action in inaction, that is, actions with no vested interest:

Surrender all actions to me,
and fix your reason on your inner self;
without hope or possessiveness,
your fever subdued, fight the battle!
(Gita 3.30)

and

Abandoning attachment to fruits
of action, always content, independent,

he does nothing at all
even when he engages in action.
                    (Gita 4.20)

By trusting in God, renouncing the fruits of action, and pausing for silent reflection, one acts, not for God, but through God, performing a
sort of action in inaction. This was the modus vivendi described by the
Gita that resonated with Weil's own philosophy, and she often repeated
the phrase "action non agissante," her version of "action in inaction."
Paradoxically, in certain cases, this precept could mean actually harming one's fellow man.

From the Gita, Weil took the idea that Krishna, or the supernatural, ensured immunity from contamination when one was not able to
avoid doing evil, but only within the rigid confines of total devotion to
the "infinite spirit" and an absence of egotistical desires. Krishna tells
Arjuna:

Men who always follow my thought,
trusting it without finding fault,
are freed
even by their actions.
                    (Gita 3.31)

and

A man who relinquishes attachment
and dedicates actions to the infinite spirit
is not stained by evil,
like a lotus leaf unstained by water.
                    (Gita 5.10)

In her mystical philosophy, Weil stressed the same two ineluctable
requirements: first, that one reject all base actions, and second, that
one love God.[22] Thus she highlighted the way of salvation preached in
the Gita, which was action in total devotion and obedience, as well as
the accomplishment pure and simple of prescribed acts, no more no

less, in willing obedience. She wished to offer guidance in difficult times, but she never implied it would be easy for her contemporaries, who were being trampled under the heavy boots of occupying troops.

A PAUSE BEFORE ACTION

One must do one's best to substitute more and more,
in the world, efficacious nonviolence for violence.

Weil, Notebooks

Krishna and Arjuna's pause for reflection before the confrontation corresponded to Weil's idea that a just reading of any peril requires a pause before taking action. To achieve a just reading meant seeking in silence the truth of a situation, which Weil referred to as the third reading, an objective one that came through the supernatural. The reversal in Arjuna's thinking takes place during a critical and voluntary respite before the opposing sides clash, giving him time to attend to his inner self. Weil wrote: "Arjuna paused before acting. That is why his action is good. Pausing is not hesitating. There are two ways of stopping [before acting]."[23] She added that Arjuna would fight all the same because his "nature" ordained it but that he would fight poorly if he neglected Krishna. The supernatural entered just at the instant that the balance weighing the forces came to a standstill and remained suspended. After the pause, the *same forces* entered into play, but the balance between them was more just.[24] She noted: "Let all activity have at its center some moments of stillness."[25]

Weil's Gita entries indicate a radical reorientation of thought and practical attitudes following her rejection of an absolute pacifist ideology. The Gita's central ideas echoed her philosophy, based on faith, obedience, action, discipline, and equanimity. Weil, agonizing over the possibility of committing base actions that harmed others, dialogued rhetorically with herself: "I may carry out an action if I can do so without lowering myself. Yes, but what if I do evil to another? Precisely, but the most precious and the most desirable measure is that I must know (know with my whole soul!) that the other really exists."[26]

WEIL AND GANDHI'S NONVIOLENCE

*Nothing inefficacious has value. The pernicious
seduction of force creates a formidable difficulty.*

Weil, Notebooks

Gandhi, a lifelong admirer of the Bhagavad-Gita, also based his theory of nonviolence on a deep respect for the existence of the other. But Weil had examined the effectiveness of Gandhi's early proposal for nonviolent resistance to aggression with mixed approbation for its effectiveness. Her statement "Nonviolence is good only if it is efficacious" pointedly referred to the Mahatma's response to an inquiry over how a man might best protect his sister and her virtue from the violent aggression of a passionate suitor.[27] Weil had reservations that Gandhi's plan for action would achieve the results necessary for blocking brute force.

Gandhi had suggested that the brother/protector, by the peaceful action of placing himself between the assailant and the woman, might extinguish the depraved passion of the suitor. If, nevertheless, brother and sister died while defending her virtue, Gandhi concluded that they would "be in a good position before the Supreme Tribunal." Weil's reaction to the anecdote was "Use force, unless you are sure that you can defend [the sister] with as much probability of success without violence."[28] Still thinking of the risk facing France, she believed that much of value would be irrevocably lost if the counterforce were not sufficiently effective. Weil had begun, however, to have confidence that the radiant force of goodness could, under certain circumstances, burn away in small increments the evil contained in oppressive force. But she had not yet discerned the guidelines for activating sufficient energies to bring this counterforce to bear in real-life situations, and she did not find what she sought in Gandhi's early counsel.

Gandhi had recounted his anecdote in an essay of 1921 that was republished in France in 1925. Weil made her notebook entry in late 1941 when she was obsessed with the fall of France. One imagines that she would have wholeheartedly concurred with Gandhi's successful campaign of civil disobedience against the British imperialists had she lived to see its success in ejecting the colonizers from India in 1947. His movement had five positive elements with which she would have agreed: opposition to illegitimate authority, apprenticeship in discipline, detachment from selfish desires, expulsion of subjugators with a minimum of violence, and virtuous example.

Weil's belief in the existence of an intangible radiation of energy had the caveat that to be effective it must equal the energy contained materially in the muscles. She considered Saint Francis as a person with radiant energies, and, perhaps, in the long run, she would have conceded that the energy in Gandhi's nonviolence movement equaled that of the opposing British physical force. Weil felt that one should strive to have this kind of radiation of energy in order to practice nonviolence, but any situation also depended on the adversary and on the force at his command. Her caution was to "endeavor to substitute *more and more efficacious* nonviolence for violence in the world," yet to remain aware: *"Nothing inefficacious has value.* The pernicious seduction of force creates a formidable difficulty."[29]

WEIL'S ASSIMILATION OF HINDU PHILOSOPHY

The meeting of Simone Weil with India has nothing fortuitous
about it; one can discern a pre-established harmony.

Lakshmi Kapani, "Simone Weil, Reader of the Vedic
Upanishads and the Bhagavad-Gita"

Weil did find good counsel in the Gita. In her commentary, one senses the reassurance she gained from the Indian philosophical concept that human beings could gather the energies to oppose force and remain free of contamination. The Hindu understanding of human nature gave her rich words to express her observations about human behavior, such as the three strands of the *guna: rajas, tamas,* and *sattva* (inertia, entropy, and life or harmony).[30] She accepted the idea of the *atman* (eternal soul of the universe, spirit) as the "inner-most reality of a person, the animate, spiritual principle of life," and that of the *dharma* as one's sacred duty, order, or law, implying a moral governance that sustained the individual, society, and cosmos.[31] As the

Indologist Barbara Stoler Miller explains, the Hindu concept of *dharma* is based on the principle that "if each unit or group in the manifold and complex universe performed his own function correctly, the whole (the individual, the society, and the cosmos) would be harmonious and ordered."[32]

"Nature," the mix of *guna* within individuals, nevertheless, held sway over situations, whether one followed or refused to follow one's *dharma*. In reality, events would unfold all the same; however, they had the potential to open the mind to something higher than oneself, for the outcomes or effects could, at fleeting moments, be channeled into less destructive patterns, thus engaging a better result for everyone involved.

In Hindu religious thought, one has a *dharma* or duty because one's soul is part of the *atman* or universal nature: spiritual and immortal. Weil connected the significance of an individual *dharma* to her concept of necessity, which she saw as the inexorable operation of the laws of the universe and of social interaction. Weil subsumed the idea of each living soul having a personal *dharma* according to his or her caste, birth, and previous incarnation into her concept of "duty" or "obligation," which, she felt, everyone had in relation to the universal order of the world. Not only did human beings have to live within set limitations, but, for Weil, true liberty came by accepting these limitations imposed by one's material existence within the universe and by one's relationships within a social structure.

Because of his initial lack of confidence in Krishna and his inability to perceive the truth, Arjuna had refused to accept his sacred duty. In her translations, Weil emphasized Krishna's revelation of the one truth to Arjuna as the means for him to know his obligations. The message of the Gita, as she read it, was that Arjuna needed to believe in God and then do as he saw fit. Weil took on Arjuna's model of obedient love for the divine Krishna by merging it into her understanding of humankind's relationship with God.

An obedient love for God, the creator of the universe, allowed one to fulfill one's sacred obligations. In her staccato notebook-entry fashion, she noted: "Obedience is the supreme virtue. One must love necessity. Necessity and *dharma* are one and the same. *Dharma* is necessity loved. . . . To consider *dharma* not as a duty, but as necessity, means

to raise oneself to a higher level."³³ All persons have obligations in-
cumbent not only on their position within a specific society but also on
their many determining choices that lead up to critical decision points.
She warned: "Be attentive to future moments when one might no longer have a choice. That's when one's *dharma* becomes apparent."³⁴ All
decisions, however small, affected future possibilities, so it was essential to maintain a state of meditative contemplation, commingled with
uncertainty, and to keep an attentive, impartial perspective on the situation, while preparing to do better in the future.³⁵

Weil's concept of necessity, with its insistence on reflection before
acting and on indifference to personal profit, merged with the Hindu
idea of acting according to one's *dharma*. She noted: "Necessity. Accept submission to necessity: only act by uniting with it. War. Gita."³⁶
The real question concerning Arjuna's obligation to fight involved his
manner of accepting necessity, that is, with obedience and renunciation of any fruitful outcome from the actions. Weil wrote in her last
notebooks: "Arjuna's fault is to have said that he would not fight,
instead of imploring Krishna—not at that instant, but a long time
before—to prescribe to him what was necessary for him to do. Who
knows what would have been the response."³⁷

Weil prized the concept of *dharma* as an all-encompassing rule,
noting: "In a given situation, all possible actions comprise a certain
proportion of good and evil, or rather a certain mixture, since the proportion is not measurable. The *dharma* would be a rule for a person
choosing a suitable mixture."³⁸ In her mind, one must have a clear
view of one's duties and then act with discipline and love. In the Gita's
fixed society, Krishna instructs Arjuna firmly in his personal and irre-
vocable sacred duty, which requires discipline, dispassion, and presence of mind:

Look to your own duty;
do not tremble before it;
nothing is better for a warrior
than a battle of sacred duty.
(Gita 2.31)

and

Perform actions, firm in discipline,
relinquishing attachment;
be impartial to failure and success—
this equanimity is called discipline.

(Gita 2.48

But Weil worried that such advice might be valid only for a stable society; no rules that she knew of existed for unstable societies. She then noted the need for further inquiry: "What became of the *dharma* in a conquered country? What duties were owed conquerors?"[39]

Weil, delighting in the good of all creatures, made every effort to indicate paths where justice and love held sway, but she worried whether having a clear image of one's *dharma* would be enough to counter the weight of evil that pervaded the world. If all actions here below were a composite of good and evil, what could be sufficient to limit the spread of evil? She maintained that any unjust or evil act deemed necessary for desired goals must be equally applicable to those one loved and even to oneself. One had to assume any evil consequences as one's personal responsibility. "If the accomplishment of the *dharma* envelops injustices, which is always the case, one must be ready to commit the same injustice, for the *dharma*, against what one loves the most."[40] Strict parameters must be acknowledged for participation in war, such as being willing to accept for oneself any evil resulting from unleashing violence. That is why one had to detach oneself from either success or failure and discipline one's nature in full awareness of the *guna*.

DETACHMENT, ACTION IN INACTION, AND DECREATION

To renounce out of love for God the illusory
power that he gives us to say: "I am."

Weil, Notebooks

Weil considered the *guna* as the source of forceful actions both positive and negative. The three strands of the *guna*, interwoven in varying proportion within the individual, formed the dominant characteristics of each person's nature. The quality in human nature that deflected one away from a higher good came from the lower *guna*, a notion that paralleled Weil's concept of moral gravity. The highest *guna, sattva*, implied unity in wisdom. The philosopher A. L. Herman describes the three ideal types of self-nature in Hinduism: "A self where the *guna* of *sattva* dominates the other two *gunas* will be a self exemplifying the qualities of knowledge, illumination, and goodness. . . . A self in which the *guna* of *rajas* dominates the other two *gunas* will be a self exemplifying the *qualities* of activity, craving, excitement and perhaps the love of physical danger. . . . A self where the *guna* of *tamas* dominates the other two *gunas* will be a self exemplifying the qualities of lethargy, heaviness and dullness."[41] Weil often expressed her own shortcomings in terms descriptive of the lowest *guna*, the *tamas*, which for her represented inertia, obscurity, and aberration. Her counsel for protection against the dangerous vacillation of the *guna* was in her theories of detachment and decreation.

Detachment, for Weil, implied rising above the three *guna* of one's nature and refusing enslavement to passions, desires, lethargic inclinations, or even one's desire for wisdom. An individual had to struggle constantly to maintain equilibrium among the three strands within human nature; a perfect equilibrium of the three natural tendencies, although infinitely desirable, was extremely rare. Weil spoke of these qualities of "nature" within each person as the determinants for the multiple choices made in a lifetime, which could contribute to either well-being or disarray, not just for the individual, but for all members in a society.

Reflecting on her own feelings of humiliation over past errors, particularly concerning her advocacy of pacifism and her sense of culpability for her crimes of lethargy and inertia, she felt that she ought to have dominated both tendencies. Weil wrote: "Accept what one is, at a given moment, as a fact, even shame."[42] In her final notebooks, she attributed her former obtuseness to the physical pain that had burdened her, explaining: "What made a screen between that evidence and me was the sin of sloth, the temptation of inertia." She confessed that in her state of health she ought to have abstained from any actions that could influence others, since the crushing weight of the physical pain prevented her from seeing clearly.[43] Every effort must be made from early consciousness on to achieve detachment from material motivations or gains, so that the *guna* would not lead one to behave in thoughtless ways. Weil entered a pertinent and severe personal reminder in her intimate reflections: "Detach oneself from the three *guna* (even *sattva*), act for the act, not for its fruit (even the fruit of interior perfection)."[44]

In the dialectic between Krishna and his pupil, the three composite qualities of "nature" (the *guna*), inertia, passion, and lucidity, which have a dominant influence on behavior, became important tools of expression for Weil. She felt that persons who believed that they personally controlled their behavior and who assumed full credit for their many characteristics, both good and bad, suffered egoistic delusion. She knew that each person held a certain influence over his or her actions but that such control was in reality limited by a multitude of determining factors put in place prior to any point of decision. Krishna informs Arjuna:

> Actions are all effected
> by the qualities of nature;
> but deluded by individuality,
> the self thinks, "I am the actor."
> . . . .
> Those deluded by the qualities of nature
> are attached to their actions.
>
> (Gita 3.27, 29)

She warned herself: "Where nature operates mechanically through me, it is wrong that I think that I am the author." In her way of thinking, detachment opened the way for a person to limit the influence of the lower *guna* and attain a higher spiritual level. In an early supplementary notepad, labeled *Petit Carnet noir,* she stated, "What is absolutely sure is that no soul can give itself to God while remaining attached to material things."[45] She preferred to keep a wary eye on all three threads of her own "nature," which she knew were deeply fallible. Relinquishing attachment to personal advantage was a way of performing "action in inaction," or, in Weil's formula "action non agissante," which she defined in capital letters in her notebook: "Doing only what one cannot not do. *Action non agissante.*"[46] She considered her theory of detachment and decreation to be closely related to the Hindu religious concept of action in inaction.

In the process that she called decreation, the "I" in the statement "I am the actor" was diminished so that a person could read situations and the self more objectively, in a manner closer to the truth. In the Gita, Krishna refers to the condition that permits a person to read situations in a detached or more truthful way. His advice privileges the worthiness of the action.

> When he can discriminate
> The actions of nature's qualities
> And think, "The qualities depend
> On other qualities," he is detached.
>
> (Gita 3.28)

Decreation, for Weil, was associated with *sattva,* the highest *guna,* or unity in wisdom. "A reasonable creature is a creature who contains within him the seed, the principle, the vocation of decreation. *Sattva* is that tendency toward decreation."[47] The effort to eliminate the "I," or the self, that formed a screen between the divine being and the sacred inner part of the human being could achieve a sort of "spiritual nudity," requiring great humility. Decreation had the goal of an eventual assimilation into God, or the eternal soul of the universe. "Spiritual nudity" contained the two correlative truths: "I am nothing. I am everything (all)."[48] The first "I" was the egoist self, which was base, but the second "I" referred to the higher self, the *atman* that existed outside one's being.[49] According to Indian thought, the attempt to meditatively weave together the mutual relationship of the two opposing selves—"the gross individuality" and the "animate spiritual principle of life"—though never easy, could lead one toward the supreme unity that was their source.[50] Weil noted: "*Sattva* is something in nature that permits the supernatural, in a certain sense, to exist. But it is something in nature."[51]

Sattva implies the idea that one acts because one must act, that is, because it is the right thing to do. Weil returned many times to this pivotal idea in the Gita. She noted for her own reflection: "To act not *for* an object, but *by* necessity. I cannot do otherwise. It is not an action but a sort of passivity. *Action non agissante.*"[52] The passivity referred to here had no resemblance to lethargic inaction; on the contrary, Weil was deeply committed to positive action that furthered the good of the individual and of society.

Weil attributed to delusion Arjuna's initial compassion and inability to act: he lived in a dream, in a world where he could not discern the reality that constituted necessity for him at that time. At first, unable to detach himself from his emotions, he suffered because of what he had to do. All the same, according to Weil, it was Arjuna's sadness and pain that incited Krishna to open Arjuna's mind to the reality of existence and to his sacred obligation. She explained: "Arjuna's moment of pity is due to his dream world. His weakness before killing is comparable to weakness before dying. At a given moment, one is not free to do whatever one wants. One must accept this internal necessity."[53]

For Weil, Arjuna, with divine guidance, overcame his dismay and, through loving obedience, ultimately accepted Krishna's command that he fight to restore concord in the world. His sacred responsibility to preserve social order in the world with the necessary force could not be renounced but had to be done for a greater good and without any personal attachment. In the Gita, Krishna tells Arjuna, "Seeing the way to preserve / the world, you should act" (Gita 3.20) and "So wise men should act with detachment / to preserve the world" (Gita 3.25). Krishna explains that this motivation is a form of action in inaction, which has its reward in immunity from contamination, but only if one performs the necessary acts to maintain order in the world with confidence in Krishna's guidance and renunciation of any personal benefit.

> Abandoning attachment to fruits
> of action, always content, independent.
> He does nothing at all
> even when he engages in action.
>
> He incurs no guilt if he has no hope,
> restrains his thought and himself,

Abandons possessions,
and performs actions with his body only.
(Gita 4.20–21)

Once again, Krishna explains to Arjuna that the wise man realizes
that it is not the deluded self that would act but "nature." He says,

He really sees who sees
that all actions are performed
By nature alone and that the self
is not an actor.
(Gita 18.29)

Weil warned that an even worse alternative to believing oneself in
control was that of imagining that the Holy Spirit authored our actions. Nothing could be further from the truth to her mind. "There is
no greater danger than to attribute an effect of 'nature' to grace. Vigilance with regard to this danger could furnish a criterion for the choice
of a conduct."[54] Weil refused any claim of providential interference in
the world by the divine. In her view, God had created the universe by
an act of withdrawal, after which, for love of his creation, he did not
interfere in its events or movements. Human beings had the obligation to love God and to see to their fellow creatures' needs, both physical and psychic. In that way, each person had the capacity to disengage
voluntarily from any attachment to the outcome of his or her actions.

THE GITA AND THE LEGEND OF JOAN OF ARC

I love those who give themselves to me [Krishna to Arjuna].

Gita 4.11, Weil's translation

In specifying the strict differences between actions produced by one's
nature and those inspired by a transcendent contact, Weil evoked once
again Joan of Arc's historical image to counterpose Joan's exploits with
those of Arjuna. Weil's contrast between Arjuna's duty to evict his

usurpers and the Maid of Orleans' motivation to fight the invaders of French soil exemplified Weil's absolute rejection of divine alteration of the laws of necessity inscribed in the world from its creation. For Weil, images that extolled Saint Joan as a partisan of force and God as a partisan of France were false, misleading, and dangerous. God would never be a partisan of a nation.

Since her concept of God was one of transcendence that was not circumscribed by any one religion, Weil believed that Arjuna had experienced a transcendent contact with the avatar Krishna. That contact, according to Weil, was diametrically opposite to Joan's imperative need to dislodge the enemy from her homeland. Joan's motivation had its origin in "nature" *(prakrti)*, not in the supernatural. The Maid's behavior in the story illustrated for Weil the action of "nature" because of the juxtaposition of circumstances and the many decisions Joan made before entering into battle. Weil acknowledged that God might well have inspired the young shepherdess to mount an army to fight in France's military struggle that was already under way. But Weil adamantly insisted that God did not intervene either to save France or to defeat the interlopers.

Weil believed that transcendence was a true contact with the divine and thereby was incapable of being fabricated or exploited. She noted that the experience of the transcendent could seem contradictory, so other rationales could be falsely taken as indicating a mystical union. "Yet the transcendent can only be known by contact, since our faculties are unable to fabricate it."[55] She stated categorically, "Gita and the legend of Joan of Arc. To fight the English was the *dharma* of Joan of Arc, although woman and shepherdess (if one does not take the system of castes in a strictly social sense), but it was nature motivating her actions *(prakrti)*, not God *(atman)*. . . . One does not lower God to the level of being a partisan in a war."[56] Her objection to the patriotic folklore created around Joan's accomplishment that attributed Joan's action to supernatural interference clarifies one facet of her concept of *dharma:* all men, women, and children have the inherent obligation to rise to the defense of their homeland when its existence is imperiled.

The shepherdess did qualify as an example of being detached from the fruits of her actions in the heroic feat of challenging the foreign intruders. For the ultimate goal of total detachment, "the soul must submit to the equivalent of what Job underwent or Christ on the cross."[57] Every indication of Joan's motives revealed a detachment from the desire to see herself as the center of the universe or to gain material goods. She was an exemplar of the challenge to subdue the carnal self in order to perfect oneself in the love of God, despite what that task might entail.

Weil's ideas of selflessness or detachment, expressed in the paradoxical phrases "action in inaction" and its reverse, "inaction in action," applied to Joan's courageous inspiration to lead the army of King Charles VII with no reward expected for herself.[58] Joan's actions entailed suffering, but they held the implicit recompense that came with total obedience to God's will. On the contrary, the ultimate joy in desiring pure good did not obtain when one harbored selfish motivations. Krishna describes this plenitude, or supreme success, in the detachment of oneself from the fruits of action:

His understanding everywhere detached,
the self mastered, longing gone,
one finds through renunciation
the supreme success beyond action.

(Gita 18.49)

Weil intuited the vital and intimate rapport between Arjuna and Krishna as analogous to the tender love between a human soul and the divine being, which was quite consistent with the primacy she gave to love as the essential bond between humankind and God and between man and his neighbor. Arjuna, in his uncertainty had, at first, persistently questioned Krishna. But once the divine and mysterious revelation overwhelmed him, he proffered a tender, respectful, and total homage to Krishna, manifesting his submission with voluntary, loving, and intimate consent.

I bow to you
I prostrate my body,
I beg you to be gracious,
Worshipful Lord—
as a father to a son,

a friend to a friend,
a lover to a beloved,
O God, bear with me.
                                     (Gita 11.44)

According to Degrâces, Weil fully empathized with Arjuna's dilemma on hearing Krishna speak about his obligation to use force.
Simone Pétrement, her friend and biographer, recounted that Weil's
thoughts and actions had become suffused by the idea of the God
Krishna.[59] When she spoke of God, she used the name Krishna. She
described her plan to work on a farm in a letter to Pétrement: "I am
transforming myself—if Krishna agrees—into a farmworker or a milkmaid this autumn."[60] Her reference to herself as a milkmaid in love
with Krishna during her stint of farmwork could have been playful
without disrespect, or it could have indicated a reluctance to speak directly of God in relation to herself, as Pétrement suggested. Degrâces
was more interested, however, in seeing Weil's reverential references
to Krishna as a result of her bringing together two very different ways
of thinking: that of Hindu mysticism and Christianity.[61] Weil's loving
letters in the last months of her life, sent from London to her parents
in New York, support Degrâces's interpretation, for they gently reminded her mother, anguishing over her daughter's absence, to "think
of Krishna."[62]

Weil harmonized Western beliefs with those of the Indian religion
in her effort to find fragments of truth pertaining to the human condition. The constraints or liberties that Hindus might attribute to a caste
and thus to a preceding incarnation she attributed to prior choices
made by the individual. As she explained: "Gita, Note that the *dharma*,
depending on caste, thus on birth, thus on preceding incarnations, depends on anterior choices. It is not that one has no choice, but that, at
any given moment, one no longer has a choice. One cannot do otherwise. It is vain to imagine doing anything else; it is good to raise oneself above what one has to do. In that way, one chooses, for later,
something better."[63]

For Weil, the "something better" in the future referred to here had
implications for society and for the individual: more harmonious social relationships, limited force, and lives enlightened by the love of

God. All decisions had sequels, so at every point one had to assess a situation with the aim of making choices that had positive ramifications for humankind. Consequently, to choose wisely, it was necessary to keep oneself insulated from evil with discipline and self-mastery, as the Gita instructed:

> Seers who can destroy their sins,
> cut through doubt, master the self,
> and delight in the good of all creatures
> attain the pure calm of infinity.
>
> (Gita 5.25)

Lakshmi Kapani, a professor of Sanskrit and of Indian civilization, analyzed Weil's reading of the Gita and praised the common denominators Weil had uncovered within the three religious traditions: Christian, Greek, and Indian. Nevertheless, Kapani also pinpointed major differences, such as Weil's adaptive interpretation of *dharma,* her lack of comment on the transmigration of souls, and the Christian image that she had given Krishna. All the same, Kapani concluded, "The meeting of Simone Weil with India has nothing fortuitous about it; one can discern a pre-established harmony."[64] Kapani saw Weil's concept of acting while maintaining a detachment from the fruits of one's action and her insistence on the decreation of one's desirous self in order to submit fully to God's love as true to the main message of the Gita. Despite Weil's personal and innovative reading of this Hindu sacred scripture, in which she credited the *dharma* with permitting the force of the weaker to counterbalance the force of the stronger, Kapani confessed: "I can only repeat my admiration for Simone Weil and her profound comprehension of the texts of my country."[65]

Other harmonies between Weil's thought and Indian philosophy exist: the emphasis on the value of a pause before action, on enlightenment or education, and on the spiritual importance of beauty. Before going into battle, Arjuna paused to reflect on his inner anguish over the coming bloodshed. In that moment of quiet suffering, Krishna gave lessons of enlightenment to Arjuna, so that he could achieve a true reading of his obligation in the difficult situation before him. The language and poetic form of the *Gita,* transmits the spiritual message with extraordinary beauty. Beauty for Weil served to entice a soul into willing obedience to divine love, which is what happened to Arjuna.

Weil drew a parallel between her countrymen's need to use force to take back their country and Arjuna's plight in having to use force, despite its terrible toll. She concluded that the moment for deflecting violence had passed; force had to be deployed to bring order and harmony back to the world and to save the precious heritage established over the past centuries. "[Arjuna] no longer has a choice. The two armies are drawn up face to face. His responsibility for his people forbids him to abandon them to the enemy's weapons. . . . There is scarcely enough time to demonstrate to Arjuna that he must fight because even before the dialogue has begun, it is beyond doubt that Arjuna will fight. . . . Arjuna is no longer at the moment of choice." Then she wondered: "What is the moment of choice?"[66]

For Weil, Arjuna could no longer ponder his options. On the field of battle, the moment for that had passed. In Arjuna's moment of piercing distress, he had seen Vishnu, the supreme god and preserver of the universe, through his avatar Krishna, and that vision had brought clarity to his understanding and dissipated the veil of illusions. For Weil, the encounter of Arjuna with the supernatural opened insights into the ways our actions were influenced by the lucidity or the obscurity of our thinking. The pause for dialogue was also an example of the third kind of reading, where one's personal biases were suspended and one achieved true vision through belief in the supernatural. Weil explained:

> As with error and clear, distinct thoughts, there are conceptions of actions that—if one fixes them with the regard of the soul, suspending judgment—vanish like air bubbles. . . . Others, on the contrary, become real, fastening onto reality through the intermediary of the body. . . . Arjuna's impulse of pity, at the moment when it appeared in his soul, was apparently of the first kind. He was torn between pity and the necessity to fight. After having seen Vishnu in his true form (which, it appears, he would not have seen if he had not been racked with suffering), his second thought alone remained.[67]

Arjuna's suffering, and his contact with the transcendent, had made him privy to the truth of the situation, which then inspired him to follow his inner sacred duty, that is, his *dharma*, which could include killing to prevent evil from spreading to others. Weil even accepted the act of killing for herself, in very limited cases: "If I am ready to kill some Germans in case of strategic necessity, it is not because I have suffered by their hand. It is not because they hate God and Christ. It is because they are the enemies of all nations on earth, my country included, and because unhappily, to my great pain, to my extreme regret, one is not able to prevent them from doing evil without killing a certain number of them."[68]

But any act of force, far from being a decision taken through passion, must be surrounded by imperative constraints, as Krishna delineated in the Gita: one must renounce the fruits of the action, abandon all personal goals, offer the action in devotion to God, ask that all evil consequences fall back on one's self, and vow total obedience to a higher law. It is not difficult to imagine that a valorization of these constraints would create impediments for many contemporary conflicts.

The Gita offered Weil guidelines for achieving a destiny that she ardently desired for all human beings—a destiny that stressed individual liberty in the choice of goals, once one's confidence was placed entirely in the divine. She felt assured that a person obliged to exercise force, who kept within immutable constraints, would not suffer contamination but rather would live within God's eternal existence. Krishna, in his instruction to Arjuna concerning the truth of his sacred duty, promises him an eternal place in the unchangeable beyond:

> Always performing all actions,
> taking refuge in me,
> he attains through my grace
> the eternal place beyond change.
> (Gita 18.56)

and again,

> If he listens in faith,
> finding no fault, a man is free

and will attain the cherished worlds
of those who act in virtue.

(Gita 18.71)

Weil exerted all her energy to convince her contemporaries that a way, however arduous, was open to them to save the future of France and Europe without contaminating their own souls. She recommended keeping a steadfast confidence in the long-term efficacy of the "good" with its foundation in the divine, a guideline she had found in the Bhagavad-Gita as the path toward serving justice. She found in "this treasure of an inestimable price" a manner of manipulating force in view of a greater justice—without ever entirely eliminating the risk of corruption for both sides.[69] Souls that could qualify as being sufficiently pure, disciplined, detached from the fruits of the action, and devoid of any egotistical intention approached sainthood, a state of being for which she felt that everyone should strive. Perfection was for God alone, but keeping the ideal of perfection permanently in sight was vital for every person.

CHAPTER SEVEN
Justice and the Supernatural

*Force is in everything that is social, only the
scales of justice can vanquish force.*

Weil, Notebooks

In the late spring of 1942, Simone, preparing to accompany her parents to New York, was counting on getting permission from the Free French Forces in London to reenter France so she could participate in the struggle of freeing her country. Her writings during this period between her agricultural work in southern France and the final months of her life in London testify to the crystallization of her thoughts around the power of charitable actions inspired by supernatural love. Confidence in the spiritual efficacy of love had now fully replaced the reliance on rationality that had motivated her early militant activism in the 1930s. Her intellect was operating simultaneously on several levels as she worked through the themes we explore in this chapter: love of neighbor, obligations toward meeting basic needs of others, and the hypocrisy of France's calling for ethical behavior from others while doing violence to the dignity of the indigenous population in its own colonies.

The following essays show the fundamental importance Weil gave to love of neighbor as a springboard for the revitalized social institutions that she wanted Frenchmen to imagine for their postwar existence. She had little trust in Charles de Gaulle's ability to lead France in the direction that would lead to the spiritual well-being of its people.

Only justice infused by love of others could prevent the spiraling devastation of vengeful force. These conditions required leaders who had a true regard for the people under their jurisdiction and who were willing to make a public affirmation of their moral commitment to meet the needs—of both bodies and souls—of all members of their community. Weil called this affirmation a profession of faith and specified its wording. Nevertheless, she felt that the people had the ultimate obligation to see that their country acted morally toward everyone, inside and outside the national borders. Fifty million people lived in its colonies, many of whom responded to France's appeal to defend the mainland under assault from the Nazis. Weil wanted the French people to acknowledge the shameful conditions in their colonies and to begin treating all subjects in the empire as their equals. The essays in this chapter reveal the next step in her thinking, in which she developed the rationale for justice administered with compassion and explained the role of supernatural love.

LOVE OF NEIGHBOR COUNTERS NATURAL JUSTICE

When a strong and a weak person meet, there is no need to unite them, for there is only one will, that of the strong. The weak obey.

Weil, "Forms of the Implicit Love of God"

On the eve of embarking for America, Weil gave her friend Hélène Honnorat a heartfelt piece entitled "Forms of the Implicit Love of God" to be delivered to Father Perrin. In it, she described for her beloved friend and mentor, who had wished for her to be baptized in the Catholic Church, her theory that God revealed his divine love universally to all persons throughout time and not just to those within the Christian tradition. This concept meant that all persons, the powerful as well as the disinherited, merited equal and compassionate treatment. Her opening section, entitled "Love of Neighbor," provided the basis for her belief that "the supernatural virtue of justice consists, if one is the superior in the unequal relationship of force, in behaving exactly as if there were equality."[1] Only by sincerely treating others as equals could one mitigate the aggressive reactions that led to forceful confrontations.

In composing "Forms of the Implicit Love of God," Weil wished to show that proof of the "grand Revelation . . . God's apparent absence yet secret presence here below" resided in the compassion, gratitude, friendship, and love for the beauty both of the world and of religious practices present in every known century and country.[2] To verify this affirmation, she cited the biblical statement: "Wisdom penetrates every-where because of its perfect purity."[3] She often brought in evidence from ancient Egypt that humankind had always inherently cried out for God's love in the hope of receiving it within the sacred part of the soul. In her reading, once again, the millennia-old Egyptian Book of the Dead testified to the long-standing virtue of benevolence toward others. "I never made anyone cry. I never spoke haughtily; I never caused anyone to fear. I never gave a deaf ear to just and true words."[4] For Weil those lines signified the act of attending to the downtrodden and administering just punishment for acts that harmed others. They implied the same virtues of living in peaceful harmony as were hon-ored in Christian morality.

The argument in "Love of Neighbor" stemmed from an under-lying concern for the devastating effects of brute force on individual souls. True faith, she argued, meant giving sincere attention to the less fortunate and loving them for themselves, not commanding wher-ever one had the power. God was the supreme model of true love of neighbor when he created the universe by retracting his own power, allowing human beings the freedom to choose or refuse obedience to supernatural love. This divine paradigm stressed the importance of preserving one's own ability and that of others to choose freely. When individuals became equivalent to inert matter, their soul's ability to orient itself toward God's illuminating love was diminished. Conse-quently, the many ways persons could be reduced to "things" or "matter" by internal and external social forces had to be flagged for elimination. Persons enlightened by supernatural love exhibited true compassion through charitable actions that alleviated the suffering of others—whatever their condition or place.

Weil intensely desired to make her position on the "Grand Reve-lation" clear to Father Perrin. Her letter built on their many conversa-tions about human existence as a selfless gift from God. Her skills and experience as educator and writer make "Love of Neighbor" significant for all readers who care to understand her foundational belief that the essence of supernatural love was abundantly available to all. She be-lieved that God was secretly present in all acts that arose from unself-ish love of neighbor and that he elevated the contact between souls to the level of a sacrament. For Weil, unconditional love of neighbor equaled justice. Christ had said, "I was hungry and you gave me to eat," and he referred to those who attended to the afflicted as "the just." Persons who honored justice by applying laws fairly, and those who benefited from the good effects of justice, received what Weil consid-ered the sacrament of supernatural justice.

To highlight supernatural justice, Weil contrasted it with natural justice, exemplified by the incident in Thucydides' well-known his-torical account of the Peloponnesian Wars when powerful Athenians confronted the hapless inhabitants of the little island of Melos. Tradi-tionally allied with Sparta, the Melians wished to remain neutral in this bloody war, but the invaders offered their captives the choice of joining forces with the Greek invaders or dying. The islanders refused to cooperate, pleading for justice and pity for their beloved city; never-theless, the Athenians, confident in their superior strength, razed the city, killed the men, and sold the women and children as slaves. Weil focused on the verbal exchange between the strong and the weak, in which the conquering Greeks, rejecting any consideration of justice, framed the situation coldly in terms of the possible. They replied to the Melian plea for justice with "Let us rather deal with what is possible. . . . You know as well as we, the human spirit is so constituted, that what is just is examined only if there is equal necessity on both sides. But if there is a strong and a weak, what is possible is imposed by the first and accepted by the second."[5]

The Melians countered that the gods would be with them in battle because their cause was just, an argument that the Athenians dis-missed out of hand. They asserted disdainfully that their way of be-having was none of their making; they were simply conforming to what was in their best interest. "We have the belief, with regard to the gods, and the certitude with regard to men, that always, by a necessity of nature, each one commands everywhere he has the power to do so. We didn't establish this law, nor are we the first to apply it; we found the law already established, so we conserve it as deserving to last forever, and that is why we apply it. We know well that you also, as would all the others, once having arrived at the same degree of power, would act in the same way."⁶

Weil suggested that the clarity of their logic, although impressive, set up pitiless guidelines in which charity had no place. She likened the Athenians to the Romans and to all others who believed their cause was just because they were the stronger. Weil was adamant that such talk banished all considerations of justice. Where a stronger will opposed a weaker will, there was no need to reconcile the two wills. The weak obeyed as if they were no more than inert matter, and the strong ran roughshod over them. The lucidity of their own argument led the powerful to suppose that they could go to the extreme limits of what seemed within their reach. But in so doing they inevitably overextended their powers, paving the way for their own downfall. Such an illusion, said Weil, illustrated the mechanism of necessity as it operated in social relationships where the weak, posing no obstacle to the dominant, were regarded as nonpersons.

Another time, Weil evoked the symbol of the balance with its scales poised in equilibrium as a representation of social justice built on mutual consent. Applied to human behavior, this image indicated conditions in which, under the influence of grace, unequal forces could miraculously become equal: a situation in which one side could dominate the other but acted in every way as if real equality existed was nothing short of supernatural. She wrote, "Anyone who treats as equals those whom the relationship of force places far below him offers them the true gift of that quality of human beings of which fate has deprived them."⁷ Caring attention given to one of society's pariahs represented true compassion in the literal sense of participation in the suffering of the other. Transporting oneself in thought and sympathy into the consciousness of one's suffering neighbor and giving personal attention to his needs became tantamount to baptizing him, according to Weil.⁸

Weil reminded her reader that Christ's parable of an outcast who stopped to give his love and attention to an anonymous bloody body abandoned in a ditch illustrated the exchange of compassion and gratitude that could occur between two beings. The Good Samaritan was a person who renounced his own immediate needs to restore dignity to a mutilated victim of violence. By listening attentively to the afflicted and ministering selflessly to their needs, a person could elevate suffering souls who had been debased. The acts of a person imbued with compassion revealed the quality of his faith and the real presence of supernatural love. The prevailing drag of moral gravity in human nature hindered unselfish behavior; thus, according to Weil, acts of compassion could not occur without the presence of supernatural love. Although one could not precisely identify the moment when the phenomenon of supernatural love took effect within a person, it was present in every situation where someone loved the afflicted for their very existence as human beings. For Weil, this reality checked the self-perpetuating aspect of violence because brute force could not contaminate the type of love in which God was present.

Because showing compassion for the afflicted was an exceptional act, Weil recognized the necessity at times to use force against force. Punishment was needed for those who violated the order of the community and its trust. But all punishment had to be just, carrying no tinge of vengeance. As Christ resided in an afflicted person whom another had nourished, he also dwelt in the felon who submitted to punishment. Consequently, from the beginning to the end of the criminal process, all involved—judges, jailers, police, and prisoners—had to remain aware of Christ's presence by paying attention to the accused not as a thing but as a human being. They had to sincerely desire that his faculty of free consent be respected and preserved. Both administrators and perpetrators had to perceive the punishment as just and legitimate: that is, carried out according to the law adapted to the situation. The primary purpose of the punishment was rehabilitation of the wrongdoer. When a thirst for dominance or retribution drove the punishment, the evil effects of violence began a self-perpetuating vicious spiral. On the contrary, criminals justly punished were strengthened by submission. This phenomenon was evident in international relations as well as in domestic relations. Weil offered the paradigm of

Christ, who in accepting his death on the cross provided the perfect example of submission to social necessity and of refusal to seek personal redress.

Unfortunately, the scorn that came too easily to custodians of the penal system almost automatically reduced the prisoner to a vile rejected object in the same category as a "thing" or matter. Weil conceded that the act of respecting transgressors could be challenging and contrary to natural justice. Corruption polluted those who came in contact with it, and sincere attention could be difficult to sustain in penal environments. But for Weil, all attitudes of disdain had an equal capacity to damage the soul, whether they involved brutality, flippancy, or one's manner of speaking and listening, or of not listening. The harm inflicted was proportional to the innocence that remained intact in the soul, for all souls harbored the innocent belief that no harm should come to them. Only infinite goodness could have contact with evil without suffering contamination. Supernatural love generated this kind of purity.

Weil believed that a human being's ability to punish another was double-edged: it could bring good or evil to the body and to the soul. By way of illustration, she evoked the material objects of bread and steel, which, devoid of good and of evil in themselves, could transmit good or evil depending on the intention of the one in command. This twofold ability also applied to societal punishments, which could be implemented with or without justice. Censure, justly imposed, could increase the wrongdoer's vital energies and be analogous to the food for which Christ thanked the just. Unjustly imposed, sanctions increased the quantity of evil in the community. Even when authorities illuminated by supernatural love enjoined just laws with rigor and charity, they could not fully eliminate the effects of moral gravity inherent in human nature. They could, however, check the contamination of force, which spread like ripples over water to all segments of society.

Ultimately, Weil sought to offer her compatriots guidelines for treating their conquered transgressors and for reforming their social institutions to meet postwar needs. Liberation from the enemy's yoke would provide a fresh opportunity to reassess customs, attitudes, mores, and official agencies with an eye to bolstering those that could further a better society and to imagining new ones that could serve that purpose well. She also wanted them to embrace the essential criterion by which they measured the value of each organization: that is, whether it encouraged a profound respect for all the members under its dominion or failed to do so. Valuing this standard would affect not only her compatriots' expectations for postwar reparations but also their treatment of their huge indigent colonial populations.

PROFESSION OF FAITH

Each action involving a relationship of one human being with others,
or of a human being with things, envelops, in truth, an original
and specific relationship with God that needs discovering.

Weil, Notebooks

During the few months left to Weil, ideas for postwar policy in France flowed from her pen. All her policy suggestions had as their base a deep concern for the needs of the individual's body and soul. Philosophically, she laid a foundation for offering compassion to human beings in distress, whether that distress was imposed by natural forces in the physical universe or by exploitative persons dragged down by moral gravity. The ravages of the European conflict intensified her desire that France make a fresh start after the war and be an inspiration to other nations. Despite her disquiet about Charles de Gaulle's postwar intentions, she hoped that he and others would put aside their personal ambitions and leave the way open for leaders who aspired to restore France's grandeur by creating institutions that nurtured virtuous civic harmony. Among her papers from this London period she left a personal memorandum subtitled "Profession of Faith," under a main heading, "Draft for a Declaration of Obligations toward the Human Person."[9] This declaration set out parameters by which leaders could judge their capacity to lead well. If they could not meet the criteria, they should not seek to govern. It also laid out the ways that a people should hold their leaders accountable. Weil later developed the "Draft" into guidelines for human relationships that would minimize force as a factor in human behavior. She used this document as a "Prelude" for her final work, *The Need for Roots.*

In her "Profession of Faith," Weil charted a rationale for the regard that was due the human person, along with inalienable obligations that this regard enjoined on every other person's actions, but particularly on the decisions of leaders. As she pursued her personal inquiry into the conduct of persons who believed in the reality of absolute goodness, her words revealed the primacy she gave to Arjuna's question to Krishna concerning perceptible signs in the behavior of people who had recognized the truth. In her attempt to answer that question, Weil made an original contribution to our understanding of the human condition by identifying and placing the terrestrial needs of the human soul on an equal plane with the needs of the body. Her mystical perspective had illuminated the teleological end of human beings, which required attention in the physical world. The needs of the soul gained validity from their link with a reality outside this world.

Weil established her principles in the opening statement:

> There is a reality situated outside this world, that is, outside space and time, outside man's mental universe, outside any domain that human faculties can attain.
>
> This reality responds to an urgent need in the center of the human heart for an absolute good that always resides there and never finds its object in this world. . . .
>
> Just as the reality of this world is the unique basis for facts, so the other reality is the unique basis for good.
>
> Only from this reality can there descend into this world all the good capable of existing, all beauty, all truth, all justice, all legitimacy, all order, and all subordination of human conduct to obligations.[10]

Throughout this succinct summary of her faith composed for readers of many different beliefs, she used the term *reality* instead of speaking of either "God" or the "supernatural," although both were certainly implied. In her mind, the supernatural had an essential role to play in the vicissitudes of ordinary life, for it responded to the radical demand for good found in the hearts of all human beings. She was specific as to its accessibility: "Although [this reality] remains outside the reach of all human faculties, human beings have the power to turn their attention and love toward it."[11]

Weil believed that this power of orienting ourselves to the good was fragile and required protection because it maintained a sacred link with the other reality, the supernatural. Brute force gained its terrible power from the fragility of this human potential.[12] In her notebooks, she insisted that attention to the supernatural reality meant, not that one added God to all things, but that each thing needed elaboration and transformation to render it transparent to the light of the supernatural. God offered his love and waited attentively like a beggar for consent, giving the individual freedom of choice to obey or to refuse. Consent gained its legitimacy by being freely given. Without openness to supernatural enlightenment, people became more likely to succumb to the imperious tow of moral gravity and seldom heeded the cry of distress issuing from their dispossessed neighbors.

Weil saw the mental, physical, and spiritual elements of the human condition intertwined within the structure of the human body. Human nature had the capacity within its very composition to be enlightened by supernatural love, yet only persons who turned their attention and love toward God could be intermediaries between the divine and their fellow beings. The exchange of mutual consent allowed the "good" to descend and to radiate out toward others. No one lacked the power to turn his or her love and attention to the reality outside the world in a willing consent to God's love. The virtual link to a reality outside this world was co-natural for all. It made up the sacredness of the individual and hence demanded esteem. No other motive for universal respect of all human beings rested on something identical in all. Only the presence of this tie with the other reality remained constant, incorruptible, and immutable in all persons.

Because of the ethereal, invisible, and undemonstrable quality of the bond between the reality of this world and a reality outside the world, the respect this bond merited could be shown only indirectly by way of meeting the needs of the material aspect of the human being. Physical or psychic harm damaged the material and mental self, but even worse, both these kinds of damage impaired the person's aspiration for the "good" that dwelt in the sacred or uncreated part of the soul. Consequently, depriving another person's body and soul of essential needs became a sacrilege. Persons who turned their attention and love to the reality that existed outside this world recognized their sacrosanct obligation to correct any deprivation. Each of the needs of the body and soul created an obligation on the part of others to furnish what was required to fill the lack. No circumstances whatsoever relieved another from the responsibility to repair deficient conditions, in so far as possible, so that all essential needs were met.

The consent or refusal to recognize this principle of sacredness governed a person's conduct and contributed to the ratio of good to evil in a society. Weil felt that this ratio depended on two components: the number of the society's members who accepted or rejected this principle, and the distribution of power between those who consented and those who refused.[13] For a society that prized its members' well-being as its guiding principle, those in power and their electors had to acknowledge in principle and in practice their duty to be mindful of others' needs. Weil made clear that the object of public life was to put power in the hands of those who promised to carry out their obligation to see to the basic needs of their fellow human beings. While this profession of faith revealed her deepest convictions, she considered its ultimate use to be an oath for leaders to take as they assumed their official duties. A refusal to accept one's responsibilities to others was a crime that became even more heinous and overwhelming when perpetrated by persons in positions of leadership. In those cases, the governments run by such leaders had no legitimacy. Nor did members of that community escape from being accomplices to that crime if they did not impeach their leaders for criminal negligence. In situations where freedom of opinion was suppressed, the accusations against those in charge had to be circulated by whatever means possible.[14] Her strictures are strong, but history has sadly shown the rampant misery under leaders whom no one holds accountable for their neglect of the well-being of their countrymen.

Weil understood that at times little could be done to redress the anguish of others. Those who tried and failed to ameliorate conditions had to explain, if possible, to the afflicted exactly what was irremediable and why. The afflicted persons, in turn, sometimes had to accept the moral gravity governing their persecutors' behavior, making every attempt not to become bitter or seek unbridled retribution. Weil knew that at times nothing could uproot the causes of suffering, but hating the enemy or indulging in violence for the sake of vengeance or frustration only increased the level of savagery. A perpetually renewed escalation of violence was what she feared might be in store for her compatriots.

For Weil, once again, the paradigm of perfect acquiescence to what could not be helped was Christ's cry, "Father, forgive them, for they know not what they do." We can find a moving contemporary example in a Tibetan monk who avowed that his greatest fear during torture by the Chinese was that of losing his compassion for the Chinese people.[15] This type of acceptance exemplifies the attitude that Weil earnestly desired for herself and for her fellow Frenchmen in view of Nazi cruelties. Employing a counterforce, however intangible, to the insidious spread of violence and evil demanded an attitude that reaffirmed the tie to the eternal, thus magnifying the pure good available to humankind.

Weil recognized the challenge of constantly orienting one's love and attention toward the eternal "good," which exacted unselfish attentiveness to others' needs. Nevertheless, she was confident that the good desired for oneself and others would unfailingly descend in response to persistence. She wrote, "Whoever consents to orient his attention and his love outside this world toward the reality situated beyond all human faculties will succeed. Sooner or later the good will descend on him and radiate through him to others around him."[16]

Having stated clearly her firm belief in the importance of showing respect for the sacred aspect of the human being by honoring the obligations created by the earthly needs of body and soul, Weil distinguished those needs and juxtaposed each one with its opposite. She set parameters for their validity in order to establish guidelines for public and private behavior. Although others had introduced similar ideas before, Weil's skill in expressing her insights gives the reader fresh ways to look at age-old questions of ethical behavior. Human needs were subordinate only to the hazards of nature and to the legitimate needs of others, considering that the same degree of attention to basic needs had to be given to all. Physical needs were apparent—food, warmth, sleep, sanitary conditions, rest, exercise, and pure air—but the needs of the soul were more elusive. Her list coupled needs that balanced, completed, and limited each other. Some are self-evident, but others need clarification, which she undertook to give in her "Prelude" to *The Need for Roots.*

The brief itemization that follows will suffice to clarify Weil's point that once one accepts and carries out the obligations entailed by others' needs, imagination and attention can move humankind in a more humane direction. For Weil, this kind of attention could constrain the effects of moral gravity through which imperious force wreaked havoc on living souls. Essential to the satisfaction of all the basic needs was a natural milieu or community operating in an orderly and just fashion so that one could send down roots in a distinct locality, language, culture, shared history, and profession.

The sixteen needs in their most concise form are italicized below:

Equality in the degree of attention and *hierarchy* in the scale of responsibilities

Consenting *obedience* to legitimate authority and *liberty* in the power of choice—within the margins of natural forces and of accepted authority

Pursuit of *truth* and *freedom of expression*—uncontaminated by propaganda or self-serving manipulation

Solitude and *social interaction*

Private property, such as a home and tools for working, and *communal property* that gives the sense of belonging to a particular human milieu

Criminal *punishment* where merited and *honor* for valued contributions to the community

Participation in disciplined *work* that contributes to the public good and opportunities for personal *initiatives*

Security and *risk*

Weil wanted very much to inspire in her readers the conviction that appropriate models existed for functioning societies in which people's aspirations could thrive. Well-formulated principles served as their foundation. She believed that the behavior of a "just" person revealed its guiding source and that the way a community honored obligations to individual persons indicated the proportion of good and evil it harbored. Where human needs found satisfaction, there was fraternity, joy, beauty, and happiness; in contrast, sadness, ugliness, and self-absorption predominated in situations of deprivation.

Despite her declining health, Weil wrote out a full description of these principles in her manuscript *The Need for Roots* to present to General de Gaulle—who did not receive it graciously. He had his own plans for the future of France, with him at the center of government, and had no patience with her alternative plan. Albert Camus, however, in admiration for the message in *The Need for Roots,* published the manuscript in 1949 as the first of eleven volumes containing Weil's writings for the Gallimard publishing company.

While Weil's preoccupation with the effects of suffering on individuals echoed the general horror of a world in chaos, she had the originality to blend her reflections with her mystical and political insights and the skills to set them down in an accessible style. She was far from being alone in her anxieties about the integrity of the individual in wartime and the impossibility, given new and deadly technologies, of protecting noncombatants. Her life ended in August 1943 before the full horror of the Nazi concentration camps was disclosed. Within two years after her death, the Allies firebombed Japanese urban areas, carried out obliteration bombing of Dresden, and dropped atomic bombs on Hiroshima and Nagasaki. Though Weil had come to accept a warranted use of force and even killing in specified circumstances, she had laid down carefully thought-out parameters for justifying the ways this force had to be applied to avoid the contamination of its inherent evil. She would have been deeply saddened by the unlimited use of force on the part of both sides. Force could be used as a punishment to encourage sincere repentance, she believed, but it should never be used against the innocent or as a tool of vengeance.

After the devastation of the Second World War, world leaders strove to establish international rules for the protection of noncombatants from wanton behavior in war. Five years after Weil's death, forty-eight nations signed the Universal Declaration of Human Rights, which defined and guaranteed human rights to all peoples, a document that Eleanor Roosevelt referred to as an international Magna Carta.[17] Had Weil lived to contribute to the wording, she would have fought tenaciously for terms that prioritized obligations over rights, and she would have found support in the terse statement attributed to Mahatma Gandhi apropos the Declaration: "The Ganges of rights originates in the Himalayas of responsibilities."[18] At the time, Gandhi and leaders of the colonized nations understood that little in this document directly pertained to them as imperial subjects. Since 1948 there have been several initiatives to codify a Responsibility Charter, of which the latest is the 2008 Universal Declaration of Human Responsibilities, guided by Hans Küng.[19]

COLONIZATION AND WAR

The problems regarding colonization can be stated above
all in terms of force. Colonization nearly always begins by the
exercise of force in its purest form, that is, by conquest.

Weil, "New Facts about the Colonial Problem in the French Empire"

During Weil's short stay in America, she formulated her most complete censure of conditions of slavery in the French Empire. Weil considered relationships between colonizing powers and the colonized, founded on force, to be among the worst of oppressive relationships. Wanting this fact to be the starting point for any analysis of the situation within the French Empire, she composed two major theoretical statements on colonialism: one published in 1938 and the other written for the Free French Forces in 1943 but published posthumously. Her commentaries on colonialism, never published during her lifetime, include lecture notes from her philosophy classes, drafts of letters, projected essays, and two articles written in English during her four-month stay in New York. Two polemics published in 1937 include a scathing denunciation, imbued with irony, of France's hypocrisy in

claiming the "right" to keep Moroccan territory from Germany's preda-
tory grasp, as well as a harsh indictment of the French public's indifference to the "manifestations of wretchedness" rising from an
"abyss of slavery and affliction" in Tunisia.[20] We see in her reactions to
the evils she perceived in colonialism a vibrant example of how she
thought a responsible citizen should react to wrongs perpetrated by his
or her country.

Weil's initial commentaries on colonial problems and their potential solutions in the lecture notes had a philosophical tone. As her outrage flared she became accusatory, but the final writings during the
Occupation show a rational, persuasive, and pragmatic approach as
France's viable options in her colonies diminished and the risks of up-
risings increased. Only in her last piece, entitled "The Colonial Question," did she give a prominent place to the ideas of spirituality, grace,
and the supernatural. Her arguments about the immorality involved
in maintaining the empire stressed the grave risk to France's security
posed by its need to control a huge population of oppressed subjects
while it struggled for survival. The fragility of France's continued existence in the face of Nazi imperialist ambitions made prudence indispensable in the immediate policies toward the millions of persons in
the colonies.

Weil's many statements on colonization reveal an inquiring but
increasingly critical attitude toward realities in France's Empire. The
class notes of a former student from her 1933–34 philosophy lectures
in Roanne highlight her initial conclusions as a professor: "Colonization has often been initiated by admirable people, explorers, missionaries. The problems come from the interior workings of the state.
Things will continue to be thus as long as men are subordinated to
things. . . . One could nevertheless try to reduce these horrors with a
little more humanity."[21]

These lecture notes show Weil's philosophical approach as she acknowledged the economic basis of colonialism, which favored com-
mercial interests over the well-being of the colonized. She summed up
advantages and disadvantages for the colonized: "Benefits: roads, rail-
ways, factories, hospitals, schools, destruction of superstitions and
family oppression (the yoke that burdens women)." The "disadvantages or horrors" included "corporal punishments, massacres, bomb-

ings, forced labor." She lamented the casual attitude of the French people toward the price paid in loss of life, the humiliation of individuals, and the destruction of native cultures. The essential point that underlay all her philosophical thought was expressed in her statement: "Saying: 'Colonization must be reformed' is the same as saying: 'The social regime must be transformed'; you must see men, and not just things."[22]

Weil recognized the potency of the national myth cherished by the French as a rationale for their vast colonial holdings: that of being charged with a *mission civilisatrice*. In *The Need for Roots,* she called it a *vocation universelle* and commented, "France's universal vocation cannot, without falsehood, be evoked with unmixed pride. If one lies, the words betray it; if one remembers the truth, shame must be mixed with the pride, for there is something troubling in all the examples from history one can furnish."[23]

Weil partially concurred with the idea that the French, who proudly took credit for the "rights of man" doctrine in 1789, had the obligation to share this democratizing concept with all who lacked the advantages of civilization and lived in societies that did not recognize human rights. Two centuries earlier, this concept had been clearly enunciated by a French statesman who made one of the many pretentious justifications of colonization by loftily declaring, "Since we have found the right way of administering European countries, why should . . . we deprive the colonies of it?"[24] As the empire developed, the self-appointed mission to spread the French language and culture alleviated the consciences of French citizens who might otherwise question their country's de facto treatment of native populations. This conceit led to passivity as cruel policies ravaged the lives of millions of the colonized. Weil's indignation exploded: "When one assumes, as France did in 1789, the role of thinking for the whole universe to define its notion of justice, one does not become the owner of human flesh."[25]

Weil knew that dispelling the comforting illusion of bringing civilization to the supposedly unenlightened would be difficult. The idea of a civilizing mission had changed over time to become an ideology, permitting the French citizenry to be oblivious to the shameful abuses that occasionally became public. They could remind themselves of the generous, edifying gifts by which they had enriched their subjects' existence. Weil deplored her countrymen's tendency to disregard the rampant injustice: "The French are so convinced of their own generosity that they do not seek to be informed of the evils that far-off populations suffer through them, while constraint deprives those populations of the capacity to complain."[26]

Weil often referred to her abrupt awakening on reading about the Yen Bay massacre in 1930, as recounted by journalist Louis Roubaud in *Le Petit Parisien*. The incident took place on the night of February 9, 1930, when, as part of a planned rebellion, a garrison of Tonkinese troops murdered six French officers. This act incited a yearlong retribution exacted against a vast net of suspected perpetrators, taking an exorbitant toll in lives. Roubaud's vivid description of the vindictive retaliation by the French military became pivotal for Weil, jolting her into an awareness of the brutal treatment of the indigenous population. His description of the pitiable lives led by the native people aroused her anger and compassion.

In deep anguish over Roubaud's newspaper exposé, Weil was beside herself with exasperation and disbelief that more of her compatriots did not demand better conditions for the colonies. Yet indignation was obviously the last thing on their minds. Just a year following the Yen Bay massacre, the 1931 Colonial Exhibition in Paris took place to commemorate the centennial year of the conquest of Algeria. At this huge celebration, Weil was shocked to see her fellow citizens, oblivious to the harm they had done to the indigenous people, marveling at the recreation of African, Arab, Polynesian, and Asian buildings, as well as a massive scale model of a Cambodian temple.

Weil wanted everyone to know that French colonial practices caused the Annamites to suffer destitution, slavery, and multiple forms of degrading treatment, out of all proportion to any benefits they might have received.[27] In a open letter to the people of Indochina, composed in 1936–37 but never published, Weil recounted her chagrin at this display of indifference to hardship: "At the Colonial Exhibition, I saw the crowd, many of whom read *Le Petit Parisien,* contemplating the reproduction of the temple of Angkor with foolish admiration, mindlessly indifferent to the sufferings caused by the regime thus represented. Since that time, I have never been able to think of Indochina without feeling ashamed of my country."[28] To her compatriots she gave a terse and prescient warning: "Wherever men are oppressed, revolt is prompted as inevitably as compressing a spring brings about its recoil."[29]

In another piece that same year, Weil expressed horror at the police in Tunisia indiscriminately firing into the crowd of striking workers, who were protesting the twelve-hour workday forced on them even during the Ramadan fasting. She especially incriminated the political parties on the left, who rallied around the slogan, "Bread, Peace and Liberty" for themselves, yet did not protest the treatment of the workers in the colonies.[30] "And we, too, French people of 'the Left,' we are responsible for the same burden of constraint and terror that has been weighing down the natives of our colonies for so many years; and we believe that the silence that we impose on them, and which they are forced to observe, is an adequate excuse for our not thinking of them."[31]

Repeating this accusation against the "French State, which acts in the name of all French people and therefore to a small degree in my name," Weil confessed, "I cannot but feel that I have crimes to atone for."[32] She stressed France's dishonor in using force against the vulnerable. Scandalously hypocritical, it reduced colonial subjects to slaves, then used them as cannon fodder, depriving them of "their dignity, their freedom and their fatherland, that they might go and die for the dignity, the freedom, and the fatherland of their masters."[33] Weil compared France's treatment of its colonies to war between two radically unequal opponents, writing: "If the population of the colony has the feeling that the conqueror wants to prolong indefinitely the relationship of conqueror to conquered, a state of peace sets in that differs from war only in that one of the protagonists is deprived of arms."[34]

She drafted a bitter complaint to the novelist and playwright Jean Giraudoux for not having told the truth when, as general commissioner for information, he made a public statement asserting that France's colonies were attached to it by bonds other than subordination and exploitation. She avowed: "I would give my life and more if it were possible to think that this were the case, since it is painful to feel oneself to be guilty through involuntary complicity."[35] She reminded him of France's conquest of Annam, the dismantling of their culture, and the imposition of French culture on them instead. The Annamites were beaten, overtaxed, and tortured. Starving parents were forced to sell their children. In evoking the blatant shooting of the striking Muslim miners in Tunisia during their religious period of fasting, Weil asked: "How would Muslims accept these and similar things if they were not subjected to them by force?"[36]

Weil wanted her readers first to accept their complicity in this relentless violence perpetrated on the colonial peoples and then to pursue ethical policies to address the terrible suffering caused by the inhumane treatment. Her compatriots' primary collective responsibility was to oppose injustice. She knew, however, that a plea targeting self-interest would have a greater psychological impact, so she stressed the danger to French security. "What threatens security speaks quite differently to the imagination, especially the collective imagination, than that which threatens simply the purity of the conscience."[37] All the same, she noted, "A man is sometimes moved by justice, even when it demands that he act against his own interest; a collectivity, whether it be nation, class, party or group, is hardly ever moved by justice, except when it is itself wronged."[38] Personally preferring to argue for justice, she bowed, nevertheless, to the realities of human nature.

This same awareness of human psychology rendered her reasoning increasingly pragmatic as war inched closer. She felt the urgent necessity to convince her compatriots that soon they would be limited to only catastrophic options for the future. The humiliation imposed by the Munich Accords allowed Germany and its allies to openly covet the empire that France had amassed primarily for reasons of worldly glory. If France's loss of status encouraged the colonies to support her adversaries in the hostilities, the ensuing chaos would be intensified. Misinformed illusions that the colonized peoples felt tied to the mainland through bonds other than pure hate could lead to dangerous inaction on the part of the French administration.

Weil dearly wished for her country's honor to be restored through just actions that were consistent with the doctrines of human dignity proclaimed by the French Revolution and not through unethical exploits, such as those used to conquer and subdue the colonies. The barbarous force exerted against the subjugated native peoples could easily rebound, bringing immanent and painful justice. In this instance, France's behavior well exemplified Weil's observation that those in control, facing little opposition, seldom foresaw that force might not always prevail. As a result, the masters enjoyed with apparent impunity the exploitation of others' labor, reinforcing their belief that such benefits were their due. Their subjects' submission encouraged the exploiters to imagine that their self-assumed superiority met with others' approval. Such was the case with the French administration of the colonies. To Weil's mind, this unethical state of affairs had to be redressed if France were to stave off impending disaster and foster an honorable and positive image for the French people.

Weil was confident that if her fellow citizens took the time to inform themselves of the true horrors of colonial oppression, they would, as she had after her own awakening, become conscience-bound to seek better conditions for tyrannized peoples. The first step was an honest appraisal. To make her point, she stated categorically in her initial sentence of "New Facts about the Colonial Problem in the French Empire," composed just prior to the outbreak of the war, that colonialism equaled conquest by force.[39] "The problems regarding colonization can be stated above all in terms of force. Colonization nearly always begins by the exercise of force in its purest form, that is, by conquest. A people, overcome through force of arms, suddenly has to submit to the control of foreigners of another color, another language, a completely different culture, and convinced of their own superiority."[40]

For analytic purposes, Weil proposed three possible strategies to address the problem. First, ideally there could be a change of heart in the colonizing nation that would encourage a more generous treatment of the colonized. She considered this hypothesis highly unlikely from her observation of the innate human resistance to acknowledging injustices committed by one's own people. Second, there could be a revolt in the colonies. This presented a scenario "too dreadful to contemplate," given the defenseless conditions of the colonized peoples who had been deprived of the advantages of technology and modern weapons. In a world governed by force, they would be prey to stronger combatant nations externally and to ruthless dictatorial struggles for power internally. The third strategy, clearly Weil's preferred alternative, was to give the subjects in the colonies something of their own: a progressive elevation of their status from subject to citizen, making them partners with administrative autonomy, collaborators in political and military power, and full participants in the decisions concerning their economy and natural resources. The specifics would vary according to the culture and conditions of the individual colonies.[41]

Weil believed that France's reputation rested on the option of transitioning colonial subjects into becoming what she called associative autonomous members of the French community of nations. In this article, she insisted that states must be held to the same moral criteria as individuals; there was "no reason to establish in this respect a different scale for national problems than for individual ones."[42] She foresaw that any forced liquidation of the empire would be costly, traumatic, and demoralizing and that it would most likely push the former colonies into new disasters for which they were totally unprepared.

In Weil's rationale, the alternative of citizenship or its equivalent for members of the empire would best serve France's self-interest and that of the colonies, as well as restore human dignity to the people involved. She worried, however, that the colonized had become so embittered that little could repair the relationships. She noted that nine out of ten families among the millions of people in Northern Annam and Tonkin had lost at least one of their members from the repression of the Yen Bay mutiny alone. This bitter memory would not be easily effaced from the Annamite consciousness. But she argued that in the long run the policy offering an elevated national status had the best chance of allowing France to merit once again a deserved place in the community of great nations. This course of action would make any increase in prestige creditable and could begin the healing process.

Although immediate independence might appear to be a moral priority, Weil saw serious impediments to acting too quickly because of the French government's stance and the colonies' weakened position. Unfortunately, independence for the colonies had been placed beyond the range of solutions envisioned by the French, who were unwilling to give up easily the cheap human labor, the resources, and the military conscripts that the enslaved populations provided. Equally problematic was the unarmed colonies' lack of preparedness to make a quick transition to full independence after long years of subjugation. The absence of powerful weapons for their defense left them at the mercy of force exerted from inside or outside their country. They were vulnerable to the impact of fanatical nationalism, fierce militarism, exaggerated industrialism, and autocratic state control of the whole of social life.

THE COLONIAL QUESTION AND THE DESTINY OF THE FRENCH PEOPLE

Freedom, like happiness, is defined first and foremost
by the feeling that one possesses it.

Weil, "The Colonial Question and the Destiny of the French People"

In her last piece dedicated to colonialism, "The Colonial Question and the Destiny of the French People," written in London for the Free French Forces in 1943, Weil wrote with two new perspectives: that of the real violence raging around her and that of the transformation of her thinking due to her mystical experiences. She widened the scope of her treatment of the colonial question to include in a more general fashion the overall responsibility of the European nations. The destiny of the whole human species now depended on the European peoples' finding a way to protect vulnerable populations and to lead them toward an independence that truly allowed them to feel free. An abundance of freedom that brought out the best in human nature required, in her words, an intensity of moral life because "freedom, like happiness, is defined first and foremost by the feeling that one possesses it."[43]

France's future and that of her colonies depended on the French people's refusal to own human flesh and on the quality of freedom that they offered the colonized. Nothing must be said or done too quickly to affirm any policy before the opportunity was taken to think out all possibilities. Suitable social and political solutions required openness to what was just and in keeping with the will of all parties. Order was given top priority, as can be seen in her list of the needs of the soul that she created as a prelude to *The Need for Roots*. Always mindful that the social scales could quickly tip toward a more cooperative relationship or instead toward utter chaos, she warned insistently against declarations that risked irreparable upheaval. At the same time, statements and actions had to nourish the hope of improved living conditions for the millions of afflicted colonized subjects whose desolation could drive them to the enemy's side.

Weil saw her country at a critical crossroads. France could reorient itself to make principled moral choices and create a model for others in similar dilemmas, or it could fruitlessly and disastrously try to maintain a no-longer-viable status quo. Since France no longer had the power to impose its will on its colonies—and since, in Weil's mind, it had never had the right to do so—it had to rethink its imperial stance and remember with humility the damage it was wreaking on others even while harboring fears of being colonized by the Germans. In her style of direct confrontation, Weil made clear to her readers that the past choices would no longer hold the empire together and that the question of how the realignment would proceed was primary. She asserted bluntly: "If it is force that decides, France has lost hers; if it is a question of rights, France never had the right to determine the destiny of non-French peoples. In no sense, either in terms of rights or of fact, can one say that the territories inhabited by these peoples are France's property."[44]

Weil argued that her compatriots had to seek means of ethically rectifying their past lapses of moral responsibility before time ran out for reasonable options. She stressed the grim conditions that France had created in the colonies, saying, "By depriving peoples of their traditions, of their past, and thus of their souls, colonization reduces these people to a state of matter, but matter that is human."[45] She reiterated the terrible insight she drew from the *Iliad:* force turns human beings into things. France could change its direction with regard to the colonies and take new inspiration from its past greatness that had sprung from a spiritual influence and from an aptitude for opening up new pathways for the human species.

Total war brought painful uprooting from the past, with the terrible result, according to Weil's mystical political philosophy, of rendering people rudderless and reducing them to objects to be manipulated. Ironically, Weil intimated that France's loss of its own past might be regarded as its just deserts for indifferently casting aside the heritage of many other cultures by forcibly yoking them into an empire. But Weil knew that the loss of a people's past was a disaster of monumental proportions, since a past once lost could never be found again; man could create in part his future, but never his past. For her, "The loss of the past is equivalent to the loss of the supernatural,"[46] since the past was indispensable for spiritual rooting. The past contained spiritual treasures, and only the spiritual heritage of the past could incline the soul to receive the operation of grace that allowed direct contact with the other reality.

Weil's fundamental conviction of the need for enlightenment from a reality outside this world came strategically near the end of her essay, where she contrasted it to the secularists' position that praised human faculties as sufficing for addressing all human problems. She conceded that if the Encyclopedists' theory were right, humankind would not need to worry about the obliteration of the past, for the human resources of will and intelligence could rise to the occasion. But she knew that her compatriots were pushed to the extreme by events, and she anguished over their incapacity to protect either their past or their country. They understood, some more than ever before, that the treasures of their heritage could disappear forever.

Weil's lengthy essay encompassed her social, political, and philosophic concerns about finding a solution to France's unethical and unjust control of her imperial subjects. The ethical solution and its rationale that she constructed in this article relied on implicit spiritual connections between human beings and proposed a progressive elevation of colonial subjects from their conditions of abject slavery to a bona fide equivalent level of citizenship. Above all, she counseled prudence and caution against premature decisions, which could set one side irretrievably against the other before all conceivable attempts had been made to find specific points of agreement.

All Weil's proposals, however, were ignored; as the war was propelled forward, conflicting emotions preoccupied everyone's attentions and inhibited the generous and selfless acts that could have been undertaken in favor of distant colonies. The French colonies almost unanimously temporarily shelved their own demands and fought on the side of France in the misplaced confidence that a well-earned independence would be theirs after the war. That they preferred, for the most part, to tie their destinies to the democracies in this time of great peril revealed the solid grounds of Weil's proposals to elevate the colonized to a desirable equal status as a potential for cooperation in the future.

Unfortunately, Weil's anxiety that France would not grant independence to the colonies, even after their enormous contributions to the mainland's defense, was borne out by the terrible and demoralizing post–World War II conflicts in Indochina and Algeria. The struggle in Indochina lasted from the Japanese defeat in 1945 through a costly Viet Minh victory over the French Expeditionary Forces nine years later in 1954 at Dien Bien Phu. That same year, the Algerian war for independence flared up in earnest and continued for eight bloody years until a referendum called for by President Charles de Gaulle resulted in Algeria's independence in July 1962. The determined resistance on both sides led to enormous loss of life and to the abandonment of all moral restraint, particularly with the use of state-sanctioned torture. The force deployed to keep Algeria under French control instigated an equivalent violence on the part of the Algerians to break free. The resulting bitter enmity on both sides and the loss of irreplaceable cultural heritage would have surely shattered Weil, who had tried so hard to warn against just such an outcome.

The ultimate resolution of the colonial question, settled under duress, brought out the worst aspects in human beings on all sides of the conflicts. In retrospect, many historians single out moments when compassion and compromise could have halted the bloodshed but note that the press of events redolent with violence did not allow a moment of pause for sensible reflection, or, as Weil would put it, for grace to descend. The paucity of successful smooth transitions in history from dependence to independence is painfully revealing. In truth, the catastrophic results that Weil had imagined became part of the discordant moves toward independence in one insufficiently prepared but determined country after another. The struggles that ensued unhappily illustrated her contention that force is an entity with a capacity of self-perpetuation that spirals out of control until it is spent or until a higher force of love and compassion activates a countering force. Both alternatives entail great sacrifice, but the second ensures a better, more stable future.

The refusal to accord human dignity to the less powerful unless compelled to do so has carried implications of violence—religious and secular—into the twenty-first century. Too many strong, well-armed industrialized nations appear unable to learn from the unspeakable suffering in the past and thus are incapable of setting in motion effective methods of directing energies toward peaceful cooperation. Weil's was one voice among the many that have tried to warn against unleashing violence without very careful forethought, strict limitations, and a definite, achievable goal untainted by selfish desires. She described the need for revitalized social institutions administered by leaders who were firmly and openly committed to principles founded on a compassionate love of neighbor. But the world has not heeded that message or learned from the past terrible failures to even begin to create harmony among peoples. Archbishop Desmond Tutu, international peace activist and Nobel Peace Laureate, expressed the truism best when he declared that if there is one thing we learn from history, it is that we don't learn from history. In contrast, Weil wanted very much for all of us to learn vital lessons from history.

CHAPTER EIGHT
Neither Victim nor Executioner

*The worst possible betrayal always consists in
willingly subordinating oneself to the state machinery of
the administration, the police, and the military and serving it
by trampling on one's own and others' human values.*

Weil, "Reflections on War"

Weil's thinking is occasionally treated as idealistic and out of touch
with the reality of human interaction. However, three mid-twentieth-
century moral philosophers of very diverse backgrounds and cultures
paid explicit homage to her insights into force and their applicability to
contemporary social conditions. In so doing, they also signaled implicit respect for her faith in the existence of a powerful "good" beyond
material existence. The American editor Dwight Macdonald and the
French author Albert Camus recognized in Weil a kindred spirit who
agonized at the thought of others' suffering. Their mutual friend the
Italian humanist Nicola Chiaromonte was instrumental in bringing
Macdonald and Camus together in New York in 1946. He had already
brought Weil's essay "The *Iliad*, or the Poem of Force" from France
and to the attention of Macdonald. In this final chapter, the ways each
man fused Weil's philosophy into his understanding of human nature and subsequently introduced her writings to a wider readership in
America and France in the mid–twentieth century serve as examples
of her relevance to the twenty-first century.

In the framework of World War II, each of the three men wrestled with the same question that preoccupied Weil: How did one keep moral values from disintegrating in the struggle against more powerful brute forces? Although all of them esteemed Weil's intense assent to supernatural love, they did not share her confidence in supernatural grace. Nevertheless, they did not temper their admiration for her keen observations of human nature and for her unflagging respect for the individual person. They believed profoundly in common values that were accessible to all human beings. Though they were avowed rationalists, their writings imply a hesitant openness to the existence of a nonmaterial positive force for good in the universe.

These unique individuals were endowed with strong independent personalities and deep empathy for the suffering of others. In the autonomy of their thinking and the fervor of their dedication, they had risen above what Weil called the collective beast mentality. Her words resonated profoundly with their understanding of human existence. Each had incorporated into his philosophy of life ideas that Weil had brought to the fore, particularly those concepts that underpinned moral consideration for others and revealed the damage that violence does to the human psyche.

To the brief encounter in New York, in the first spring after World War II, each man brought indelible impressions of the terrible wartime violence. Their personal observations of human behavior had undermined prior optimistic expectations that humankind would live in greater harmony, and they groped for sources of hope for the future. The international scene was far from promising: the immediate joy in the United States over the declaration of peace had given way to ominous forebodings of a Third World War. Tensions due to the cold war were enabling manipulative political leaders to exploit people's fears. Even after victory was declared, the governmental restriction of civil liberties persisted, creating a climate of distrust. In their common concern over how to maintain moral values when confronted with immoral abusive force—social, political, or physical—the three thinkers persistently tried to alert their readers to the dangers of submitting to irrational fear and abandoning precious freedoms. But their energies had been sapped by the struggle against the dehumanizing behavior they had recently observed. Camus, in particular, appeared worn out by his Resistance fighting and by disagreements with fellow partisans who thirsted for postwar vengeance.

Each man, independently coming upon selections of Weil's writings long before she gained public recognition as a thinker and writer, had the immediate reaction of discovering a voice that spoke the truth. Despite the recent wartime savagery, her thought inspired in them some hope for the future of humanity. In France, Camus had read a few of her earlier works published in limited-circulation journals but had made little note of them. Dwight Macdonald was impressed by her essay "Reflections on War," which he had found in a small anarchist bulletin in the early 1930s. Nicola Chiaromonte had read the "The *Iliad*, or the Poem of Force," in its original printing in southern France and had cared enough to keep it with him on his flight from fascism. Making a brief stop in North Africa on his way to America, Chiaromonte joined Albert Camus's theatrical group in Oran, Algeria. There he and Camus began a lifelong friendship, which took on fresh importance when they met again in New York.

Camus's springtime arrival in the United States coincided with Macdonald's reprinting in his political review several of Weil's essays on war, so her ideas were on his readers' minds. Macdonald frequented a circle of New York intellectuals that included Hannah Arendt, also an admirer of Weil's ideas. On his return to France, Camus, as editor, began to bring Weil's writings to an international audience by publishing a series of volumes of her writings in his special imprint entitled L'Espoir (Hope) for Gallimard, a publishing house in Paris. Jean Grenier, Camus's philosophy professor and long-term correspondent, wrote that Weil's thought was a major key to Camus's work. Camus particularly admired the value she gave to both mystery and the sacred without ever abandoning the need for revolt.[1]

The three writers were explicit about their indebtedness to Weil's thought, particularly to her insights into the contagious, objectifying effect of brute force and the importance of fully understanding that force could not be controlled. Macdonald quoted Weil extensively in his polemics against war and in the furious editorial he wrote on learning of the bombing of Hiroshima and Nagasaki. Chiaromonte used Weil as a model in his literary essay on Tolstoy's *War and Peace,* which he called the "second 'poem of Force,'" and Camus, though not citing Weil in his talk "The Human Crisis," given at Columbia University, nevertheless showed through this lecture how deeply his thoughts on the human condition converged with hers. He developed these ideas into an eight-part essay, "Neither Victims nor Executioners," for his journal *Combat*.[2]

DWIGHT MACDONALD

Must we not now conclude with Simone Weil, that the technical aspect of war today is the evil, regardless of political factors?

Dwight Macdonald, "The Decline to Barbarism"

Macdonald saw his role as that of a gadfly, an activist who gave full primacy to the individual conscience. His model for a society that harmonized opposing elements without destroying the contradictory forces of motion and inertia was a gyroscope. Weil's preferred image was the balance that symbolized the continual effort needed to assess and correct injustices in society. Macdonald insisted that only constant self-scrutiny could uproot hypocrisy in oneself and in others and protect one's right to think independently. His voice on the radical left called out to the American conscience for vigilance concerning the ever-present dangers to civil liberties and the slippery slope of violence. He tried in every way to signal overextensions of power by authorities, whatever their rationale, and complicity in offenses against humanity.

Macdonald admired Weil's writing style in her 1933 essay "Reflections on War"[3] for being "devoid of all rhetoric, of all literary 'effects.'"[4] He had fortuitously come across the piece in a small review privately owned by a New York schoolteacher, who had translated Weil's essay, giving it the title "The Coming Revolution." When Macdonald later republished the piece in his own journal, he restored the title to its original "Reflections on War." In that essay Weil laid the initial groundwork for the image of a perpetual cycle of violence, which she described more fully a half-dozen years later in "The *Iliad*, or the Poem of Force."

Macdonald often referred to Weil's writings in his numerous harangues against intellectuals, oppressive power, hollow slogans, and violence imposed on the vulnerable. In a 1939 article for the *Partisan Review* entitled "War and the Intellectuals: Act Two," he cited extensively Weil's attack on illusory thinking, applying her arguments to the vacuous reasoning of his intellectual colleagues. He upbraided intellectuals who swallowed whole the propaganda that war would make the world safe for democracy and increase domestic social justice. These declarations, he reminded them, had been disproved in the First World War, and by circulating them again one nourished the futile hope that a second try might be successful. Macdonald, feeling that the cost in lives, civil liberties, and democratic values was far too great for such elusive goals, highlighted the contradiction between a second war for democracy and the disintegration of democratic principles within the nation. Weil had steadfastly warned that a nation gearing for war undermined bit by bit the democratic rights enjoyed by its citizens. Macdonald described how the U.S. campaign for exporting democracy masked the weakening of democratic procedures at home: "The closer the second great crusade for democracy draws near, the feebler grow the forces of democracy inside the country; the more the battleships, the lower the relief standards; the bolder the President's utterances against Hitler, the more conciliatory his attitude towards our own business rulers."5

Weil had similarly warned her worker-readers not to capitulate to the forces that would eventually destroy them. She wrote: "The great error of almost all studies concerning war, an error to which the socialists have particularly been prone, is to consider war as an episode of external politics, when it constitutes above all a matter of internal politics and the most atrocious of them all."6

Macdonald deplored the cooperative compliance of liberal thinkers even before the hostilities began, for he feared, as did other critical thinkers in America, that a careful analysis of the effects of war on society was being purposefully deflected by simplistic slogans. He blamed a hidden agenda on the part of the authorities and wanted his readers to reflect on the dichotomy between seductive wartime rallying cries and the fragility of democracy. He reminded them: "[A] modern war cannot be fought without universal conscription, without outlawing strikes and shackling the unions, without suppressing all dissenting opinion and handing the national economy over to the ruling class."7

Weil had insisted that no problem relative to war could be resolved or even correctly posed without a detailed analysis of how social, economic, and technological relationships were altered when a government accorded priority to the military. For Weil, the essential question was not "What are the ends pursued, but what are the means employed and what are their material and social consequences?"8 The means to be employed in any coming war similarly preoccupied Macdonald. He wanted to engage intellectuals in a careful study of how domestic politics changed when the military called the shots. His insistent voice, evoking precious freedoms that could disappear, was drowned out by the patriotic clamor about fighting fascism to protect democracy. In response, he echoed Weil's claim, stating that both advocates of war and isolationists "fail to understand that the war drive is primarily a matter of domestic rather than foreign policy."9 In his view, intellectuals wallowed in the luxury of disinterested moral judgments. Since they risked neither their property nor their lives, they could avoid with impunity their social responsibility for the coming devastation.

In his diatribe against disengaged intellectuals, Macdonald cited Weil at length to show his agreement with her suggestion that war was manifestly a matter of political manipulation on the home front. Weil had concluded: "War in the last analysis appears as a struggle led by all the state apparatuses and their general staffs against all men old enough and able to bear arms." She then made the following analogy, which Macdonald quoted in its entirety: "In the same way, war in our days is distinguished by the subordination of the combatants to the instruments of combat. The armaments, the true heroes of modern warfare, as well as the men dedicated to their service, are directed by those who do not fight. And since this directing apparatus has no other way of fighting the enemy than by sending its own soldiers, under compulsion, to their death, the war of the State against another State evolves into the State using the military apparatus to wage war against its own army."10

Macdonald agreed with Weil's conclusion, in which she specified that the worst possible treason consisted in one's acquiescence to a state apparatus that trampled human values underfoot. He valued her original perspectives on the futility of initiating a war to safeguard democracy without fully considering the material and psychological desolation that war would entail. Weil's repeated message was: "Arms manipulated by a sovereign state apparatus can bring liberty to no one."[11] Weil, as a voice for the oppressed and a bearer of fruitful, humane ideas, Macdonald concluded, was "a 'Utopian' thinker who combined imagination with common sense."[12]

Having infused Macdonald's thinking, Weil's writings also influenced the editorial direction of his journal. Macdonald called his review *politics* (with a small p) because he felt profoundly that every social question had at its heart a political decision. Everything was politics, which meant that "the only hope of a submerged majority to change things in their favor will rest on political action." Macdonald wanted his periodical to be partisan in favor of those on the bottom: "the Negroes, the colonial peoples and the vast majority of common people everywhere."[13] Weil also saw the necessity for the lower classes to maintain a healthy tension within a society so that power would be persistently contested and kept within limits. These sentiments expressed by Weil and Macdonald were far from being common currency at the time, either in Europe or in the United States.

Macdonald's review insistently needled the American people about the strategies deployed by the Allies as well as by the Axis forces. He did not limit his accusations to the atrocities done by the "other," however monstrous. The articles in *politics* juxtaposed the Nazi barbarities committed against noncombatants with the Allies' "saturation" bombing of German communities and the firebombing that had virtually incinerated sixty-four Japanese cities and their inhabitants. No shameful "episodes" were left out: the mass slaughters by the white race against the black race in the Belgian Congo, in the Amazon, and in Australia, along with violence against the Negro in America, and the decimation of the American Indians. Macdonald repeatedly pointed out that the U.S. Army was still segregated, to the consequent humiliation of the Negro.[14] His persistent theme was that "military necessity" apparently ruled "us" as absolutely as it ruled "them."

Echoes of Weil's thought can be detected throughout Macdonald's lament over the degradation of the individual by the "mechanism" of society. He evoked her image of society as a machine running on its own, beyond humankind's ability to control it: "Modern society has become so tightly organized, so rationalized and routinized that it has the character of a mechanism that grinds on without human consciousness or control. The individual, be he 'leader' or mass-man, is reduced to powerlessness vis-à-vis the mechanism."[15]

This summation of Macdonald's thought appeared in March 1945, in the issue just after the one reprinting Weil's "Reflections on War." Then in August came the detonation of the atomic bomb, that product of "scientific progress," first in Hiroshima on August 6, then three days later in Nagasaki. Macdonald was in a paroxysm of rage over the bombs dropped on the civilian centers of two Japanese cities. This unconscionable act confirmed for him the moral decadence of both adversaries in the war, as well as the truth of Weil's warnings about the two-edged contamination of force. On hearing the heartrending news of Hiroshima, he rushed back to New York from New England, stopped the presses, and inserted a biting, terse expression of outrage on the front page of the August issue of *politics*. His rhetoric resembled Weil's at its most caustic and sardonic. He announced the facts in short staccato rhythm: twenty thousand tons of TNT, 343,000 human beings presumably destroyed.[16] "No warning whatsoever was given. This atrocious action places 'us,' the defenders of civilization, on a moral level with 'them,' the beasts of Maidanek." He emphasized his points with capital letters: 1) "THE CONCEPTS: WAR AND 'PROGRESS' ARE NOW OBSOLETE. . . . 2) THE FUTILITY OF MODERN WARFARE SHOULD NOW BE CLEAR. . . . 3) ATOMIC BOMBS ARE THE NATURAL PRODUCT OF THE KIND OF SOCIETY WE HAVE CREATED." At the very center of the tirade he asked: "Must we not now conclude, with Simone Weil, that the technical aspect of war today is the evil, regardless of political factors? Can one imagine that the atomic bomb could ever be used 'in a good cause'? Do not such means instantly, of themselves, corrupt ANY cause?"

In his editorial, he insisted that everyone had to assume responsibility: "'We,' the American people are just as much and as little responsible for this horror as 'they,' the German people." He concluded with an urgent appeal for a "fraternity of all men everywhere" who would stand solidly together and say "No" to the present direction of Western society, since this new source of energy entrapped everyone into being a potential victim or executioner. He scorned faith in "Science and Progress," which had allowed the antihuman dynamics that produced the bomb; he also scorned those who treated the discovery of atomic fission as another step in man's long struggle to control the forces of nature. Macdonald asked his readers to analyze the content in notions like "democracy" and "government of, by and for the people" in a society where over 125,000 construction and factory workers had constructed this bomb without even knowing what they were producing.[17] He repeated: "The social order is an impersonal mechanism, the war is an impersonal process, and they grind along automatically." As he imagined the full potential of atomic fission, he recalled Weil's persistent reminder of Nemesis: "the old Greek notion of *Hubris,* that lack of restraint in success, which invites the punishment of the gods." Weil had often denigrated the modern faith in both science and progress that undermined any real safeguarding of human values. How the retribution of Nemesis might eventually come about from the disregard for limits, the editors of *politics* did not venture to guess. But they felt the need to bear witness to the dehumanization of triumphal victors who ignored their own vulnerability and treated others with disdain.

At this point, Macdonald and Nicola Chiaromonte, his coeditor, urged their friend the novelist Mary McCarthy to finish translating "The *Iliad,* or the Poem of Force," for the November 1945 issue of *politics.* They understood that in the excesses of this war the dignity of the human person no longer served as a criterion for political and military decisions and that the victors had exceeded their limits in the destruction of communities with all that made life worth living. Weil had observed at the central point of her essay on the *Iliad* that the powerful tended to go beyond their limits as soon as their subdued population no longer caused them to reflect before acting. Consequently, the victors concluded that destiny gave them full license and their victims none.

After the impact of the atomic bomb, Weil's depiction of force in her essay on the *Iliad* struck a profound chord with readers of *politics.* Their immediate and positive reactions pleasantly surprised Macdonald. He wrote to a friend: "The response . . . has surprised me: I thought it was a great political article, dealing with the moral questions implicit in the terrible events one reads about in every day's newspaper, which was why I played it up so prominently in the issue. But I had not expected such an overwhelming reaction from readers. Nothing I've printed yet seems to have made so deep an impression."[18]

Macdonald wanted Weil's essays to spur Americans into facing the troubling moral question of bombing civilians, and he wanted them to comprehend the disconnect between their concept of a democracy of, by, and for the people and their abdication of critical decision making. Society, as he and Weil had forewarned, had become so mechanized that it was now the subject and humankind the object. The Manhattan Project, carried to its horrendous outcome by workers kept ignorant of what they were producing, had made this transformation glaringly obvious to Macdonald.

The decision to explode the atomic bomb does unhappily exemplify the mistaken belief of some men that they could control force and of others that they could isolate themselves from the effects of force. In truth, as Weil argued, force takes on a life of its own and affects everyone concerned. Both Weil and Macdonald denounced the inherent inertia of bureaucracy that made it possible to create a separation between inhumane acts and personal responsibility. Time has proved what was apparent only to some people at the time: later generations of weapons of mass destruction have become increasingly devastating, while limitations on their production have become less and less sustainable. The arms race has made war and preparation for war the primary driving force of nations.

Weil was greatly apprehensive about the potential for a future of never-ending war; Macdonald felt he was watching the realization of war cycling into war in perpetuity, and he was not far from the truth. As the historian Martin J. Sherwin concluded in his thorough study *Hiroshima and Its Legacies*, "The technology of war was already being hailed as the symbol of peace, and it was becoming increasingly clear that instead of promoting American postwar aims, wartime atomic energy policies had made them more difficult to achieve. As American-Soviet relations deteriorated, Hiroshima and Nagasaki rose as symbols of a new American barbarism, and as explanations for the origins of the cold war."[19] Sherwin then quoted a military analyst, P. M. S. Blackett, who had pointed out back in 1948 that "the dropping of the atomic bombs was not so much the last military act of the second World War, as the first major operation of the cold diplomatic war with Russia now in progress."[20] For us in the twenty-first century, escalating force is visibly taking on a self-perpetuating life of its own. As Weil maintained in her *Iliad* essay, conquerors and conquered are destined to become brothers in the same misery, both equally innocent and guilty.

Weil's apprehension of the tendency of society to subordinate human values to science in its pursuit of technological progress was, for Macdonald, proving to be a reality. Her thought continued to thread its way through his reflections, and he sadly agreed with her para-doxical affirmation that nations went to war to defend their capacity to make war. In reaction, Macdonald took up Tolstoy's question: "What should a man live by?" In his search for a better direction for society, he looked to those he called the "Ancestors"—Socrates, Lao Tzu, Christ, Homer, and others—just as Weil had sought wisdom from past thinkers. His list of inspiring modern thinkers included Tolstoy, Camus, Weil, and Chiaromonte.

NICOLA CHIAROMONTE

The triumph of Hitler's brute force over all the promises of civilization and reason led that remarkable woman to find in Homer what cannot be found in any modern poem, novel or philosophical theory.

Nicola Chiaromonte, *The Paradox of History*

Nicola Chiaromonte, Macdonald's friend and close editorial advisor on the review *politics*, also came across Weil's writing by chance. On his flight from totalitarianism to what he hoped would be freedom, he read the original 1940–41 printing of Weil's essay "The *Iliad*, or the Poem of Force," published in two parts by the Marseilles review *Cahiers du Sud*. Although he did not know who had written the essay until some time later (since the by-line was "Emile Novis," Weil's wartime pseudonym), he cared enough about its insights into force to bring it to the attention of Macdonald. Chiaromonte immediately recognized the pertinence of the "Poem" to contemporary events. Later he described his encounter with Weil's penetrating analysis: "I did not know who Emile Novis was. The author was certainly . . . someone who had suffered in spirit and had purged through intellect the sense of defeat that had been hanging over Europe for at least four years. That this person would and could express himself through a new reading of the *Iliad* was a sign that 'humane letters' could still yield vigorous thought."[21]

In her teaching and writing, Weil had relied more and more on literature to ground her philosophy. Her friend and biographer Simone Pétrement wrote: "Like Alain, her admired Henri IV philosophy professor, Simone Weil considered that real philosophy is found not only in philosophers but also in novelists, poets, and all great writers."[22] Like Chiaromonte, Weil had an abiding concern for the individual lives that were shattered by major social upheavals exacerbated by an ill-founded belief in the benefits of progress.

To Chiaromonte, Tolstoy's portrayal of force in *War and Peace* closely paralleled Homer's in the *Iliad*. His essay, "Tolstoy and the Paradox of History" makes evident his debt to Weil in his reference to *War and Peace* as "the second great 'poem of Force' in Western literature."[23] He wrote:

> *War and Peace* is, as Simone Weil has said of the *Iliad,* "a poem about force," that leads us, like no other modern work of art, to ponder on this primary fact of human existence. . . . That remarkable woman [found] in Homer what cannot be found in any modern poem, novel or philosophical theory, that is, the world of force seen and contemplated as such "without any comforting fiction coming to modify it, without any consoling vision of immortality, without any vapid halo of glory or of patriotism." In the *Iliad,* the misfortune of the vanquished hero and the Nemesis that impends on the victor are seen in the same light, as two aspects of the same destiny.[24]

Tolstoy believed that the Napoleonic Wars had occurred because a certain number of French people had actively facilitated Napoleon's ability to seize and hold power while others remained passive. He concluded, as did Weil, that "the man who commands and the one who obeys are accomplices."[25]

After he left America in 1948 for France and then Italy, Chiaromonte continued to read Weil in the volumes published by Camus. He never hesitated to criticize her ideas when he disagreed with them. In an essay first published in *Il Mondo* in 1953, he questioned Weil's unrelenting pursuit of spiritual purity and the strange form her Christianity took, but he praised her perceptive observation that modern man's great defect was his failure to contemplate or "geometrize" force.[26] For him, Weil's judgment that "we are geometricians only of matter" revealed our inadequacies when confronted with the human world and its brutalities. We were, he said, "incapable of measuring, understanding, or 'contemplating' force when force appears in man and between men."[27] He believed that "to 'geometrize' force, to contemplate it, modern man would have to know where, in this world, the human and intelligible ended and where the divine began. He would have to have a sense of sacred limit." But, he insisted, this was difficult; even the Greeks, who were so dear to Weil, told us that these subjects had best be left unmentioned.[28] Yet they had warned of the ease with which power could be misused because people did not exercise their full responsibility of oversight, which inevitably incited a backlash of reckoning.

This idea of indirect but shared complicity was a principal theme for Weil in her "Poem of Force": "Thus violence crushes all it touches. In the long run, it appears as extrinsic to the manipulator as it does to the sufferer. And so is born the idea of a destiny under which both executors and victims seem equally innocent. The victors and the victims are brothers in the same misery. The victim is a cause of affliction for the victor, as the victor is for the victim."[29]

ALBERT CAMUS

Yes, there is a Human Crisis, since the death or torture of a human being can, in our world, be examined with a feeling of indifference, with friendly or experimental interest, or without response.

Albert Camus, "The Human Crisis"

Camus ardently pursued the question of shared responsibility for terrible things that happen in times of chaos. For his editorial series, on his immediate return home from America, he elaborated on the personal obligation to remain vigilant and to resist, in every way possible, any participation in violence. His point was that in order not to be a victim, one had to seek out and eliminate any elements in society that made one an executioner. His reintroduction to some of Weil's writings during his brief visit to the United States seems to have played a significant part in his efforts to renew his compatriots' determination to oppose anyone who would deprive human beings of their reasons for living.

In his essays, editorials, and fiction, Camus, like Macdonald and Chiaromonte, encouraged his readers to refuse conditions in which lives were "lived in haste, separated from natural truth, from intelligently ordered leisure, and from simple joys."[30] The title for his series, "Neither Victims nor Executioners," was a variation of a theme in Weil's "The *Iliad,* or the Poem of Force." Although he made few direct references to her thought in his writings, his ideas converged with hers, particularly on the dehumanization that force effected. This concurrence of ways of thinking was evident in the talk he gave at Columbia University.

As one of France's most celebrated journalists and Resistance fighters, Albert Camus disembarked in New York on March 25, 1946, from the ocean liner the *Oregon* in the same month that Weil's "The Power of Words" appeared in *politics*—though newly titled in Macdonald's translation as "War and Words." The first English translation of her essay "The *Iliad,* or the Poem of Force," had appeared four months earlier in the same journal. Chiaromonte, who had not seen Camus since their meeting before the war in Oran, Algeria, was waiting at the dock to welcome his friend on his first visit to the United States. Camus disembarked tired and discouraged. During his stay he spent a great deal of time with Chiaromonte, who shared his views on the essential quality of liberty and the vital need to reject totalitarianism in any form.[31] Much had happened since the Liberation to dampen Camus's aspirations for cooperative harmony among men.

In 1943 Camus had joined Combat, the largest and most prestigious underground Resistance network within the noncommunist Left.[32] Shortly thereafter he became editor-in-chief of its clandestine periodical, *Combat,* which in August of the following year began to appear openly on the streets as part of the newly organized and emboldened liberation press. Camus's goal with *Combat* was to awaken his readers' "critical faculties rather than allow them to nurture a spirit of complacency."[33] But while the coeditors of *politics* could criticize American society with impunity, any opposition in occupied France had to be voiced with great caution, since any confrontational approach invited a ruthless reaction from the Nazi occupiers and the Vichy police. Camus's resolute statements on freedom and justice explain the immediate close kinship Macdonald felt for his French counterpart even before they met.

During his visit to New York, Camus, a recognized publisher and moral philosopher, was immersed in a circle of admirers of Weil's work. Chiaromonte and Macdonald, still uplifted by the recent reception of Weil's "The *Iliad,* or the Poem of Force," had much to share with their fellow journalist. It is easy to imagine that Weil's ideas held an important place in the conversations of the three humanists. On Camus's arrival, Chiaromonte promptly took him to meet Macdonald and the circle of intellectuals who had attentively followed his editorials in *Combat.*

Camus was known in New York, not just formally as editor of the candid and outspoken *Combat,* but also personally. Chiaromonte had talked about him, and Hannah Arendt, an intimate in the New York intellectuals' circle since her arrival in 1941, had described the French philosopher as a new type of individual, more European than nationalist.[34] Macdonald, an avid admirer of the French revolutionary tradition, had closely followed the Resistance struggles in France and had applauded any expression of intransigence concerning human values. In the November issue of *politics,* Macdonald prominently cited Camus's statement, "Disorder is preferable to injustice," from the October 12, 1944, *Combat* editorial response to de Gaulle's evident intention of reestablishing a strong governmental authority with him holding full power. In his pointed opinion piece, Macdonald had boldly cited Camus's rationale, with which he agreed wholeheartedly, "It is not order that reinforces justice, it is justice that guarantees order."[35] One can well imagine Weil in complete agreement with Camus's insistence, in that moment of great disorder in recently liberated France, that order could not exist without a balance established between the weak and the strong that would be based on the principle of justice.³⁶

In the midst of all the turmoil of struggling against the Nazi power in France, Camus had tried to hold firmly to a high standard of moral means in the fight against the enemy—within or outside the country. The means had to be commensurate with the goal of safeguarding the dignity of people. He did not always meet with great success. Chiaromonte later described him on his arrival: "Once again I see Albert Camus in New York in 1946 on the dock where I had gone to welcome him. For me, he seemed to be leaving a battlefield; his face showed both sadness and pride."³⁷

Albert Camus had been as overwhelmed as the editors of *politics* at the announcement of the atomic bomb exploding on two Japanese cities. His response in *Combat*, on August 8, 1945, to this grim news was one of outrage and foreboding. Juxtaposing in somber disbelief the obliteration wrought by this early weapon of mass destruction on Japanese urban centers and the sensationalist reports of the event by the media, he insisted that this catastrophic atrocity required not applause but reflection and above all silence. The irrationality of an exultant response to the reality of tens of thousands of deaths resulting from a device "the size of a soccer ball, " without considering what it augured for the future, appalled him.

He made an urgent plea for people to insist that their government stay on the path to peace and to petition still more energetically in favor of an all-inclusive international organization that would honor smaller nations by according them equal status with the larger powers. The choices before humanity, he argued, were stark: an intelligent use of scientific conquests or collective suicide. Any celebration of scientific discoveries that furthered out-of-control violence was pernicious. Technology had arrived at the ultimate degree of savagery: organized murder. Hell was the alternative to not employing reason.³⁸ Weil would have concurred in deep sadness with all Camus's horror at the purposeful annihilation of cities and helpless individuals.

Camus's avidity to learn from the observation of a deeply flawed human nature surely opened his mind to embracing Weil's thought. In his postwar reading of Weil's "Poem of Force," he must have had a visceral reaction to her claim that "violence crushes all it touches. . . . Victors and victims are brothers in the same misery. The victim causes affliction for the victor, just as the victor does for the victim." The idea that force exercised through physical violence and social humiliation left no one untouched or innocent was evident throughout his talk, "The Human Crisis," given at Columbia University in March.

In that speech, Camus stated that humanity was in crisis because the war had debased people to the point of indifference to human dignity, bureaucratic accountability, and love of neighbor. Fear had created an atmosphere in which homicide was legitimized and human life regarded as insignificant. A society that truly respected life, liberty, and justice would reject killing as punishment and would embrace compassion as vital to human relationships.

The text of his talk reveals Camus's anxieties and his attempt to resolve them. Roger Quilliot, editor of Camus's *Essais,* remarked that Camus's conference in the United States represented an important step in his long history of reflecting on violence, legitimized murder, and the drive for power. The out-of-control violence reigning in the aftermath of the Liberation because of the purge trials in France against perceived collaborationists inspired him to develop his ideas into a full essay for *Combat* and then republish them in another review: *Caliban.*[39]

Chiaromonte, who knew the contours of his friend's thought, wrote later about his talk at Columbia: "It appears to me now that this discourse—which is a sort of autobiography—contains the germ of all the themes running through *The Plague, The Rebel,* and 'The Just Assassins.'" Chiaromonte depicted Camus during his visit as "sad, tenebrous, misanthropic, avid for communication—a man, who, putting the entire world up for questioning, also questions his own position. By that attitude, he witnesses fully to his personal vocation."[40]

For his talk at Columbia, Camus asked to speak in his native tongue. In New York, at that time, there were many French exiles, and French was the preferred second language of intellectuals. Unfortunately, the original French text of his speech has been lost, but an English version still exists. Lionel Abel, a writer and critic in the *politics* circle, translated Camus's remarks for a small review called *Twice a*

Year. Not mentioning either place or university, Abel situated Camus's text simply as having been delivered in "America—Spring—1946." Since Camus spoke several times on "the Human Crisis" and often strayed from his written notes, a reasonable speculation can be made that the translation in English is most likely a composite of his conference talks.[41] Quilliot regretted not being able to include the talk in his collection of Camus's essays, since he didn't have the actual words in French. Consequently, the text we have remains one step from the original and is relatively less well known among Camus's readers. In his editorial series entitled "Neither Victim nor Executioner," written for *Combat* immediately on his return to France, he developed further the ideas touched on in his talk.

In his message, Camus focused on the anguish manifest in the contemporary world, pointing to the atmosphere of stifling terror, provoked by a corruption of values, as one of the clearest symptoms of the crisis. He appealed to the audience by suggesting that if "that unhappy man, the Job of modern times," was not to die of his painful indignities on the dunghill, then the encumbrance of fear and anguish had to first be lifted from him. Without liberty of thought none of the problems set for modern consciousness could be solved.[42]

For his audience, he first gave the background of his generation, which was Weil's generation who were "born just before or during the first Great War, reached adolescence during the global economic crisis, and were twenty years old the year Hitler took power."[43] The sequence of tragic events during that time included the Spanish Civil War, the appeasement in Munich, the war of 1939, and the defeat, followed by four years of occupation and secret conflict. The shame over the defeat and occupation of their country had taught his peers rebellion. Weil's rebellion is evident in her rejection of illusions nourished by empty propaganda and in her unending struggle to speak truth to her fellow human beings.

To provide a context for his remarks to young Americans, who had not known the disorientation of living under the harsh rule of the enemy, Camus briefly narrated three poignant events from the occupation of France. For him, these episodes demonstrated the dehumanization of the modern world and the detachment by which people sought to distance themselves from its horrors. All three incidents involved the kind of disengaged and alienated person that Weil very much feared would be the by-product of a society that did not refuse to glorify force.

In the first anecdote, an impassive French concierge was cleaning a room around two tightly bound, bloody men accused of sabotage. Reproached by one of the men for cooperating with their German persecutors, she replied indignantly that she never meddled in the affairs of her tenants. Camus commented that "when death or torture of a human being can, in our world, be examined with a feeling of indifference, with friendly or experimental interest, or without response, there is a Human Crisis."44

In the second, a German officer, who had mutilated a prisoner the prior evening by ripping his ears to shreds, inquired in a tone of solicitude the following day: "How are your ears now?" Camus reproached the German officer's obliviousness of his own dehumanization resulting from torturing a fellow human being. The tormentor belonged to a bureaucracy created through orders written on paper by government functionaries who were not answerable for what was being done and felt no obligation to know the end purpose of the orders.

Last, Camus told of a Greek mother whose three sons, taken hostage, were to be shot. When she begged for mercy, a German officer consented to spare one, but only on the sadistic condition that she decide which son would live. By choosing one, she condemned the other two. The officer's heartless, unconscionable requirement meant that the mother would suffer unending torments of guilt from whichever choice she made. When Weil delineated the needs of the soul, she specifically condemned situations in which conflicting obligations, equally requiring obedience, tore up the soul's need for order. This, in her mind, was a violation of every human being's obligation to care for another's deepest needs.

In each situation, neither victims nor perpetrators escaped the insidious effects of brutality imposed by the dominant power. The victims became objects to be abused and discarded, while the victors destroyed part of their own humanity. This was an example of the double-edged contamination of force about which Weil was warning her compatriots. Camus's principal theme concurred with Weil's insight, for if the individual was no longer protected by a respect for hu-

manity based on human values, the only alternative henceforth open
to him was to be the victim or the executioner.[45] But he told his audience, who still lived in this "happy America," that his generation de-
spised both alternatives since they knew deep in their hearts that "even
this distinction was illusory, and that at bottom all were victims, and
that assassins and assassinated would in the end be reunited in the
same defeat."[46]

In his later editorials, Camus commented that the spectacle of
the years his countrymen had just lived through had destroyed their
confidence that a human being would respond to the common language of humanity. This observation echoed Weil's conviction that
the trust that every human being held in the secret inner recesses of
the heart that good, not evil, would be done to him was precious but
very fragile. A violation of this trust brought out the piteous lament,
"Why am I being hurt?" which only attentive listeners could hear. To
bring on this cry was to perpetrate an injustice, and to persist in the
degradation of another was to commit a sacrilege. Camus wrote, "In
the face of lying, belittling, degrading, killing, deporting, torturing, it
was not possible to persuade those who were doing it not to do it. They
were sure of themselves, and one does not persuade an abstraction,
that is, the representative of an ideology."[47]

Camus faulted situations in which a collective bureaucracy controlled individual lives. This misguided priority eliminated the ability
to communicate among persons and shut down the capacity to share
common values, such as the beauty of the world and of human faces.
He elaborated: "We live in a world of abstraction, one of offices and
machines, of absolute ideas and of fanatic zealots. We are suffocating
amid people who believe they are right without question, be it in their
machines or in their ideas. For those who can live only with dialogue
and friendship, this absence is the end of the world."[48] For Weil, who
believed that friendship, one of the implicit signs of God's love for his
creation, was to be treasured as a rare gift, the absence of friendship
would make human life untenable.

Camus mourned the loss of human warmth in an organization
where men came in contact with one another only through a maze of
formalities. He saw this form of bureaucracy taking over modern society, and he claimed sardonically that instead of his filling out all the

paper forms in order to come to America he could have simply printed up his talk and then sent it on. But he insisted that people who admired a "good organization" that allowed persons to die, love, or kill by proxy posed a great risk for society.[49]

Camus condemned the dangerous lack of principles that led to the idea that everything was possible for those who held power because then success or failure, rather than morality, became the criterion for the value of an action: in nihilist ideologies, everything was permitted and what counted was to succeed.[50] He speculated that even intelligent persons could imagine that if by chance Hitler had won this war, History would have honored his cause and sanctified the atrocious pedestal on which he stood.[51] But such persons would have been accepting the illusion of success for reality, for the idea of possessing power was deceptive. "We are all responsible for Hitlerism."[52]

Weil had developed this idea and spelled it out in detail in her essay "The Origins of Hitlerism," which portrayed Hitler as a product of Europe's adulation of the power displayed by the Roman Empire. She too was sure that a victorious Hitler would win praise for bringing civilization to the uncivilized, just as France claimed to have brought civilization to its colonized nations. She also held that a society's legitimizing the destruction of peoples or cultures under its dominion contaminated any criterion for justice. Weil believed that the sense of justice that enlightened the works of Homer, Aeschylus, and Sophocles, who never glorified force in war or politics, provided an alternative to the idolization of power. Force appeared in their works with a cold hardness, accompanied by dire effects from which no one escaped—neither the manipulators nor the manipulated. In the Greek works, the humiliation of the subdued soul was not disguised, scorned, or enveloped in facile pity.[53] Camus's admiration for Greek culture and literature paralleled that of Weil.

In his tirade against legitimized murder, Camus identified an enduring cycle of injustice: "We live in a world where murder is legitimized; it is up to us if we do not wish to live so. But it appears that one cannot change the system without running the risk of murder. Murder reverts to murder. We will continue to live in terror, either because we accept it with resignation or we wish to suppress it by substituting another terror."[54]

In his youth in Algeria and during the Occupation, Camus had witnessed the capacity of fear to alter the self, and he understood why it was the preferred tool of anyone seeking to dominate others. Unscrupulous leaders inculcated fear on purpose to forestall any clear analyses of the actual situation. In 1933, Weil expressed this atmosphere of hovering fear in her opening statements in "Reflections on War": "We live today in the perpetual expectation of war. The danger may be imaginary, but the atmosphere of danger exists. . . . We run the risk, if we do not make a serious effort of analysis, that one day, sooner or later, war will find us powerless, not only to act, but even to judge."[55]

Those who spread fear and who remained impervious to persuasion, in Camus's eyes, bartered their humanity for a mess of ideologies, abstractions, and absolutes. They repeated clamorous words without dissecting them to verify either their true meaning or their vacuity, causing great suffering for themselves as well as others.[56] Weil, too, condemned slogans that incited people to frenzy while robbing them of their humanity and negating the value of life. She wrote: "If, in this manner, one were to analyze all the words, all the formulas that have incited, throughout history, the spirit of sacrifice and of cruelty both together, one would find them all, without doubt, similarly empty. Nevertheless, all these entities avid for human blood hold essential ties to real life."[57] She concluded this same essay with: "Hordes of empty entities not only impede perception of the facts of the problem but dull the sense that there is a problem to resolve and not a fatality to suffer."[58]

Weil and Camus wanted humankind to rationally think out realistic options in order to avoid being duped by men who sought power by intimidation and demagoguery. Both moral philosophers believed in the obligation to resist complicity in actions that ruined human lives. Camus proposed working toward an international democracy through dialogue as a positive and fruitful project for the future of mankind. Weil urged her readers to confront without illusions the pernicious and intractable nature of force and to rethink the means and ends of their social institutions by imbuing them with a spirituality that would give primacy to love of neighbor. Force deployed by the devastating weapons available to modern unconscionable leaders, who proposed ill-defined goals and hid their intention under catchy slogans, posed a fatal danger to everyone everywhere.

According to Weil, when the mechanism of social power led to the trampling of human dignity, men of goodwill had to be encouraged to struggle relentlessly against those who commanded. For Camus, a "No" to abstractions and ideologies that menaced existence by creating a civilization of death signified a "Yes" to a world in which humankind could embrace values that established the dignity of human beings as a solid basis for action. He told his audience that the stake in their present collective tragedy was "common dignity, a communion of men which was important to defend and sustain. . . . For if this communication of men with one another in the mutual recognition of their dignity rested on being able to seek out the truth, then it was this communication itself that was the value to be supported."[59] The freedom of the individual to say "No" to oppressive conditions remained the sine qua non of the struggle toward human dignity for Weil and for all three of the moralists presented here as supporters of her ideas.

While Weil, in her mystical political philosophy, relied strongly on the importance of the supernatural, Camus constructed his vision on reason in a world lacking grace and justice. He claimed that one was an assassin because one reasoned poorly, suggesting that everyone was implicitly an assassin. First, things must be called by their true names, "for if nothing is true or false, good or bad, if the only value is that of efficiency, then the only rule to follow is the one enjoining us to be the most efficient, that is to say, the strongest. The world is then no longer divided into the just and the unjust, but into masters and slaves. He is right who dominates."[60] He concluded that judging a country in terms of power only reinforced and sustained a conception of humankind that logically led to its mutilation. Encouraging the thirst for domination, in the long run, legitimized murder. Saying or writing that the end justified the means, and that greatness went with power, was responsible for the hideous accumulation of crimes that had disfigured the contemporary world.

Camus knew that individuals who struggled for human dignity were most often subjected to great suffering and humiliation, even though they, and not the powerful and violent, should be the admired heroes. He recognized that only solidly motivated men, moved by passion and ready for sacrifice, could banish the fear and silence that separated souls. His statement about individuals who struggled for human dignity equally described the persons "mad with love for their neighbor" that Weil insisted were necessary to bring about just conditions in society.[61]

Camus's American speech resonates with a heartfelt lament, yet one detects a renewed vigor animating his belief in humankind. His comrades in the Resistance had offered a positive affirmation for him. By choosing to struggle against wrong, they had all learned that they had struggled, not for themselves alone, but for something common to all men. "All of us, by the mere fact of living, hoping, and struggling, were affirming something."[62] Despite the many disappointments following the Liberation, this belief seemed to take on new life in his argument for solidarity and dialogue as a verification that something greater than man's material life existed.

Neither Macdonald nor Chiaromonte noted down the details of their discussions during Camus's brief visit. But all three staunchly independent spirits habitually honed an idea by measuring its validity against the ideas of others, so one must imagine the give and take of their discussions. Does the above concordance of ideas between Weil and Camus demonstrate conclusively that the latter took a refreshed enthusiasm for Weil from her war pieces? Perhaps the question is superfluous, given the profound truth echoed in their compassion for others, their anguish over the savagery of the times, and their steadfast intellectual honesty. But we do know that shortly thereafter Camus dedicated himself to publishing Weil's works.

Roy Pierce, a political scientist, has credited the writings of Weil that "tried to deal with current problems in as concrete a fashion as possible and without regard to preconceived general principles" with making a strong impact on Camus "the liberal moralist."[63] He cites Camus's praise in two of his editorials for the journal *Les Nouveaux Cahiers*, published by a study group, in which Weil discussed contemporary problems with others. Pierce suggests that Camus most likely read Weil's essay "The Power of Words" in the spring 1939 issue of the journal, which he praised for its lucidity. About the journal, Camus also wrote: "In the light of good sense, many truths are difficult to accept. Reading *[Nouveaux Cahiers]* demands therefore that one lay aside a certain number of [preestablished] prejudices and habits of thought."[64]

On his return to Paris, Camus received with gratitude the lengthy Weil manuscript of *The Need for Roots* from Weil's close friend Boris Souvarine.[65] It became the first of Weil's writings published in Camus's L'Espoir series for Gallimard. Camus began the major project of publishing Weil's works in as direct and unadulterated a fashion as possible, but unfortunately, his premature death in 1960 at the age of forty-seven, due to a car accident outside Paris, curtailed the full project as he had conceived it. Chiaromonte, after joining Camus briefly in Paris, returned to Italy to continue writing as a drama critic and editor and died in 1972.[66] To the end of his days, Macdonald relentlessly followed his personally assumed vocation as gadfly to the American political establishment. He died in 1982.

The three radical humanists each considered Weil's writings as a beacon for his thought, and each understood the applicability of her social and political philosophy to the contemporary scene of violence and manipulation. As moral humanists, they knew that in the headlong drive of technological progress, Western society had to stay focused on the needs of human beings in the workplace, in the market, and on the battlefield in order to avoid a catastrophic future for humankind.

Although these moral philosophers had pacifist inclinations, their experiences had shown them that at times force had to be used, most particularly when outsiders usurped one's country. All of them accepted strictly limited conditions that justified strong-arm opposition to an invasive enemy, but never at the cost of giving up one's freedom of conscience or of forgetting that the means had to be commensurate with the final goal. In Weil's philosophy, a compassionate concern for the dignity of the individual set the parameters for the means to be employed when struggling against a powerful antagonist. Only this condition could justify using force to stop an implacable enemy. She came to believe that the supernatural origin of the sacredness of the individual person created the moral obligation to protect everyone's freedom to act in obedience to God's love. Her conviction that acts inspired by grace would increase the amount of good in the world and decrease the effect of evil gave an explicit spirituality to her beliefs, which the three men admired even though they did not wholly subscribe to it.

Macdonald, Chiaromonte, and Camus's attachment to Weil's thought testifies to its value for humanity as a whole, particularly in modern times, when technological advances and multiplying layers of bureaucracy have distanced people from the reality of their innate complicity in the self-perpetuating capacity of force. Weil worked tirelessly to remind all thinking persons of their responsibility to actively foster political and social harmony. Love of the divine could be explicitly and implicitly acknowledged by seeing to one's neighbors' basic needs; no religious attachment was needed to hold true love of neighbor as the driving impetus for one's actions. She believed that many atheists by their actions were closer to God than professed practicing Christians; but without a willingness to see themselves as participants in the perpetuation of violence in social interaction, ordinary people of every stripe would have little chance of counteracting the unleashed forces that could annihilate all that they held dear.

Weil's desire to dispel the illusion that force could be controlled has validity for us in the twenty-first century. Her description of the force that shreds the soul aptly fits the scourge of torture, which continues to be employed and sanctioned by authorities. Despite worldwide condemnation and the existence of treaty provisions that forbid inflicting severe pain or suffering on others, torture is still practiced today in far too many countries. This fact subverts any wishful thinking that similar horrors cannot occur in modern, civilized countries or that progress has rendered them a vestige of the past. The Universal Declaration of Human Rights categorized torture as an extreme violation of human rights, and state signatories to the Third and Fourth Geneva Conventions agreed not to intentionally inflict severe pain or suffering on anyone to obtain information or a confession or to punish them. Yet torture, a form of force that reduces a human being to a thing without killing him or her, is still practiced. Weil's insights into the willful transformation of human persons into things—by subjecting them to physical duress or the intangible stress of humiliation—offers a valuable criterion for judging one's behavior toward perceived enemies.

Many persons today are working toward the goals of peace that Weil considered crucial, including those who continue the discussion of the limited conditions that could justify the use of force against individuals and against nations. Weil offered her cogent version of a just-war theory, with very strict parameters laid out to keep the means in close accordance with the ends. Hans Küng's effort to codify a charter of responsibilities was referred to in chapter 7. Another activist is the political scientist Gene Sharp, founder of the Albert Einstein Institute, which studies and promotes the use of nonviolent action and pursues questions about using nonviolent force to achieve peace.

Like Weil, Sharp accepts that "violence shapes our societies in many ways, through war, dictatorships, social oppression, genocide, political assassinations, and terrorism." Nevertheless, brutish despots, who have no intention of negotiating in good faith, still need to be deterred, and so do misguided leaders who think that force is a quick and easy solution to international problems. Sharp's methods also correspond to Weil's in his attempts to educate the public about realistic alternative "mechanisms of change," which, "if understood accurately and applied intelligently, wisely, and courageously, . . . offer great hope for a better future for our world."[67] While Weil rejected a pacifism that could not stop hostile violence, she earnestly sought effective means, such as education and negotiation, to increase the potential for a positive outcome in incipient conflicts.

Education through accurate public information and rational persuasion was the goal of the 2009 Panel of Eminent Jurists, formed in 2005 as an independent branch of the International Commission of Jurists to study the global aftermath of the deadly crash into the World Trade Center's Twin Towers in New York City on September 11, 2001.[68] Concerned that "the international legal order based on respect for human rights was in jeopardy," the jurists identified the "war on terror" paradigm initiated by the U.S. administration, with its flawed application of the laws of war to a criminal act, as a provocation for a callous indifference to humanitarian laws. In their three-year study, they found that the cumulative impact of the free-ranging counterterrorism policies adopted since that attack had imperiled the international legal structure, so assiduously assembled over six decades, to safeguard human rights.

According to their interviews, this conflation of criminal acts with acts of war has weakened the hard-earned respect for human rights and has led to illicit use of force, such as extraordinary rendition, secret detentions, enforced disappearances, and torture.[69] Weil had deplored all such practices for their ability to turn human beings into things. By officially sanctioning ill treatment of suspected "terrorists," the U.S. government undermined its moral standing, allowing other states that routinely violated human rights to justify their own wrong-doing by comparisons with the United States.[70]

That powerful nations would violate with impunity international agreements to respect the dignity of individuals evokes Weil's reflec-tions about the strong assuming that they have the right to do as they please because nothing in their human environment appears to im-pose limitations. But Weil commented that the strong are never ab-solutely strong, just as the weak are never absolutely weak, although neither of them realizes it. Such a realization would require thought, self-reflection, and a necessary pause to seek a true reading of the situ-ation. Weil's persistent warning is that where thought has no place, neither do justice or prudence.

The panel has urged the global community to understand the seis-mic change that policies such as sanctioned torture have brought about and to repeal all policies inconsistent with the obligations implied in humanitarian law.[71] They insist that the prohibition against torture is a non-negotiable safeguard. "Torture violates the principle of human dignity that lies at the heart of the broader international human rights framework, and as such is never acceptable."[72] The present world situ-ation illustrates Weil's claims about the ability of brute force to con-taminate the victim and the perpetrator and to self-generate beyond original intentions.

––––––

Throughout this book, we have followed the thread of Weil's warnings against the self-perpetuating capacity of force and her advocacy for a silent, intangible force that empowers individuals to counter evil through selfless acts that seek justice. Human-destroying force, once loosed on the world, spirals out of control until spent, leaving a trail of mangled lives and eviscerated cultures. Through her reading, reflec-tions, and mystical experiences, Weil intuited that an accessible coun-terforce inspired by God's grace, available to all, could offset brute force. Such a positive force had its source in supernatural love. But empowering this love required sacrifice and generosity through compassionate attention to the needs of others, which for Weil constituted an indispensable element of justice. Justice, when inspired by love of neighbor, became a vehicle for spreading and increasing the amount of pure good in society.

Weil devoted her energies to informing others about the meaning of merciful justice and the dedication required to realize a just society. The legitimacy of any social structure depended, she wrote, on the freely given consent of the governed. She believed that the ability of an individual soul to consent to God's love had to be safeguarded by legitimate social institutions based on an impartial, equitable, and spiritual structure of laws and by leaders committed to guaranteeing that the needs of individuals' bodies and souls would be met. Her concept of justice, enlightened by her mystical experiences, reveals the extent to which the spiritual and the political converged in her philosophy.

Weil interpreted the Parable of the Sower as an indication that God continually spreads his grace to all persons who answer his call to consecrate themselves in obedience to him.[73] Supernatural grace energizes persons to strive for social justice even in the face of overwhelming odds and is essential to becoming a just person because the constant interplay of forces within society and between nations requires courageous vigilance to balance the needs of the less powerful against those of the powerful. The task is neither easy nor appreciated, but it is vital. She wrote, "Just as one cannot expect a man without grace to be just, by the same token, a society must be organized so that injustices continually correct each other in a perpetual oscillation."[74]

Five weeks before her death, she wrote to her mother:

Darling Mime.

You think that I have something to offer . . . I too have a growing interior certainty that there is a deposit of pure gold in me that needs transmitting. Only, experience and the observation of my contemporaries persuade me more and more that there is no one to receive it.

Receiving it would take such an effort! And an effort is so tiring. . . .

What else could one expect? I am persuaded that even the most fervent Christians don't pay much more attention when they pray or read the Gospels. . . .

As for posterity, should there even be a future generation with vigor and thought, the books and manuscripts from our time will have without doubt substantially disappeared.

That doesn't grieve me. The mine of gold is inexhaustible.[75]

This motherlode of pure gold—radiating in Weil's writings and in her life lived with rigor and tenacity in conformity to an idea—resides in her insights into the seductive appeal of raw force and into the counterforce that can be elicited through receptivity to supernatural love.

On August 24, 1943, Weil departed from the "world here below" because of a severely weakened physical state that brought on cardiac arrest. She died believing that no one was listening to the message of "pure gold" that she had gleaned from many sources: observations of human behavior, the Gospels, ancient sacred texts, Greek philosophy, and the Bhagavad-Gita. She had not published much of her work, but she left behind pieces scattered among various friends, doing what she could in the time allotted her. She knew that the truth she had discovered concerning the use of force and the gift of supernatural grace was universal and abundantly available to anyone who loved humankind. We would do well in the twenty-first century to heed the legacy of thought left us by Simone Weil.

APPENDIX
English Translations of Simone Weil's Essays

English translations of the French essays referred to in this book are listed below with the title of the collection. Weil's better-known essays are found in a variety of collections; occasionally, the titles differ according to the translator. Many of Simone Weil's early polemics have not yet been translated.

"Agonie d'une civilisation vue à travers un poème épique." Translated as "A Medieval Epic Poem," in *Selected Essays, 1934–1943*, ed. and trans. Richard Rees (New York: Oxford University Press, 1962).

"Autobiographie spirituelle." Translated as "Spiritual Autobiography," in *Waiting for God*, ed. and trans. Emma Craufurd (New York: Harper Colophon Books, 1973).

"Désarroi de notre temps." Translated as "The Distress of Our Time," in *Formative Writings, 1929–1941*, ed. and trans. Dorothy Tuck McFarland and Wilhelmina Van Ness (Amherst: University of Massachusetts Press, 1987).

"En quoi consiste l'inspiration occitanienne?" Translated as "The Romanesque Renaissance," in *Selected Essays, 1934–1943*, ed. and trans. Richard Rees (New York: Oxford University Press, 1962).

"Essai sur la notion de lecture." Translated as "Essay on the Notion of Reading," in *Philosophical Investigations* 13 (October 1990): 297–302, ed. and trans. Rebecca Fine Rose and Timothy Tessin.

"Étude pour une déclaration des obligations envers l'être humain." Translated as "Draft for a Statement of Human Obligations," in *Simone Weil: Writings Selected with an Introduction*, ed. Eric O. Springsted (New York: Orbis Books, 1998).

"Formes de l'amour implicite de Dieu." Translated as "Forms of the Implicit Love of God," in *Simone Weil: Writings Selected with an Introduction*, ed. Eric O. Springsted (New York: Orbis Books, 1998).

"La personne et le sacré." Translated as "Human Personality," in *The Simone Weil Reader*, ed. George A. Panichas (New York: David McKay, 1977).

L'enracinement: Prélude à une déclaration des devoirs envers l'être humain. Translated as *The Need for Roots: Prelude to a Declaration of Duties toward Mankind,* trans. A. F. Wills (Boston: Beacon Press, 1955).

"Lettre à Georges Bernanos." Translated as "Letter to Georges Bernanos," in *The Simone Weil Reader,* ed. George A. Panichas (New York: David McKay, 1977).

"Lettre à Jean Giraudoux." Translated as "Letter to Jean Giraudoux," in *Seventy Letters,* ed. Richard Rees (New York: Oxford University Press, 1965).

"Lettre à Jean Posternak." Translated as "Letter to Jean Posternak," in *Seventy Letters,* ed. Richard Rees (New York: Oxford University Press, 1965).

"Lettre à Joë Bousquet." Translated as "Letter to Joë Bousquet" (May 12, 1942), in *The Simone Weil Reader,* ed. George A. Panichas (New York: David McKay, 1977).

"Lettre à un religieux." Translated as *Letter to a Priest,* trans. Richard Rees (New York: Penguin Books, 2003).

"Lettre aux *Cahiers du Sud* sur les responsabilitiés de la literature." Translated as "The Responsibility of Writers" in *The Simone Weil Reader,* ed. George A. Panichas (New York: David McKay, 1977).

"L'Europe en guerre pour la Tchécoslovaquie?" Translated as "A European War over Czechoslovakia?" in *Formative Writings, 1929–1941,* ed. and trans. Dorothy Tuck McFarland and Wilhelmina Van Ness (Amherst: University of Massachusetts Press, 1987).

"L'Iliade ou le poème de la force." Translated as "The *Iliad,* or the Poem of Force," pamphlet, trans. Mary McCarthy (Wallingford, PA: Pendle Hill Publications, 1956).

"Luttons-nous pour la justice?" Translated as "Are We Struggling for Justice?" in *Simone Weil: Writings Selected with an Introduction,* ed. Eric O. Springsted (New York: Orbis Books, 1998).

"Méditation sur l'obéissance et la liberté." Translated as "Meditation on Liberty," in *Oppression and Liberty,* ed. and trans. Arthur Wills and John Petrie (London: Routledge and Paul, 1972).

"Morale et littérature." Translated as "Morality and Literature," in *The Simone Weil Reader,* ed. George A. Panichas (New York: David McKay, 1977).

"Ne recommençons pas la guerre de Troie." Translated as "The Power of Words," in *Selected Essays, 1934–1943,* ed. and trans. Richard Rees (New York: Oxford University Press, 1962).

"Pour la Ligue." "For the League," not yet translated into English.

"Quelques réflexions autour de la notion de valeur." Translated as "A Few Reflections on the Notion of Value," forthcoming in the *Cahiers Simone Weil,* trans. E. Jane Doering and Bernard E. Doering.

"Quelques réflexions sur les origines de Hitlérisme." Translated as "The Great Beast: Some Reflections on the Origins of Hitlerism," in *Selected Essays, 1934–1943*, ed. and trans. Richard Rees (New York: Oxford University Press, 1962).

"Réflexions à propos de la théorie des quanta." Translated as "Reflections on Quantum Theory," in *Science, Necessity, and Love of God*, ed. and trans. Richard Rees (New York: Oxford University Press, 1968).

"Réflexions concernant le service civil." "Reflections on the Civil Service," not yet translated into English.

"Réflexions en vue d'un bilan." Translated as "Cold War Policy in 1939," in *Selected Essays 1934–1943*, ed. and trans. Richard Rees (New York: Oxford University Press, 1962).

"Réflexions sur la barbarie." Translated as "Reflections on Barbarism," in *Selected Essays, 1934–1943*, ed. and trans. Richard Rees (New York: Oxford University Press, 1962).

"Réflexions sur la guerre." Translated as "Reflections on War," in *Formative Writings, 1929–1941*, ed. and trans. Dorothy Tuck McFarland and Wilhelmina Van Ness (Amherst: University of Massachusetts Press, 1987).

"Réflexions sur le bon usage des études scolaires en vue de l'amour de Dieu." Translated as "Reflections on the Right Use of School Studies with a View to the Love of God," in *Simone Weil: Writings Selected with an Introduction*, ed. Eric O. Springsted (New York: Orbis Books, 1998).

"Réflexions sur les causes de la liberté et de l'oppression sociale." Translated as "Reflections on the Causes of Liberty and Social Oppression," in *Oppression and Liberty*, ed. and trans. Arthur Wills and John Petrie (London: Routledge and Paul, 1972).

"Réponse à une question d'Alain." Translated as "A Reply to One of Alain's Questions," in *Formative Writings, 1929–1941*, ed. and trans. Dorothy Tuck McFarland and Wilhelmina Van Ness (Amherst, University of Massachusetts Press, 1987).

"Science et perception dans Descartes." Translated as "Science and Perception in Descartes," in *Formative Writings, 1929–1941*, ed. and trans. Dorothy Tuck McFarland and Wilhelmina Van Ness (Amherst: University of Massachusetts Press, 1987).

"Un mouvement revendicatif dans l'armée romaine de Germanie." "A German Tribal Conquest against the Roman Army," not yet translated into English.

NOTES

The following are abbreviations used in the notes:

K [no.], ms [no.]   For Weil's Notebooks: K, an abbreviation used by the *OC* editors, and the number following it refer to the number of the original notebook in which Weil wrote; "ms" and the number following it refer to the manuscript page in that original notebook.

OC   Simone Weil, *Oeuvres complètes,* gen. ed. André Devaux and Florence de Lussy (Paris: Gallimard, 1988–).

OSW   Simone Weil, *Oeuvres / Simone Weil,* ed. Florence de Lussy (Paris: Gallimard, 1999).

INTRODUCTION

The chapter epigraph from Weil's "Of What Does the Occitanian Inspiration Consist?" ("En quoi consiste l'inspiration occitanienne?") is in her *Écrits historiques et politiques* (Paris: Gallimard, 1960), 80.

     1. Simone Weil, "Autobiographie spirituelle," *OSW,* 771.

     2. Ibid.

     3. Ibid.

     4. Ibid., 771–72.

     5. Ibid., 777.

     6. See the many fine scholarly articles in the journal *Cahiers Simone Weil.*

     7. See Ann Pirruccello, "'Gravity' in the Thought of Simone Weil," *Philosophy and Phenomenological Research* 57 (March 1997): 73–93.

ONE. SIMONE WEIL'S REJECTION OF PACIFISM

The chapter epigraph from "Reflections on the Civil Service" is translated from "Réflexions concernant le service civil," *OC*, vol. 2, pt. 1, 47. The first section's epigraph, also from "Reflections on the Civil Service," is on the same page. The second, third, and fourth sections' epigraphs, from "Reflections on War," are translated from "Réflexions sur la guerre," *OSW*, 453, 457, and 466, respectively. The fifth section's epigraph, from "Let Us Not Recommence the Trojan War," is translated from "Ne recommençons pas la guerre de Troie," *OC*, vol. 2, pt. 3, 51. The sixth section's epigraph, from Weil's Notebooks, is translated from K 9, ms 16, in *OC*, vol. 6, pt. 3, 164. The seventh section's epigraph, from "Europe at War for Czechoslovakia?" is translated from "L'Europe en guerre pour la Tchécoslovaquie?" *OSW*, 499.

1. Simone Weil, "Réflexions concernant le service civil" [Reflections on the Civil Service], *OC*, vol. 2, pt. 1, 48.

2. The Civil Service Organization was founded in 1920 by a Swiss, Pierre Cérésole. On Weil's loss of interest in participating, see Simone Pétrement, *La vie de Simone Weil* (Paris: Librairie Arthème Fayard, 1973), 93.

3. In 1894, Captain Alfred Dreyfus, a high-ranking Jewish artillery officer in the French army, was falsely accused, tried, and convicted of treason, charges on which he was later exonerated after much suffering and humiliation.

4. Simone Weil, "Pour la Ligue" [For the League], *OC*, vol. 2, pt. 1, 55.

5. Gabriella Fiori, *Simone Weil: An Intellectual Biography*, trans. Joseph R. Berrigan (Athens: University of Georgia Press, 1989), 45.

6. Pétrement, *La vie de Simone Weil*, 695.

7. Jacques Cabaud, *Simone Weil: A Fellowship in Love* (New York: Channel Press, 1964), 37.

8. Fiori, *Simone Weil*, 44.

9. Pétrement, *La vie de Simone Weil*, 97.

10. Fiori, *Simone Weil*, 82.

11. Simone Weil, "Réflexions sur la guerre" [Reflections on War], *OSW*, 451–61.

12. Ibid., 456.

13. Ibid., 461.

14. Simone Weil, "Lettre à Georges Bernanos" [1938], *OSW*, 406.

15. Ibid., 408.

16. Simone Weil, "Réponse à une question d'Alain" [Response to a Question from Alain], *OC*, vol. 2, pt. 2, 329–32.

17. Raymond Poincaré, president of the French Third Republic, 1913–20.

18. "World War I," in *The New Encyclopædia Britannica* (Chicago: Encyclopædia Britannica, 2005), table 4, 29:987. The statistics were reported by the U.S. War Dept. in February 1924.

19. See her first version of the article, "Pour un peu de clarté," *OC*, vol. 2, pt. 3, 283; on the reaction of the pacifist press to Giraudoux's play, see *OSW*, 470. In English, the literal translation of the play's title is "The War of Troy Will Not Take Place." English playwright Christopher Fry translated the title as "The Tiger at the Gates."

20. Weil, "Ne recommençons pas la guerre de Troie" [Let Us Not Recommence the Trojan War], *OC*, vol. 2, pt. 3, 49.

21. Ibid., 51.

22. Ibid.

23. Ibid., 52.

24. Ibid., 51.

25. Ibid., 64.

26. Ibid., 53.

27. Ibid., 54.

28. Ibid., 65.

29. Simone Weil, Notebooks, K 3, ms 112–13, *OC*, vol. 6, pt. 1, 354.

30. Simone Weil, "Méditation sur l'obéissance et la liberté" [Meditation on Obedience and Liberty], *OSW*, 489–94.

31. Weil, Notebooks, K 9, ms 16, *OC*, vol. 6, pt. 3, 164.

32. Weil, "Méditation sur l'obéissance," *OSW*, 489.

33. Simone Weil, "Lettres de Simone Weil à Jean Posternak," *Cahiers Simone Weil* 10 (June 1987): 124.

34. Weil, "Méditation sur l'obéissance," *OSW*, 491.

35. Inhabitants of French Indochina, a colony, at that time, of the French Empire.

36. Estienne de La Boétie, *The Politics of Obedience: The Discourse of Voluntary Servitude*, trans. Harry Kurz (New York: Free Life Editions, 1975), 51.

37. Ibid., 59.

38. Ibid., 55–56.

39. Ibid., 60.

40. Ibid.

41. Ibid., 64.

42. Ibid., 61.

43. Ibid., 60–61.

44. Ibid., 65.

45. Frederick Douglass, an American slave, is an excellent example of such an individual. At great risk, he taught himself to read, after which he underwent great suffering to become free. Later, as a free man, he was named consul-general to the Republic of Haiti for the U.S. government.

46. Weil, "Méditation sur l'obéissance," *OSW*, 492–93.

47. Cornelius Tacitus, *The Annals and The Histories*, ed. Moses Hadas, trans. Alfred John Church and William Jackson Brodribb (New York: Modern Library, 2003), 20–21.

48. Simone Weil, "Un mouvement revendicatif dans l'armée romaine de Germanie" [A German Tribal Conquest against the Roman Army], *OC*, vol. 2, pt. 3, 167.

49. Weil, "Méditation sur l'obéissance," *OSW*, 494.

50. Simone Weil, "L'Europe en guerre pour la Tchécoslovaquie?" [Europe at War for Czechoslovakia?] *OSW*, 497–502, first published in *Feuilles Libres de la Quinzaine* 4, no. 58 (May 25, 1938).

51. Ibid., 502.

52. "Sudetenland," in *New Encyclopædia Britannica* [2005], 11:352, 1a.

53. Gordon Wright, *France in Modern Times*, 3rd ed. (New York: W. W. Norton, 1981), 402.

54. Ibid., 397.

TWO.   THE EMPIRE OF FORCE

The chapter epigraph, from Weil's Notebooks, is translated from K 1, ms 11, in *OC*, vol. 6, pt. 1, 79. The first section's epigraph, from Weil's "Reflections on Barbarity," is translated from "Réflexions sur la barbarie," *OSW*, 506. The second section's epigraph, from Weil's "Reflections in View of an Assessment," is translated from "Réflexions en vue d'un bilan," *OSW*, 524. The third section's epigraph, from Weil's "The *Iliad*, or the Poem of Force," is translated from "*L'Iliade* ou le poème de la force," *OSW*, 552. The fourth section's epigraph, from Weil's Notebooks, is translated from K 3, ms 22, in *OC*, vol. 6, pt. 1, 304.

1. Simone Weil, "Réflexions sur la barbarie" [Reflections on Barbarity], *OSW*, 505–7.

2. Ibid., 506.

3. Ibid.

4. Simone Weil, "Désarroi de notre temps" [The Distress of Our Time], *OC*, vol. 2, pt. 3, 93.

5. Ibid., 93–94.

6. Simone Weil, "Réflexions en vue d'un bilan" [Reflections in View of an Assessment], *OSW*, 511–26.

7. Ibid., 512.

8. Ibid., 515.

9. Gabriella Fiori, *Simone Weil: An Intellectual Biography*, trans. Joseph R. Berrigan (Athens: University of Georgia Press, 1989), 155. This explanation was given to Fiori by Simone Pétrement in a letter of January 12, 1978. See Fiori, *Simone Weil*, 342 n. 39. Habituating people to the thought of war was also a concern of the American social activist Dorothy Day in the 1950s when she protested against the mandatory air raid drills in New York City.

10. Weil, "Réflexions en vue d'un bilan," *OSW*, 526.

11. Simone Weil, "L'Iliade ou le poème de la force" [The *Iliad*, or the Poem of Force], *OSW*, 542.

12. Ibid., 543.

13. Ibid.

14. Simone Pétrement, *La vie de Simone Weil* (Paris: Librairie Arthème Fayard, 1973), 497.

15. Simone Weil, "Lettres à Jean Posternak," May 1937 [no day given], *OSW*, 648.

16. Weil, "L'Iliade," *OSW*, 552.

17. Ibid., 542–43.

18. Ibid., 545.

19. Pètrement, *La vie de Simone Weil*, 529.

20. Weil, "L'Iliade," *OSW*, 529.

21. Ibid., 549.

22. Ibid., 540.

23. Ibid., 529.

24. Ibid.

25. All English translations of the *Iliad*, except where noted, are from Homer, *The Iliad*, trans. Robert Fagles (New York: Viking Press, 1990).

26. Ibid., 545.

27. Ibid., 533.

28. Ibid., 549.

29. Ibid., 535, 536.

30. Ibid.

31. Ibid., 537.

32. Ibid., 537.

33. Ibid., 548.

34. Matt. 26:52.

35. Simone Weil translated this verse, "Ares est équitable, il tue ceux qui tuent," directly from her Greek text. Homer's line (*Iliad* 8.309) follows

Hector's response to Polydamas that he will continue the battle. Weil, "*L'Iliade*," *OC*, vol. 2, pt. 3, 235 and 319 n. 194.

36. Weil, "*L'Iliade*," *OSW*, 551.

37. Malou Blum, "Ma rencontre avec Simone Weil," in *Le choix de la Résistance* (Paris: Cerf, 1998), 111.

38. *OC*, vol. 6, pt. 1, 215.

39. Fiori, *Simone Weil*, 73.

40. Introduction to Weil, Notebooks, K 18, *OC*, vol. 6, pt. 4, 359.

41. Weil, Notebooks, K 4, ms 17, *OC*, vol. 6, pt. 2, 69.

42. Weil, "Réflexions en vue d'un bilan," *OSW*, 517–18.

43. Simone Weil, "Formes de l'amour implicite de Dieu" [Forms of the Implicit Love of God], in *Attente de Dieu* (Paris: Fayard, 1966), 127.

44. Simone Weil, "Quelques réflexions sur les origines de l'Hitlérisme" [Some Reflections on the Origins of Hitlerism], *OC*, vol. 2, pt. 3, 194.

45. Weil, "Formes de l'amour," 131.

46. Weil, Notebooks, K 3, ms 25, *OC*, vol. 6, pt. 1, 306.

47. Ibid., K 3, ms 11, *OC*, vol. 6, pt. 1, 297.

48. Certain post–World War II analysts suggest that Roosevelt's insistence on Germany's unconditional surrender and on the British area bombing was exploited propagandistically by the German High Command to keep the German people motivated to fight, implying that they would be destroyed as a people if the Allies won.

49. Weil, Notebooks, K 3, ms 22, *OC*, vol. 6, pt. 1, 305.

50. Ibid., K 3, ms 22–25, *OC*, vol. 6, pt. 1, 304–7.

51. Carl von Clausewitz, *On War*, ed. and trans. Michael Howard and Peter Paret (Princeton: Princeton University Press, 1984), 20.

52. Weil, Notebooks, K 3, ms 24, *OC*, vol. 6, pt. 1, 306.

53. Ibid.

54. Ibid., K 5, ms 44, *OC*, vol. 6, pt. 2, 198–99.

55. Ibid., K 4, ms 37, *OC*, vol. 6, pt. 2, 88.

56. Ibid., K 9, ms 56, *OC*, vol. 6, pt. 3, 197.

57. Ibid., K 1, ms 11, *OC*, vol. 6, pt. 1, 79.

58. Ibid., K 3, ms 19, *OC*, vol. 6, pt. 1, 303.

THREE.   LOVE OF NEIGHBOR VERSUS TOTALITARIANISM

The chapter epigraph, from Weil's "Spiritual Autobiography," is translated from "Autobiographie spirituelle," in *Attente de Dieu* (Paris: Fayard, 1966), 55. The first section epigraph, from Simone Weil's letter to Joë Bousquet, May 12, 1942, is translated from *Correspondance*, by Simone Weil and Joë

Bousquet, ed. Jil Silberstein (Lausanne: Éditions l'Age d'Homme, 1982), 45. The second section epigraph, from Weil's *Random Thoughts Concerning the Love of God*, is translated from *Pensées sans ordre concernant l'amour de Dieu* (Paris: Gallimard, 1962), 47. The third, fourth, fifth, and sixth section epigraphs, all from "Some Reflections on the Origins of Hitlerism," are translated from "Quelques réflexions sur les origines de Hitlérisme," *OC*, vol. 2, pt. 3, 217, 172, 181, and 203–4 respectively.

1. Maurice Schumann, "Présentation de Simone Weil," quoted in *Simone Weil: Philosophe, historienne et mystique*, ed. Gilbert Kahn (Paris: Aubier Montaigne, 1978), 18–19.

2. Simone Weil, "Autobiographie spirituelle," in *Attente de Dieu* (Paris: Fayard, 1966), 36–37.

3. Simone Weil to Joë Bousquet, May 12, 1942, in *Correspondance*, by Simone Weil and Joë Bousquet, ed. Jil Silberstein (Lausanne: Éditions l'Age d'Homme, 1982), 45.

4. Weil, "Autobiographie spirituelle," 43. "God's fool" is a reference to the title of Julien Green's book *God's Fool: The Life and Times of Francis of Assisi*, trans. Peter Heinegg (San Francisco: Harper and Row, 1987).

5. Simone Weil, "Brouillon du Prologue" [Draft of the Prologue], in Notebooks, K 11, ms 75–77, *OC*, vol. 6, pt. 3, 445–47.

6. Weil to Bousquet, May 12, 1942, in Weil and Bousquet, *Correspondance*, 45.

7. Simone Weil, *La connaissance surnaturelle* (Paris: Gallimard, 1950), 255.

8. Weil, "Autobiographie spirituelle," 16.

9. Ibid., 55.

10. Meister Eckhart, a Dominican, was one of the great Christian mystics with an original manner of expounding on eternal mysteries. In the fourteenth century he was accused of heresy and has never yet been fully rehabilitated by the Church.

11. Weil, "Autobiographie spirituelle," 55.

12. Ibid., 37.

13. Weil, Notebooks, K 9, ms 66, *OC*, vol. 6, pt. 3, 205.

14. Jean Riaud, "Simone Weil et l'Ancien Testament," *Cahiers Simone Weil* 3 (June 1980): 83–84.

15. Ibid., 89 n. 64. Riaud cites Charpentier's "Méthodes d'analyse et de lecture de la Bible," *Bulletin du Secrétariat de la Conférence Épiscopale Française*, no. 13 (September 1978): 6.

16. Simone Weil, *Pensées sans ordre concernant l'amour de Dieu* [Random Thoughts Concerning the Love of God] (Paris: Gallimard, 1962), 47.

17. Weil, Notebooks, K 4, ms 49, *OC*, vol. 6, pt. 2, 95.

18. Ibid., K 6, ms 65, *OC*, vol. 6, pt. 2, 339.

19. Emmanuel Levinas, "Simone Weil contre la Bible," *Evidences* 24 (February–March 1952): 9–12, 44.

20. Martin Buber, "Bergson et Simone Weil devant Israël," *Cahiers Simone Weil* 6 (March 1983): 46–54.

21. David Tracy, "Simone Weil and the Impossible: A Radical View of Religion and Culture," in *Critical Spirit: Theology at the Crossroads of Faith and Culture*, ed. Andrew Pierce and Geraldine Smyth (Blackrock: Columba Press, 2003), 214.

22. Wladimir Rabi, "Simone Weil entre le monde juif et le monde chrétien," *Sens* 7 (1979): 169–74.

23. Simone Weil, *Lettre à un religieux* [Letter to a Priest] (Paris: Gallimard, 1951), 8.

24. Ibid., 17.

25. Ibid., 10.

26. Ibid., 16.

27. Ibid., 92.

28. Ibid., 45–46.

29. Simone Weil, "Quelques réflexions sur les origines de Hitlérisme" [Some Reflections on the Origins of Hitlerism], *OC*, vol. 2, pt. 3, 168–219.

30. Ibid., 207.

31. Ibid., 179–80.

32. Ibid., 174.

33. Ibid., 197.

34. Ibid., 316 n. 102.

35. Ibid., 316 nn. 111, 112.

36. Ibid., 189.

37. Ibid., 198.

38. Ibid., 203–4.

39. Ibid., 204–5.

40. Ibid., 209.

41. Ibid., 211 (see 317 n. 150). Translated by Simone Weil from James Breasted's *The Dawn of Conscience* (New York: Charles Scribner's Sons, 1933), 221.

42. Weil, "Quelques réflexions," *OC*, vol. 2, pt. 3, 211.

43. Ibid., 212.

44. Ibid., 218.

45. Ibid., 215.

46. Ibid., 173.

47. Ibid., 217.

FOUR. VALUES FOR READING THE UNIVERSE

The chapter epigraph, from Weil's *The Need for Roots*, is translated from *L'enracinement* (Paris: Gallimard, 1949), 165. The first section epigraph is also from that book, 360. The second section epigraph, from Weil's Notebooks, is translated from K 8, ms 100–101, in *OC*, vol. 6, pt. 3, 121. The third and fourth section epigraphs, from *The Need for Roots*, are from *L'enracinement*, 366 and 24. The fifth section epigraph, from Weil's Notebooks, is translated from K 9, ms 33, in *OC*, vol. 6, pt. 3, 179.

1. Simone Weil, *L'enracinement* [The Need for Roots] (Paris: Gallimard, 1949), 269.

2. Simone Weil, "Fragments de lettres," in *Écrits historiques et politiques* (Paris: Gallimard, 1960), 109.

3. Simone Weil, "Fragments et notes," in *Écrits de Londres* (Paris: Gallimard, 1957), 158.

4. Simone Weil, Notebooks, K 18, ms 8–9, *OC*, vol. 6, pt. 4, 365.

5. Simone Weil, Notebooks, K 3, ms 26, *OC*, vol. 6, pt. 1, 307.

6. Weil, *L'enracinement*, 305.

7. Ibid., 359.

8. Ibid., 67.

9. Simone Pètrement, *La vie de Simone Weil* (Paris: Librairie Arthème Fayard, 1973), 664–65.

10. Weil, *L'enracinement*, 285.

11. Ibid., 287.

12. Ibid., 288.

13. Ibid., 174.

14. Ibid., 238–40.

15. Joë Bousquet to Simone Weil, May 2, 1942, in *Correspondance*, by Simone Weil and Joë Bousquet, ed. Jil Silberstein (Lausanne: Éditions l'Age d'Homme, 1982), 32.

16. Ibid., 34.

17. Weil, Notebooks, K 8, ms 100–101, *OC*, vol. 6, pt. 3, 121.

18. Ibid., K 14, ms 49, *OC*, vol. 6, pt. 4, 188.

19. Simone Weil to Maurice Schumann, July 30, 1942, in *Écrits de Londres*, 192.

20. Ibid., K 6, ms 34, *OC*, vol. 6, pt. 2, 314.

21. The American Red Cross had begun a system of plasma injections on the battlefield for trauma, burns, and hemorrhaging.

22. Weil, Notebooks, K 18, ms 83, *OC*, vol. 6, pt. 4, 394.

23. Gabriël Maës, "Un repère allemand de notre histoire, ou Le Hitler de Simone Weil," *Cahiers Simone Weil* 24 (September 2001): 167.

24. Weil, *L'enracinement*, 302. As Weil translated this passage from the German, "L'homme ne doit jamais tomber dans l'erreur de croire qu'il est seigneur et maître de la nature. . . . Il sentira dès lors que dans un monde où les planètes et les soleils suivent des trajectoires circulaires, où des lunes tournent autour des planètes, où la force règne partout et seule en maîtresse de la faiblesse, qu'elle contraint à la servir docilement ou qu'elle brise, l'homme ne peut pas relever de lois spéciales."

25. Ibid., 306.

26. David Minton, "La critique weilienne de la conception de Dieu dans l'Ancien Testament," *Cahiers Simone Weil* 3 (June 1980): 113.

27. Weil, *L'enracinement*, 362.

28. Weil, Notebooks, K 9, ms 82, *OC*, vol. 6, pt. 3, 215.

29. Weil, *L'enracinement*, 361.

30. *The New Oxford Annotated Bible*, ed. Bruce Metzger (New York: Oxford University Press, 1991).

31. Weil, *L'enracinement*, 366.

32. Ibid., 305.

33. Weil, Notebooks, K 1, ms 27, *OC*, vol. 6, pt. 1, 89.

34. Ibid., K 1, ms 18, *OC*, vol. 6, pt. 1, 81.

35. Ibid., K 5, ms 50, *OC*, vol. 6, pt. 2, 203.

36. For an interesting modern study of the complex and debilitating relationships in slavery that bears out Simone Weil's statements, see Annette Gordon-Reed's *The Hemmingses of Monticello: An American Family* (New York: W. W. Norton, 2008).

37. Ibid., K 5, ms 55, *OC*, vol. 6, pt. 2, 207.

38. Ibid., K 4, ms 23, *OC*, vol. 6, pt. 2, 75.

39. Ibid., K 5, ms 93, *OC*, vol. 6, pt. 2, 246.

40. Ibid., K 5, ms 93–94, *OC*, vol. 6, pt. 2, 246–47.

41. Ibid., K 3, ms 110, *OC*, vol. 6, pt. 1, 352, and K 5, ms 108, *OC*, vol. 6, pt. 2, 260.

42. Ibid., K 8, ms 3, *OC*, vol. 6, pt. 3, 196.

43. Ibid., K 4, ms 111, *OC*, vol. 6, pt. 2, 140.

44. Ibid., K 8, ms 3, *OC*, vol. 6, pt. 3, 44.

45. Ibid., K 4, ms 95, *OC*, vol. 6, pt. 2, 128.

46. Ibid., K 14, ms 65, *OC*, vol. 6, pt. 4, 197.

47. Ibid., K 5, ms 52, *OC*, vol. 6, pt. 2, 204.

48. Ibid., K 6, ms 139, *OC*, vol. 6, pt. 2, 396.

49. Ibid., K 4, ms 95–96, *OC*, vol. 6, pt. 2, 128.

50. Ibid., K 5, ms 47–48, *OC*, vol. 6, pt. 2, 201.

51. Anne Pirruccello, "'Gravity' in the Thought of Simone Weil," *Philosophy and Phenomenological Research* 57 (March 1997): 92. I am indebted to Pirruccello for this essay's insights on Weil's notion of gravity.

52. Simone Weil, "Réflexions sur les causes de la liberté et de l'oppression sociale" [Reflections on the Causes of Liberty and Social Oppression], *OC*, vol. 2, pt. 2, 92.

53. Ibid., 92.

54. Weil, Notebooks, K 4, ms 111, *OC*, vol. 6, pt. 2, 141. Weil is referring here to the thermodynamic distinction between open and closed systems: a closed system, isolated from the rest of the environment, exchanges neither light, heat, nor matter with its surroundings; the total quantity of energy remains constant.

55. Ibid., K 5, ms 53, *OC*, vol. 6, pt. 2, 205.

56. Ibid., K 5, ms 101, *OC*, vol. 6, pt. 2, 267.

57. Ibid., 253.

58. Pirruccello, "Gravity," 89.

59. For an in-depth examination of Weil's conflation of desire, energy, and entropy, see Pirruccello, "Gravity."

60. Weil, Notebooks, K 3, ms 110, *OC*, vol. 6, pt. 1, 352.

61. Pirruccello, "Gravity," 82.

62. Weil, Notebooks, K 4, ms 86, *OC*, vol. 6, pt. 2, 120.

63. Simone Weil, "Réflexions sur le bon usage des études scolaires en vue de l'amour de Dieu" [Reflections on the Right Use of School Studies with a View to the Love of God], in *Attente de Dieu* (Paris: Fayard, 1966), 86, 92.

64. Ibid., 96–97.

65. Weil, Notebooks, K 1, ms 27, *OC*, vol. 6, pt. 1, 89.

66. Pirruccello, "Gravity," 90.

67. Simone Weil, *Sur la science* (Paris: Gallimard, 1966), 276.

68. Pirruccello, "Gravity," 92.

69. Weil, Notebooks, K 3, ms 29, *OC*, vol. 6, pt. 1, 309.

FIVE.   READING AND JUSTICE

The chapter epigraph, from Weil's Notebooks, is translated from K 3, ms 6, in *OC*, vol. 6, pt. 1, 295. The first, second, and third section epigraphs, also from Weil's Notebooks, are from K 7, ms 99, in *OC*, vol. 6, pt. 2, 483; K 6, ms 38, in *OC*, vol. 6, pt. 2, 317; and K 5, ms 121, in *OC*, vol. 6, pt. 2, 273, respectively. The fourth section epigraph, from Weil's "Some Reflections on the Idea of Value," is translated from "Quelques réflexions autour de la notion de valeur" *OSW*, 121. The fifth section epigraph, from Weil's "Agony of a Civilization Seen through an Epic Poem," is translated from "Agonie d'une civilisation vue à travers un poème épique," in *Écrits Historiques et Politiques*, 67. The sixth section epigraph is translated from Weil's *Poèmes—suivis de Venise sauvée—Lettre de Paul Valéry* (Paris: Gallimard, 1968), 47, 48.

1. Simone Weil, "Essai sur la notion de lecture," *Études philosophiques* n.s. 1 (January–March 1946): 14.

2. Simone Weil, "Science et perception dans Descartes," in *Sur la science* (Paris: Gallimard, 1966), 85.

3. Ibid., 86.

4. Weil, "Essai sur la notion de lecture," 13.

5. Ibid., 15.

6. Ibid., 13–19.

7. Marie-Magdeleine Davy, *Introduction au message de Simone Weil* (Paris: Librairie Plon, 1954), 226.

8. André Devaux, "Présence de Descartes dans la vie et dans l'oeuvre de Simone Weil," *Cahiers Simone Weil* 18 (March 1995): 21.

9. Simone Weil, Notebooks, K 3, ms 60, *OC*, vol. 6, pt. 1, 321.

10. Weil, "Essai sur la notion de lecture," 18.

11. Weil, Notebooks, K 1, ms 63, *OC*, vol. 6, pt. 1, 184.

12. Ibid., K 3, ms 51, *OC*, vol. 6, pt. 1, 315.

13. Ibid., K 3, ms 58, *OC*, vol. 6, pt. 1, 319.

14. Ibid., K 5, ms 121, *OC*, vol. 6, pt. 2, 272.

15. Ibid., K 10, ms 40, *OC*, vol. 6, pt. 3, 278.

16. Ibid., K 5, ms 55, *OC*, vol. 6, pt. 2, 207.

17. Ibid., K 5, ms 121, *OC*, vol. 6, pt. 2, 273.

18. Weil, "Essai sur la notion de lecture," 17.

19. Weil, Notebooks, K 3, ms 51, *OC*, vol. 6, pt. 1, 315.

20. Weil, "Essai sur la notion de lecture," 16.

21. Ibid., 17.

22. Commentary on Weil's preference for this reading is in *OC*, vol. 6, pt. 1, 490 n. 52.

23. Weil, Notebooks, K 3, ms 9, *OC*, vol. 6, pt. 1, 296.

24. Ibid., K 5, ms 121, *OC*, vol. 6, pt. 2, 273.

25. Ibid., K 5, ms 111, *OC*, vol. 6, pt. 2, 264.

26. Simone Weil, "Réflexions sur le bon usage des études scolaires en vue de l'amour de Dieu" [Reflections on the Right Use of School Studies with a View to the Love of God], in *Attente de Dieu* (Paris: Fayard, 1966), 87.

27. Simone Weil, "Quelques réflexions autour de la notion de valeur" [Some Reflections on the Idea of Value], *OSW*, 121.

28. Florence de Lussy, introduction to Weil, "Quelques réflexions," *OSW*, 120.

29. Weil, Notebooks, K 9, ms 52, 53, *OC*, vol. 6, pt. 3, 194, 195.

30. Weil, "Quelques réflexions," *OSW*, 121.

31. Weil, Notebooks, K 6, ms 116, *OC*, vol. 6, pt. 2, 379.

32. Simone Weil, "Étude pour une déclaration des obligations envers l'être humain" [Draft for a Declaration of Obligations toward the Human Person], in *Écrits de Londres* (Paris: Gallimard, 1957), 74.

33. Weil, Notebooks, K 4, ms 59, 60, *OC*, vol. 6, pt. 2, 103–4.

34. Weil, "Réflexions à propos de la théorie des quanta" ["Reflections Related to Quantum Theory"], *OSW*, 592. This juxtaposition was made by Florence de Lussy in her introduction to "Quelques réflexions."

35. Simone Weil, "Responsabilités de la littérature" [Responsibilities of Literature], *Cahiers Simone Weil* 10 (December 1987): 356–57.

36. Weil, "Quelques réflexions," *OSW*, 121.

37. Ibid., 125–26.

38. Ibid., 122.

39. Weil, Notebooks, K 7, ms 26, *OC*, vol. 6, pt. 2, 431.

40. Ibid., K 7, ms 13, *OC*, vol. 6, pt. 2, 422.

41. Weil, "Quelques réflexions," *OSW*, 123.

42. George Grant, "'In Defence of Simone Weil': A Review Essay of *Simone Weil: A Modern Pilgrimage* by Robert Coles," *Idler* 15 (January–February 1988): 37.

43. Simone Weil, "En quoi consiste l'inspiration occitanienne?" [Of What Does the Occitanian Inspiration Consist?], in *Écrits historiques et politiques* (Paris: Gallimard, 1960), 79.

44. Ibid., 84.

45. Grant, "In Defence of Simone Weil," 37.

46. Simone Pétrement, *La vie de Simone Weil* (Paris: Librairie Arthème Fayard, 1973), 516.

47. Ibid.

48. Simone Weil, *Poèmes—suivis de Venise sauvée—Lettre de Paul Valéry* (Paris: Gallimard, 1968), 45.

49. Ibid., 104.

50. Ibid., 45.

51. Ibid., 77.

52. Ibid., 96.

53. Simone Weil, *La connaissance surnaturelle* (Paris: Gallimard, 1950), 16.

54. Weil, *Poèmes*, 52.

55. Simone Weil, "Morale et littérature," *Cahiers Simone Weil* 9 (December 1987): 349–50.

56. Weil, Notebooks, K 1, ms 57, *OC*, vol. 6, pt. 1, 115.

57. Weil, *Poèmes*, 133–34, my translation.

58. Weil, Notebooks, K 8, ms 117, *OC*, vol. 6, pt. 3, 134.

59. Weil, "La personne et le sacré" [The Person and the Sacred], in *Écrits de Londres*, 32.

60. Weil, *Poèmes*, 7.

SIX. SIMONE WEIL AND THE BHAGAVAD-GITA

The chapter epigraph, from Weil's "Spiritual Autobiography," is translated from "Autobiographie spirituelle," *OSW*, 772. The first section epigraph, from Weil's Notebooks, is translated from K 3, ms 9, in *OC*, vol. 6, pt. 1, 296. The second and third section epigraphs, from Weil's Notebooks, are translated from K 3, ms 51, in *OC*, vol. 6, pt. 1, 315, and K 3, ms 75, in *OC*, vol. 6, pt. 1, 331, respectively. The fourth section epigraph, from the Bhagavad-Gita, is from the translation by Barbara Stoler Miller (New York: Bantam Books, 1986). The fifth section epigraph, from Weil's Notebooks, is in K 4, ms 37, in *OC*, vol. 6, pt. 2, 87–88. The sixth section epigraph is from Lakshmi Kapani's "Simone Weil, lectrice des Upanisad védiques et de la Bhagavad-Gita: L'action sans désir et le désir sans objet," *Cahiers Simone Weil* 5 (June 1982): 98. The seventh section epigraph, from Weil's Notebooks, is in K 12, ms 30, in *OC*, vol. 6, pt. 3, 402. The eighth section epigraph, from the Gita 4.11, is translated from Weil's translation from Sanskrit ("J'aime ceux qui se donnent à moi"), quoted in Gérard Colas's "Une traduction de la Bhagavad Gita annotée par Simone Weil," *Cahiers Simone Weil* 6 (September 1983): 369.

1. Simone Pétrement, *La vie de Simone Weil* (Paris: Librairie Arthème Fayard, 1973), 533.

2. Simone Weil to René et Véra Daumal (undated), quoted in Marie-Magdeleine Davy, *Simone Weil* (Paris: Editions Universitaires, 1961), 36–37.

3. Marie-Magdeleine Davy, *Introduction au message de Simone Weil* (Paris: Librairie Plon, 1954), 220.

4. Gérard Colas, "Une traduction de la Bhagavad-Gita," *Cahiers Simone Weil* 4 (December 1983): 356–69.

5. Alyette Degrâces, Avant-propos 2, "L'Inde ou le passage obligé," *OC*, vol. 6, pt. 1, 36.

6. Simone Weil, Notebooks, K 3, ms 9, *OC*, vol. 6, pt. 1, 296–97.

7. All excerpts from the Gita in this chapter are from the English translation by the late specialist in Sanskrit and Indic studies Barbara Stoler

Miller. In the citations, the first number is the lesson number and the second is the number of the (usually four-line) verse.

8. Alyette Degrâces-Fahd, "La langue des Upanishad chez Simone Weil: Une herméneutique retrouvée selon l'expérience intérieure," *Philosophie and Langage* 13 (1991): 96.

9. R. C. Zaehner, ed. and trans., *The Bhagavad-Gita* (Oxford: Clarendon Press, 1969), 5–6.

10. A. L. Herman, ed. and trans., *The Bhagavad Gita: A Translation and Critical Commentary* (Springfield, IL: Charles C. Thomas, 1973), 8.

11. Colas, "Une traduction," 364.

12. Zaehner, *Bhagavad-Gita*, 7.

13. Weil, Notebooks, K 3, ms 16, *OC*, vol. 6, pt. 1, 300.

14. Ibid., K 3, ms 79, *OC*, vol. 6, pt. 1, 334.

15. Ibid., K 4, ms 71, *OC*, vol. 6, pt. 2, 111.

16. Ibid., K 3, ms 75, *OC*, vol. 6, pt. 1, 331.

17. Ibid., K 3, ms 75, *OC*, vol. 6, pt. 1, 500 n. 181.

18. Ibid., K 2, ms 59, *OC*, vol. 6, pt. 1, 250.

19. Ibid., K 4, ms 38, *OC*, vol. 6, pt. 2, 88.

20. Ibid., K 7, ms 14, *OC*, vol. 6, pt. 2, 423. In French, the word *charité* refers to the theological virtue of the love of God embracing the love of neighbor.

21. Ibid., K 4, ms 25, *OC*, vol. 6, pt. 2, 76.

22. Ibid., K 3, ms 75, *OC*, vol. 6, pt. 1, 331.

23. Ibid., K 3, ms 90, *OC*, vol. 6, pt. 1, 341.

24. Ibid., K 4, ms 39, *OC*, vol. 6, pt. 2, 88.

25. Ibid., K 4, ms 36, *OC*, vol. 6, pt. 2, 87.

26. Ibid., K 3, ms 71, *OC*, vol. 6, pt. 1, 328.

27. Ibid., K 4, ms 37, *OC*, vol. 6, pt. 2, 87.

28. Ibid.

29. Ibid., K 4, ms 37, *OC*, vol. 6, pt. 2, 87–88. The whole citation is as follows: "La non-violence n'est bonne que si elle est efficace. Ainsi, la question du jeune homme à Gandhi concernant sa sœur. La réponse devrait être: use de la force, a moins que tu sois tel que tu puisses la défendre, avec autant de probabilité de succès, sans violence. A moins que tu ne possèdes un rayonnement dont l'énergie (c'est-à-dire l'efficacité possible, au sens le plus matériel) soit égale à celle contenue dans tes muscles. Certains ont été tels. Saint François. S'efforcer de devenir tel qu'on puisse être non-violent. Cela dépend aussi de l'adversaire. S'efforcer de substituer de plus en plus, dans le monde, la non-violence efficace à la violence. Rien d'inefficace n'a de valeur. La séduction de la force est basse. C'est là une terrible difficulté."

30. Ibid., K 3, ms 120, *OC*, vol. 6, pt. 1, 360.
31. Miller, *Bhagavad-Gita*, 168, 164.
32. Ibid., 165.
33. Weil, Notebooks, K 4, ms 36, *OC*, vol. 6, pt. 2, 87.
34. Ibid., K 6, ms 14, *OC*, vol. 6, pt. 2, 297.
35. Ibid., K 7, ms 6, *OC*, vol. 6, pt. 2, 417.
36. Ibid., K 3, ms 51, *OC*, vol. 6, pt. 1, 315.
37. Simone Weil, *La connaissance surnaturelle* (Paris: Gallimard, 1950), 306.
38. Weil, Notebooks, K 3, ms 68, *OC*, vol. 6, pt. 1, 326.
39. Ibid.
40. Ibid., K 3, ms 69, *OC*, vol. 6, pt. 1, 327.
41. Herman, *Bhagavad Gita*, 34-35.
42. Weil, Notebooks, K 3, ms 81, *OC*, vol. 6, pt. 1, 335.
43. Weil, *La connaissance surnaturelle*, 317.
44. Weil, Notebooks, K 4, ms 25, *OC*, vol. 6, pt. 2, 76.
45. Simone Weil, "Petit Carnet noir," *OC*, vol. 6, pt. 1, 399.
46. Weil, Notebooks, K 4, ms 36, *OC*, vol. 6, pt. 2, 87.
47. Ibid., K 6, ms 122, *OC*, vol. 6, pt. 2, 384.
48. Ibid., K 4, ms 81, *OC*, vol. 6, pt. 2, 117.
49. Ibid., K 4, ms 86, *OC*, vol. 6, pt. 2, 120.
50. Alyette Degrâces, comment, *OC*, vol. 6, pt. 2, 575 nn. 376, 377. The terms for the two selves are from Miller, *Bhagavad-Gita*, 168.
51. Weil, Notebooks, K 4, ms 34, *OC*, vol. 6, pt. 2, 86.
52. Ibid., K 4, ms 88, *OC*, vol. 6, pt. 2, 123.
53. Ibid., K 3, ms 81, *OC*, vol. 6, pt. 1, 335.
54. Ibid., K 7, ms 70, *OC*, vol. 6, pt. 2, 464.
55. Ibid., K 6, ms 70, *OC*, vol. 6, pt. 2, 343.
56. Ibid., K 3, ms 78, *OC*, vol. 6, pt. 1, 333.
57. Ibid., K 6, ms 22, *OC*, vol. 6, pt. 2, 305.
58. On action in inaction, see ibid., K 6, ms 22, *OC*, vol. 6, pt. 2, 566, n. 209. The expression "inaction in action" is from René Guenon, a Hindu scholar whose works Weil read.
59. Pétrement, *La vie de Simone Weil*, 566.
60. Ibid., 577.
61. Degrâces, Avant-propos 2, *OC*, vol. 6, pt. 1, 40.
62. Simone Weil to Bernard and Selma Weil, May 10 and 31 and June 6, 1943, respectively, in *Écrits de Londres* (Paris: Gallimard, 1957), 235, 240, 242.
63. Weil, Notebooks, K 3, ms 80, *OC*, vol. 6, pt. 1, 335.

64. Lakshmi Kapani, "Simone Weil, lectrice des Upanisad védiques et de la Bhagavad-Gita: L'action sans désir et le désir sans objet," *Cahiers Simone Weil* 5 (June 1982): 98.

65. Ibid., 119.

66. Weil, Notebooks, K 3, ms 76, *OC*, vol. 6, pt. 1, 331.

67. Ibid., K 3, ms 78, *OC*, vol. 6, pt. 1, 333.

68. Weil, *La connaissance surnaturelle*, 311.

69. Pétrement, *La vie de Simone Weil*, 566.

SEVEN.   JUSTICE AND THE SUPERNATURAL

The chapter epigraph, from Weil's Notebooks, is translated from K 9, ms 16, in *OC*, vol. 6, pt. 3, 164. The first section epigraph, from Weil's "Forms of the Implicit Love of God," is translated from "Formes de l'amour implicit de Dieu," in her *Attente de Dieu* [Waiting for God] (Paris: Fayard, 1966), 128. The second section epigraph, from Weil's Notebooks, is translated from K 17, ms 8, in *OC*, vol. 6, pt. 4, 315. The third section epigraph, from Weil's "New Facts about the Colonial Problem in the French Empire," is from Janet Patricia Little's translation in *Simone Weil on Colonialism: An Ethic of the Other* (Oxford: Rowman and Littlefield, 2003), 66. The fourth section epigraph, from Weil's "The Colonial Question and the Destiny of the French People," is also in Little's book, 117.

1. Simone Weil, "Formes de l'amour implicit de Dieu" [Forms of the Implicit Love of God], in *Attente de Dieu* [Waiting for God] (Paris: Fayard, 1966), 129.

2. Ibid., 132.

3. Ibid., 144.

4. Ibid., 130.

5. Ibid., 127.

6. Ibid., 126–27.

7. Ibid., 130.

8. Ibid., 132.

9. Simone Weil, "Étude pour une déclaration des obligations envers l'être humain" [Draft for a Declaration of Obligations toward the Human Person], in *Écrits de Londres* (Paris: Gallimard, 1957), 74–84.

10. Ibid., 74.

11. Ibid., 75.

12. Weil develops at length the idea of the sacred link between humankind and the supernatural in a unique revelatory essay entitled "The

Sacredness of the Human Person" [La personne et le sacré], which is beyond the scope of this study.

13. Weil, "Étude pour une déclaration," 78–79.

14. This last caveat reflects Simone's experience in Marseilles from 1940 through 1942 when she personally participated in the covert distribution of the illegal *Témoignage Chrétien*. See Malou Blum, "Ma rencontre avec Simone Weil," in *Le choix de la Résistance* (Paris: Cerf, 1998), 104–15.

15. Sharon Begley, *Train Your Mind, Change Your Brain: How a New Science Reveals Our Extraordinary Potential to Transform Ourselves* (New York: Ballantine Books, 2007), 56.

16. Weil, "Étude pour une déclaration," 75.

17. Eleanor Roosevelt, "On the Adoption of the Universal Declaration of Human Rights," address to the United Nations General Assembly, December 9, 1948, in Paris, www.americanrhetoric.com/speeches/eleanorrooseveltdeclarationhumanrights.htm.

18. Attributed to Gandhi by Pope Benedict XVI in his January 1, 2007, message for the Celebration of the World Day of Peace, www.vatican.va/holy_father/benedict_xvi/messages/peace/documents/hf_ben-xvi_mes_20061208_xl-world-day-peace_en.html.

19. See Thomas S. Axworthy, ed., *Bridging the Divide: Religious Dialogue and Universal Ethics* (Kingston, Ontario: Queens School of Policy Studies, 2008).

20. Simone Weil, "Morocco, or a Lesson in Theft," and "Blood Is Flowing in Tunisia," in *Simone Weil on Colonialism: An Ethic of the Other*, ed. and trans. Janet Patricia Little (Oxford: Rowman and Littlefield, 2003), 31–35 and 41–44 respectively.

21. Simone Weil, "Colonization," in *Simone Weil on Colonialism*, 28.

22. Ibid., 27.

23. Simone Weil, *L'enracinement* [The Need for Roots] (Paris: Gallimard, 1949), 189.

24. Rita Maran, *Torture: The Role of Ideology in the French-Algerian War* (New York: Praeger, 1989), 13.

25. Simone Weil, "Extracts from *The Need for Roots*," in *Simone Weil on Colonialism*, 124.

26. Simone Weil, "New Facts about the Colonial Problem in the French Empire," in *Simone Weil on Colonialism*, 67–68.

27. The Annamites were the people of the French protectorate encompassing the central region of Vietnam.

28. Simone Weil, "Letter to the Indochinese," in *Simone Weil on Colonialism*, 29–30.

29. Simone Weil, "Who Is Guilty of Anti-French Plots?" in *Simone Weil on Colonialism*, 47.

30. Weil, "Blood Is Flowing in Tunisia," 44 n. 6.

31. Ibid., 43.

32. Weil, "Who Is Guilty," 48.

33. Ibid., 49.

34. Weil, "New Facts," 67.

35. Simone Weil, "Letter to Jean Giraudoux," in *Simone Weil on Colonialism*, 78.

36. Ibid., 79.

37. Simone Weil, "Fragment: About the Colonial Regime," in *Simone Weil on Colonialism*, 64.

38. Ibid., 63.

39. Weil, "New Facts," 65–71.

40. Ibid., 66.

41. Ibid., 67–69.

42. Weil, "Fragment," 63.

43. Simone Weil, "The Colonial Question and the Destiny of the French People," in *Simone Weil on Colonialism*, 117.

44. Ibid., 109.

45. Ibid., 111.

46. Ibid., 116.

EIGHT. NEITHER VICTIM NOR EXECUTIONER

The chapter epigraph, from Weil's "Reflections on War," is translated from "Réflexions sur la guerre," in *OC*, vol. 2, pt. 1, 299. The first section epigraph, from Dwight Macdonald's "Decline to Barbarism," is from the front page of *politics*, August 1945. The second section epigraph is from Nicola Chiaromonte's *The Paradox of History: Stendhal, Tolstoy, Pasternak, and Others* (Philadelphia: University of Pennsylvania Press, 1985), 45. The third section epigraph, from Albert Camus's "The Human Crisis," is from Lionel Abel's translation in *Twice a Year*, Fall–Winter 1946–47, 19–33, repr., New York: Kraus Reprint, 1967, 22.

1. Jean Grenier, *Albert Camus; Souvenirs* (Paris: Gallimard, 1968), 142–43.

2. Albert Camus, "Neither Victims nor Executioners," in *Between Hell and Reason: Essays from the Resistance Newspaper "Combat," 1944–1947*, ed. and trans. Alexandre de Gramont (Hanover: Wesleyan University Press, 1991), 115–40.

3. Simone Weil, "Réflexions sur la guerre" [Reflections on War], *OC*, vol. 2, pt. 1, 288–99.

4. Dwight Macdonald, "A Note on Simone Weil," *politics*, February 1945, 56.

5. Dwight Macdonald, "War and the Intellectuals: Act Two," *Partisan Review* 6 (Spring 1939): 9.

6. Weil, "Réflexions sur la guerre," *OC*, vol. 2, pt. 1, 293.

7. Macdonald, "War and the Intellectuals," 12.

8. Weil, "Réflexions sur la guerre," *OC*, vol. 2, pt. 1, 292.

9. Macdonald, "War and the Intellectuals," 17.

10. Ibid., 18.

11. Weil, "Réflexions sur la guerre," *OC*, vol. 2, pt. 1, 294.

12. Dwight Macdonald, "A Formula to Give a War-Torn Society Fresh Roots," review of *The Need for Roots*, by Simone Weil, *New York Times*, July 6, 1952, 6.

13. Dwight Macdonald, "Why politics?" *politics*, February 1944, 6–8.

14. Desegregation in the U.S. armed services began only with President Truman's Executive Order of 1948.

15. Dwight Macdonald, "The Responsibility of the People," *politics*, March 1945, 86–87.

16. Evan Thomas reports fifty years later that "perhaps 70,000 men, women and children died instantly. An additional 50,000 died within months from radiation poisoning and burns." See Evan Thomas, "Why We Did It!" *Newsweek*, July 24, 1995, 8.

17. In fact, as ascertained later, "There were almost 200,000 people working on the project at 37 secret plants and laboratories." Thomas, "Why We Did It!" 2.

18. Dwight Macdonald to Art Wiser, January 16, 1946, in *A Moral Temper: The Letters of Dwight Macdonald*, ed. Michael Wreszin (Chicago: Ivan R. Dee, 2001, 129). Wiser was in prison at the time for his activities as a pacifist and conscientious objector.

19. Martin J. Sherwin, *A World Destroyed: Hiroshima and Its Legacies* (Stanford: Stanford University Press, 2003), 238.

20. Ibid., 270 n. 64.

21. Nicola Chiaromonte, *The Worm of Consciousness and Other Essays* (New York: Harcourt Brace Jovanovich, 1976), 184.

22. Simone Pétrement, *La vie de Simone Weil* (Paris: Librairie Arthème Fayard, 1973), 215.

23. Nicola Chiaromonte, *The Paradox of History: Stendhal, Tolstoy, Pasternak, and Others* (Philadelphia: University of Pennsylvania Press, 1985), 19.

24. Ibid., 45.

25. Ibid., 29.

26. Chiaromonte, *Worm of Consciousness*, 188.

27. Ibid.

28. Ibid., 189.

29. Simone Weil, "*L'Iliade* ou le poème de la force" [The *Iliad*, or the Poem of Force], *OSW*, 540–41.

30. Albert Camus, "The Human Crisis," trans. Lionel Abel, *Twice a Year*, Fall–Winter 1946–47, 19–33 (repr., New York: Kraus Reprint 1967), 26.

31. Fernande Bartfeld, "Le voyage de Camus en Amérique du Nord," in *"L'homme révolté" cinquante ans après*, ed. Raymond Gay-Crosier (Paris: Lettres Modernes Minard, 2001), 223.

32. James D. Wilkinson, *The Intellectual Resistance in Europe* (Cambridge, MA: Harvard University Press, 1981), 52.

33. Ibid., 59.

34. Hannah Arendt to Karl Jaspers, November 11, 1946, in *Hannah Arendt / Karl Jaspers Correspondence, 1926–1969*, ed. Lotte Kohler and Hans Saner, trans. Robert and Rita Kimber (New York: Harcourt Brace Jovanovich, 1992), 66.

35. Dwight Macdonald, "Dual Power in France," *politics*, November 1944, 290–91.

36. Albert Camus, editorial, *Combat*, October 12, 1944, in *Essais*, ed. Roger Quilliot (Paris: Gallimard, 1965), 275–77.

37. Nicola Chiaromonte, "La résistance à l'histoire" [Resistance to History], *Preuves* 10 (April 1960): 18.

38. Camus, editorial, *Combat*, August 8, 1945, in *Essais*, 291–93.

39. Roger Quilliot, "Ni victime ni bourreau," in Camus, *Essais*, 1569.

40. Chiaromonte, "La Résistance," 207–8.

41. Bartfeld, "Le voyage de Camus," 208.

42. Camus, "Human Crisis," 22.

43. Ibid., 20.

44. Ibid., 21, 22.

45. Ibid., 24.

46. Ibid., 26.

47. Camus, "Le siècle de la peur" [The Century of Fear], *Combat*, November 1946, in *Essais*, 331–32.

48. Ibid., 332.

49. Camus, "Human Crisis," 23.

50. Camus, "Le socialisme mystifié" [Socialism Mystified], in *Essais*, 336.

51. Camus, "Human Crisis," 24.

52. Ibid., 22.

53. Weil, "*L'Iliade*," *OSW*, 550.

54. Camus, "Le siècle de la peur," 334.

55. Weil, "Réflexions sur la guerre," *OC*, vol. 2, pt. 1, 288.

56. Camus, "Le siècle de la peur," 331–33.

57. Simóne Weil, "Ne recommençons pas la guerre de Troie" [Let Us Not Recommence the Trojan War], *OC*, vol. 2, pt. 3, 63.

58. Ibid., 65.

59. Camus, "Human Crisis," 27–28.

60. Ibid., 25.

61. Weil uses the phrase "la folie d'amour" with great effectiveness in her essay "Luttons-nous pour la justice?" [Are We Struggling for Justice?], in *Écrits de Londres* (Paris: Gallimard, 1957), 45–57.

62. Camus, "Human Crisis," 26–27.

63. Roy Pierce, *Contemporary French Political Thought* (London: Oxford University Press, 1966), 128–29, 122.

64. Ibid., 128–29.

65. Jacques Cabaud, "Albert Camus et Simone Weil," *Kentucky Romance Quarterly* 21 (1974): 384.

66. Joseph Frank, foreword to Chiaromonte, *Paradox of History*, xi.

67. Gene Sharp, *Waging Nonviolent Struggle* (Boston: Extending Horizons Books, 2005), 1.

68. Eminent Jurists Panel on Terrorism, Counter-terrorism and Human Rights, *Assessing Damage, Urging Action: Executive Summary* (Geneva: International Commission of Jurists, 2009).

69. Ibid., 11.

70. Ibid., 8–9.

71. Ibid., 1, 9–10.

72. Ibid., 12.

73. Simone Weil, Notebooks, K 16, ms 105–6, and K 17, ms 39–40, *OC*, vol. 6, pt. 4, 301, 337. The Parable of the Sower is in Matt. 13:3–23, Mark 4:2–20, 26–29, and Luke 8:4–15.

74. Weil, Notebooks, K 9, ms 39, *OC*, vol. 6, pt. 3, 184.

75. Simone Weil to Selma Weil, July 18, 1943, *OSW*, 1228.

BIBLIOGRAPHY

Arendt, Hannah, and Karl Jaspers. *Hannah Arendt / Karl Jaspers Correspondence, 1926–1969*. Edited by Lotte Kohler and Hans Saner. Translated by Robert and Rita Kimber. New York: Harcourt Brace Jovanovich, 1992.

Axworthy, Thomas S., ed. *Bridging the Divide: Religious Dialogue and Universal Ethics*. Kingston, Ontario: Queens School of Policy Studies, 2008.

Bartfeld, Fernande. "Le voyage de Camus en Amérique du Nord." In *"L'homme révolté" cinquante ans après*, edited by Raymond Gay-Crosier, 203–29. Paris: Lettres Modernes Minard, 2001.

Begley, Sharon. *Train Your Mind, Change Your Brain: How a New Science Reveals Our Extraordinary Potential to Transform Ourselves*. New York: Ballantine Books, 2007.

Birou, Alain. "Amour surnaturel, dynamisation vers Dieu de toute l'expérience psychologique de Simone Weil." Parts 1 and 2. *Cahiers Simone Weil* 9 (June 1986): 189–208 and 9 (September 1986): 297–303.

———. "L'articulation entre le surnaturel et le social chez Simone Weil." *Cahiers Simone Weil* 8 (March 1985): 50–66.

Blackett, P. M. S. *Fear, War and the Bomb: Military and Political Consequences of Atomic Energy*. New York: Whittlesey House, 1949.

Blum, Malou. "Ma rencontre avec Simone Weil." In *Le choix de la Résistance*, 104–15. Paris: Cerf, 1998.

Buber, Martin. "Bergson et Simone Weil devant Israël." *Cahiers Simone Weil* 6 (March 1983): 46–54.

Cabaud, Jacques. "Albert Camus et Simone Weil." *Kentucky Romance Quarterly* 21 (1974): 383–94.

———. *Simone Weil: A Fellowship in Love*. New York: Channel Press, 1964.

Camus, Albert. *Between Hell and Reason: Essays from the Resistance Newspaper "Combat," 1944–1947*. Edited and translated by Alexandre de Gramont. Hanover: Wesleyan University Press, 1991.

———. *Essais*. Edited by Roger Quilliot. Paris: Gallimard, 1965.

———. "The Human Crisis." Translated by Lionel Abel. *Twice a Year*, Fall–Winter 1946–47, 19–33. Reprint, New York: Kraus Reprint 1967.

———. *Journaux de voyage*. Edited by Roger Quilliot. Paris: Gallimard, 1978.

———. "La crise humaine." Translated from the English by Jean-Marie Laclavetine. *La Nouvelle Revue Française* 516 (January 1996): 8–29.

Camus, Albert, and Jean Grenier. *Correspondence: 1932–1960*. Translated by Jan F. Rigaud. Lincoln: University of Nebraska Press, 2003.

Chiaromonte, Nicola. "La résistance à l'histoire." *Preuves* 10 (April 1960): 17–20.

———. *The Paradox of History: Stendhal, Tolstoy, Pasternak, and Others*. Philadelphia: University of Pennsylvania Press, 1985.

———. *The Worm of Consciousness and Other Essays*. New York: Harcourt Brace Jovanovich, 1976.

Clausewitz, Carl von. *On War*. Edited and translated by Michael Howard and Peter Paret. Princeton: Princeton University Press, 1984.

Colas, Gérard. "Une traduction de la Bhagavad-Gita." *Cahiers Simone Weil* 4 (December 1983): 356–69.

Davy, Marie-Magdeleine. *Introduction au message de Simone Weil*. Paris: Librairie Plon, 1954.

———. *Simone Weil*. Paris: Éditions Universitaires, 1961.

Degraces-Fahd, Alyette. "La langue des Upanisad chez Simone Weil: Une herméneutique retrouvée selon l'expérience intérieure." *Philosophie et Langage* 13 (1991): 89–117.

Devaux, André. "Présence de Descartes dans la vie et dans l'oeuvre de Simone Weil." *Cahiers Simone Weil* 18 (March 1995): 1–24.

Eminent Jurists Panel on Terrorism, Counter-terrorism and Human Rights. *Assessing Damage, Urging Action: Executive Summary*. Geneva: International Commission of Jurists, 2009.

Fiori, Gabriella. *Simone Weil: An Intellectual Biography*. Translated by Joseph R. Berrigan. Athens: University of Georgia Press, 1989.

Grant, George. "'In Defence of Simone Weil': A Review Essay of *Simone Weil: A Modern Pilgrimage* by Robert Coles." *Idler* 15 (January–February 1988): 36–40.

Grayling, A. C. *Among the Dead Cities: The History and Moral Legacy of the WWII Bombing of Civilians in Germany and Japan*. New York: Walker, 2006.

Green, Julien. *God's Fool: The Life and Times of Francis of Assisi*. Translated by Peter Heinegg. San Francisco: Harper and Row, 1987.

Grenier, Jean. *Albert Camus: Souvenirs*. Paris: Gallimard, 1968.

Herman, A. L., ed. and trans. *The Bhagavad Gita: A Translation and Critical Commentary*. Springfield, IL: Charles C. Thomas, 1973.

Homer. *The Iliad*. Translated by Robert Fagles. New York: Viking Press, 1990.

Kahn, Gilbert, ed. *Simone Weil: Philosophe, historienne et mystique*. Paris: Aubier Montaigne, 1978.

Kapani, Lakshmi. "Simone Weil, lectrice des Upanisad védiques et de la Bhagavad-Gita: L'action sans désir et le désir sans objet." *Cahiers Simone Weil* 5 (June 1982): 95–119.

La Boétie, Estienne de. *The Politics of Obedience: The Discourse of Voluntary Servitude*. Translated by Harry Kurz. New York: Free Life Editions, 1975.

Levinas, Emmanuel. "Simone Weil contre la Bible." *Evidences* 24 (February–March 1952): 9–12, 44.

Little, Janet Patricia. "Society as Mediator in Simone Weil's 'Venise sauvée.'" *Modern Language Review* 65 (1970): 298–305.

Macdonald, Dwight. "A Formula to Give a War-Torn Society Fresh Roots." Review of *The Need for Roots*, by Simone Weil. *New York Times*, July 6, 1952, 6.

———. *A Moral Temper: The Letters of Dwight Macdonald*. Edited by Michael Wreszin. Chicago: Ivan R. Dee, 2001.

———. *Politics*. 6 vols. New York: Politics Publishing, 1944–49.

———. "War and the Intellectuals: Act Two." *Partisan Review* 6 (Spring 1939): 3–20.

Maës, Gabriël. "Un repère allemand de notre histoire, ou le Hitler de Simone Weil." *Cahiers Simone Weil* 24 (September 2001): 159–81.

Maran, Rita. *Torture: The Role of Ideology in the French-Algerian War*. New York: Praeger, 1989.

Miller, Barbara Stoler, ed. and trans. *Bhagavad-Gita: Krishna's Counsel in Time of War*. New York: Bantam Books, 1986.

Minton, David. "La critique weilienne de la conception de Dieu dans l'Ancien Testament." *Cahiers Simone Weil* 5 (June 1980): 111–24.

New Oxford Annotated Bible. Edited by Bruce Metzger. New York: Oxford University Press, 1991.

Pétrement, Simone. *La vie de Simone Weil*. Paris: Librairie Arthème Fayard, 1973.

Pierce, Roy. *Contemporary French Political Thought*. London: Oxford University Press, 1966.

Pirruccello, Ann. "'Gravity' in the Thought of Simone Weil." *Philosophy and Phenomenological Research* 57 (March 1997): 73–93.

Rabi, Wladimir. "Simone Weil entre le monde juif et le monde chrétien." *Sens* 7 (1979): 169–74.

Rees, Richard. *Brave Men: A Study of D. H. Lawrence and Simone Weil*. London: Victor Gollancz, 1958.

Riaud, Jean. "Simone Weil et l'Ancien Testament." *Cahiers Simone Weil* 3 (June 1980): 83–84.

Sharp, Gene. *Waging Nonviolent Struggle*. Boston: Extending Horizons Books, 2005.

Sherwin, Martin J. *A World Destroyed: Hiroshima and Its Legacies*. Stanford: Stanford University Press, 2003.

Tacitus, Cornelius. *The Annals and The Histories*. Edited by Moses Hadas. Translated by Alfred John Church and William Jackson Brodribb. New York: Modern Library, 2003.

Thomas, Evan. "Why We Did It." *Newsweek*, July 24, 1995, 1–8.

Tracy, David. "Simone Weil and the Impossible: A Radical View of Religion and Culture." In *Critical Spirit: Theology at the Crossroads of Faith and Culture*, edited by Andrew Pierce and Geraldine Smyth, 208–22. Blackrock: Columba Press, 2003.

Weil, Simone. *Attente de Dieu*. Paris: Fayard, 1966.

———. *Écrits de Londres*. Paris: Gallimard, 1957.

———. *Écrits historiques et politiques*. Paris: Gallimard, 1960.

———. "Essai sur la notion de lecture." *Études philosophiques* n.s. 1 (January–March 1946): 13–19.

———. *Intuitions pré-chrétiennes*. Paris: La Colombe, 1951.

———. *La connaissance surnaturelle*. Paris: Gallimard, 1950.

———. *Leçons de philosophie de Simone Weil, présentée par Anne Reynaud*. Paris: Librairie Plon, 1959.

———. *L'enracinement*. Paris: Gallimard, 1949.

———. *Lettre à un religieux*. Paris: Gallimard, 1951.

———. "Lettre aux *Cahiers du sud* sur les responsabilités de la littérature." *Cahiers Simone Weil* 10 (December 1987): 354–57.

———. "Lettres de Simone Weil à Jean Posternak." *Cahiers Simone Weil* 10 (June 1987): 124.

———. "Morale et littérature." *Cahiers Simone Weil* 9 (December 1987): 349–52.

———. *Oeuvres complètes*. Vol. 2. *Écrits historiques et politiques*. Pt. 1. *L'engagement syndical, 1927–juillet 1934*. Edited under the direction of André Devaux and Florence de Lussy. Paris: Gallimard, 1988.

———. *Oeuvres complètes*. Vol. 2. *Écrits historiques et politiques*. Pt. 2. *L'expérience ouvrière et l'adieu à la révolution, juillet 1935–juin 1937*. Edited under the direction of André Devaux and Florence de Lussy. Paris: Gallimard, 1991.

———. *Oeuvres complètes*. Vol. 2. *Écrits historiques et politiques*. Pt. 3. *Vers la guerre, 1937–1940*. Edited under the direction of André Devaux and Florence de Lussy. Paris: Gallimard, 1989.

———. *Oeuvres complètes*. Vol. 6. *Cahiers*. Pt. 1. *1933–septembre 1941*. Edited under the direction of André Devaux and Florence de Lussy. Paris: Gallimard, 1994.

———. *Oeuvres complètes.* Vol. 6. *Cahiers.* Pt. 2. *septembre 1941–février 1942.* Edited under the direction of André Devaux and Florence de Lussy. Paris: Gallimard, 1997.

———. *Oeuvres complètes.* Vol. 6. *Cahiers.* Pt. 3. *La porte du transcendant.* Edited under the direction of André Devaux and Florence de Lussy. Paris: Gallimard, 2002.

———. *Oeuvres complètes.* Vol. 6. *Cahiers.* Pt. 4. *La connaissance surnaturelle.* Edited under the direction of André Devaux and Florence de Lussy. Paris: Gallimard, 2006.

———. *Oeuvres / Simone Weil.* Edited by Florence de Lussy. Paris: Gallimard, 1999.

———. *Oppression et liberté.* 1955. Reprint, Paris: Gallimard, 1966.

———. *Pensées sans ordre concernant l'amour de Dieu.* Paris: Gallimard, 1962.

———. *Poèmes—suivis de Venise sauvée—Lettre de Paul Valéry.* Paris: Gallimard, 1968.

———. *Simone Weil on Colonialism: An Ethic of the Other.* Edited and translated by Janet Patricia Little. Oxford: Rowman and Littlefield, 2003.

———. *Sur la science.* Paris: Gallimard, 1966.

Weil, Simone, and Joë Bousquet. *Correspondance.* Edited by Jil Silberstein. Lausanne: Éditions l'Age d'Homme, 1982.

Wilkinson, James D. *The Intellectual Resistance in Europe.* Cambridge, MA: Harvard University Press, 1981.

Wreszin, Michael. *A Moral Temper: The Letters of Dwight Macdonald.* Chicago: Ivan R. Dee, 2001.

———. *A Rebel in Defense of Tradition: The Life and Politics of Dwight Macdonald.* New York: Basic Books, 1994.

Wright, Gordon. *France in Modern Times.* 3rd ed. New York: W. W. Norton, 1981.

Zaehner, R. C., ed. and trans. *Bhagavad-Gita.* Oxford: Clarendon Press, 1969.

INDEX

Able, Lionel, 226
action in inaction or inaction in
   action, *action non agissante,*
   163–64, 172–73, 177
Alain (Emile Chartier), 3, 15, 20
Albigensians/Cathars, 5, 73, 140–41,
   143
Annamites/Annam, 31, 200–204
Arendt, Hannah, 212, 224
attention
   equal, 129
   essence of, 118
   quality of, 67, 100, 101, 104,
      117–18, 129, 134, 138, 141–42,
      149, 185–89, 194–95, 238–39
   realistic, 45
   and spiritual dimension, 117
   to the supernatural, 192–94

barbarian, barbarity, 41–43
Basch, Victor, 15
beauty, 145–47
   contemplation of, 123, 134, 146
   criterion for, 139
   and Divine Wisdom, 108
   ephemeral, 147–48
   eternal value of, 64, 110, 128, 134
   God's presence in, 185
   Gospels as source of, 128
   human creation of, 5, 6, 23, 52,
      71, 134, 141, 143, 156
   human need for, 191, 196, 229

natural, 4, 107, 134, 145
   role of, 6, 123, 148, 149, 179–80
Bhagavad-Gita, 6, 11, 51, 151–82, 239
Bousquet, Joë, 71–72, 101–5
Buber, Martin, 80
bureaucracy
   anonymous, 2, 41, 90–91,
      228–29
   inertia of, 219
   layers of, 235

Caesar, Julius, 86, 100
Cahiers du Sud, 53, 61, 138, 141, 220
Camus, Albert, 84, 196, 210, 212,
   222–35
Carthaginians, 88, 91
Cathars, 73, 122, 140–43
Catholic Church
   baptism, 5, 184
   critique of, 69–82, 141
   dogma, 6
Charles V, 86
Charles VII, 177
Chiaromonte, Nicola, 53, 210, 212,
   218, 220–26, 234–35
Christianity, 144
   Alain and, 70
   heresies against, and use of
      violence, 73
   religion of slaves, 5
   Weil and, 5–6, 70–82, 152, 178
Churchill, Winston, 47

270

E. JANE DOERING

is a professor and the executive coordinator of the
Teachers as Scholars Program in the College of Arts and Letters,
University of Notre Dame.
She is the co-editor of *The Christian Platonism of Simone Weil*
(University of Notre Dame Press, 2004).